LANGUAGE AT WORK

Nigel Gough,
Language Arts Consultant,
Perth County Board of Education
Gael Tickner,
Teacher, Business Department,
Grey Highlands Secondary School,
Grey County Board of Education

Executive Editor: Maggie Goh
Developmental Editor: Barbara Muirhead
Art Director: Mary Opper
Assistant Art Director: Julia Naimska
Production Editor: Lisa Collins
Proofreader: Carol Lee
Cover Illustrator: Ken Stampnick

Holt, Rinehart and Winston of Canada Ltd. wishes to thank the following educators
for their evaluations and helpful advice:

Heather Bichan
York Board of Education

John Borovilas
Toronto Board of Education

Mark Brubacher
York Board of Education

Anthony Buzzelli
Halton Roman Catholic School Board

Mary Donlevy
York Board of Education

Mary Dunnigan
Archbishop O'Leary High School
Edmonton Separate School Board

Rick Elliot
Lennox and Addington Board of Education

Doug Hilker
Runnymede Collegiate Institute,
Toronto

Corinne Hyatt
Toronto Board of Education

Anne Katz
Halton Board of Education

Mary Ann Neely
Elgin County Board of Education

Mary Lou Souter-Hayes
Scarborough Board of Education

Canadian Cataloguing in Publication Data

Gough, Nigel.
Language at work

ISBN 0-03-922031-1

1. English language—Business English.
2. Language arts (Secondary).
3. Communication in management.
4. Vocational guidance.
I. Tickner, Gael. II. Title.

PE1479.B87G68 1986   428.2'02'4651   C86-093751-8

Printed in Canada
  3 4 5 91 90 89

► LANGUAGE AT WORK

Nigel Gough
Gael Tickner

Holt, Rinehart and Winston of Canada, Limited

DEDICATIONS:

To my wife for inspiration and consultation, and to my parents for encouragement
–Nigel Gough

To the students of my classes over the years 1984 to 1986
– Gael Tickner

► TABLE OF CONTENTS

► ALL THAT I AM CAPABLE OF BECOMING

▶ Tracking the Right Job

ALL IN A DAY'S WORK

▶ ## IN PRAISE OF ENTREPRENEURS

▶ THE FRAGILE BONDS

▶ GET A GRIP ON IT

▶ FUTURE PROMISES

▶ ## STUDENT GUIDE

►MEMORANDUM

TO: the students
FROM: Nigel Gough and Gael Tickner
RE: LANGUAGE AT WORK
DATE: 1986 09 26

THIS BOOK IS ABOUT EFFECTIVE COMMUNICATION. It contains reading selections that will stimulate new thoughts and lead you to reflect, to evaluate, and to question. The selections are accompanied by activities that invite you to express your thoughts and ideas in many different ways, to a variety of audiences, and for various purposes. In working through the book, you will develop and use your language skills to "make meaning." In other words, through reading, writing, listening, speaking, and viewing, you will be reshaping and clarifying your thoughts and finding the best ways to share them with others.

The book is organized into seven units, each of which focusses on a theme or topic. ALL THAT I AM CAPABLE OF BECOM-ING asks you to get to know yourself and then to explore the options that are available to you. TRACKING THE RIGHT JOB takes you through the whole job-search process. ALL IN A DAY'S WORK looks at the work situation—the conditions, the issues, the demands, and the rewards. The selections in IN PRAISE OF ENTREPRENEURS introduce you to some successful entrepreneurs and highlight the challenges and the satisfaction to be found in setting up your own business. In THE FRAGILE BONDS, you will reflect on the relationships in your life: with other people, with your job, and with the environment. GET A GRIP ON IT examines stress, which is part of everyone's life, and offers strategies for coping with it. The last unit, FUTURE PROMISES, speculates on what is to come and challenges you to examine your role in a world that is faced with technological revolution, scarcity of natural resources, and the threat of a nuclear holocaust. The book ends with a STUDENT GUIDE containing information that will help you work through the activities with minimum reliance on your teachers.

Neither the units nor the selections within the units are ordered sequentially. This allows you to use the book in the manner that is best suited to your needs and interests. The only exception is the unit TRACKING THE RIGHT JOB, which takes you through the process of finding and getting a job step by step. If you choose to work through this unit, it would probably be best to start at the beginning and go right through to the end.

The reading selections include articles from newspapers and magazines, short stories, and poems. Each reading selection is accompanied by two sets of activities. The READING AND RE-ACTING activities focus on the content of the selection. The activities encourage you to clarify your understanding of the information presented, and to formulate, express, and share your opinions based on the text. The REACHING OUT activities use the selection as a catalyst to lead you to explore the themes touched on from different angles; and to reach beyond the piece, to do further research, and to make contacts outside of your classroom—in your community, with your family members and friends, and in the business community.

Each unit ends with a set of COMMUNICATION PRO-JECTS. These are major projects that require a significant degree of planning and research. It is unlikely that you will have the time to do more than two communication projects in the year. However, we have included many suggestions to ensure that you will be able to find projects that interest and challenge you.

The key to a successful business is teamwork. Likewise, LAN-GUAGE AT WORK is built around the concept of cooperative team learning: while there are numerous opportunities for you to work on your own or with a partner, in many instances you will be asked to work in a small group. You will find that interacting with your classmates—sharing ideas, planning, researching, and refining one another's work—can be an enjoyable, dynamic, and rewarding way to learn.

We hope that you will enjoy working through this book and that the skills and attitudes you acquire will prepare you for a fulfilling and productive working life.

▶ COMMUNICATION MODEL

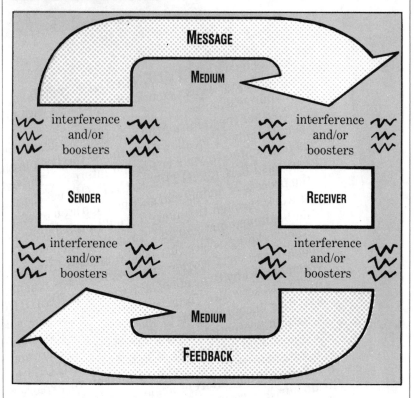

All communication processes follow a form similar to the above model and involve:

MESSAGE: information or instruction that is to be communicated by the SENDER to the RECEIVER
MEDIUM: the method by which the message is transmitted, e.g., conversation, letter, newspaper article
SENDER: the person who is sending out the information
RECEIVER: the person to whom the message is being sent
INTERFERENCE: anything that could hinder the clear transmittal of the message or the feedback
BOOSTER: anything that could help the clear transmittal and reception of the message or the feedback
FEEDBACK: the response from the receiver to the sender. Not all communication processes will result in a feedback.

Each of the activities suggested in this book involves a communication process. Before you begin to work on an activity, try to identify the sender, the receiver, the message, the medium, and the interference and/or boosters that would be involved in the process. This will give you a clear idea of the audience that you are aiming for, the purpose of the activity, and the appropriate format and tone to use.

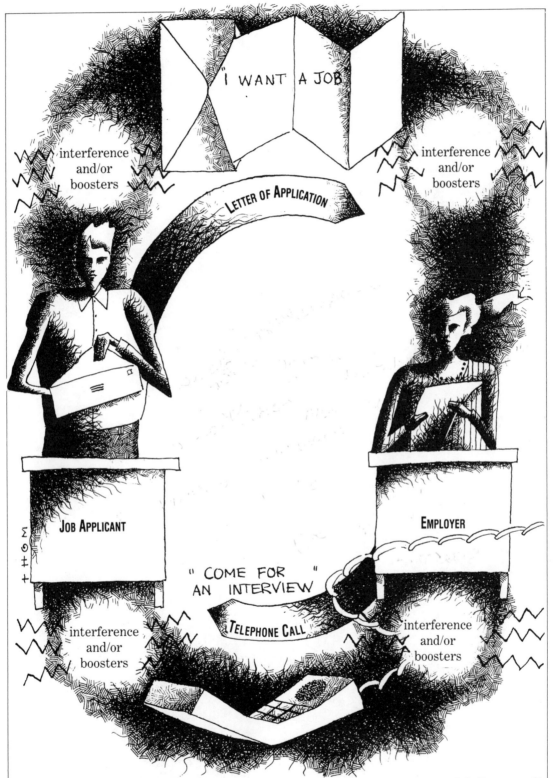

This is how the job-search process would look as a communication model. In a small group, brainstorm some of the interferences and/or boosters that could occur at each stage of this communication process.

►ALL THAT I AM CAPABLE OF BECOMING

In this unit you will be asked to get to know yourself, and to explore all the options that are open to you. The selections and activities will focus on the personal skills that you will need to realize your full potential.

JOURNAL ENTRY – KATHERINE MANSFIELD

Katherine Mansfield was born in New Zealand and established herself as a writer in Britain. These words, written by Katherine Mansfield in 1922, were the last entry in her journal. She died in 1923 at the age of 35.

1922

I want, by understanding myself, to understand others. I want to be all that I am capable of becoming ...

This all sounds very strenuous and serious. But now that I have wrestled with it, it's no longer so. I feel happy – deep down. All is well!

READING AND REACTING

1. With a partner, discuss this final journal entry in terms of what it reveals about Mansfield and how she felt about her life.

REACHING OUT

1. In a journal entry, write a brief overview of your life: note your major accomplishments and successes; describe opportunities that you missed and potential that you neglected. Conclude your journal entry with a paragraph similar to Mansfield's in which you sum up your feelings about your life so far.

2. a) List your personal goals for the coming year and briefly describe to a partner how you plan to achieve them. If necessary, try to improve each other's action plans.

   b) Write a contract that sets a timeline and an action plan for achieving your goals. Trade contracts with a partner and make a note in your journal to review them together at the end of the year to see which goals were or were not met and why.

3. a) Talk to your grandparents or elderly people in your family or community. Ask their advice on how to live a satisfying life. Inquire particularly about what they value most as they look back on their lives. If possible, tape your interviews and play the tape for a small group.

   b) Write about the thoughts and sentiments of one of the people you interviewed. Choose a format that will best express his or her feelings—a poem, a song, a short story, or a letter. With a partner, revise and polish your writing and send a copy to the person about whom you are writing.

▶ THE MUSCLE

Barry Callaghan

LIVIO WAS LATE FOR SCHOOL BECAUSE OF THE morning walk he'd taken with his father, a long walk, and in front of a Greek café with steaming chrome coffee machines in the window his father had insisted that they sit down at one of the small arborite tables and have a thimble-cup of good thick coffee, and he'd smiled and patted Livio's hand as if it were the old days in the village, and then they had hurried along the street to the school and at the door he'd said, "Livio, you listen, always listen to the teacher."

His father had been a stonemason in the Alban Hills outside Rome, and his father loved stone, the way it captured light and held it, he said, like life itself, speckled with colour, and yet it could be dead weight. But the real secret of stone, he said, like the stone he'd cut for the village fountain, was when you held it to your ear; if you listened hard you could hear water, water locked in the stone, and Livio always wondered why the village men sat hunched against the stone with their legs stretched out, never listening, not even to each other, as they laughed and joked and got quietly drunk on wine in the early evening.

When Livio got to the classroom he hung back at the door, not because he was a little late but because Mr. Beale the history teacher always made him feel small and unimportant, made him feel like a stranger who could never belong in this new world. Yet it consoled him to know that all the students felt unimportant when Mr. Beale was teaching.

He was talking about Rome. A tall and easygoing man with a confident air, he liked to amble back and forth in his tweed suit, talking in a rambling, authoritative way about history, and sometimes he would open his long arms wide as if he were offering his students all the wisdom in the world. He never doubted that his students respected him.

Livio hoped he could sneak into the room without Mr. Beale noticing. He never wanted Mr. Beale to notice him again because the last time Livio was late Mr. Beale had said sarcastically, "Where did you come from?" as if he had never seen him before. "You don't belong here, do you? Ah, you do, you do, I do believe

"You don't belong here, do you?"

4

that's true," and all the students had laughed, and later, between classes, they had called out, "Where you from, Livio boy?"

But he hesitated too long at the door and Mr. Beale saw him and cried, "Come in, come in, you're among friends," and someone at the back of the room snickered as Livio sat down, hunched forward, listening to Mr. Beale who was suddenly standing in the light in front of the big window, opening his arms.

"Livio, you should know about this, I bet you know all about Rome and Carthage, yes? So, the great question is did the Romans make a mistake, was it a mistake to kill off Carthage?"

Livio looked up, wondering, a little wide-eyed, shaking his head.

"Carthage," Mr. Beale repeated dryly.

"Yes," Livio said.

"*Delenda est Carthago*," Mr. Beale said.

"Yes."

"Was it a mistake, eh? Was it in their own interest to kill off their enemy for ever?"

"No, Carthage a no mistake," Livio said, smiling.

"Wrong," Mr. Beale said, turning away. "These things always seem so simple, but life's complex, boys," and he turned back to Livio for a moment with a wan smile and then went on to explain that the Romans should have worked out a deal with the Carthaginians in the same way the Americans had come to terms with Germany after the war. "Because you can't get blood out of a stone. You got to get your enemy in debt to you because you can't feed off yourself, which is what Rome ended up doing, and you won't find that in your books," he said. The class was over. He looked pleased with himself.

He put these difficult questions to Livio every day and Livio sometimes stared and said nothing, not sure what was going on, and one day Mr. Beale, throwing open his arms, said, "Livio, you pay attention, always a you listen, you gotta to listen," and the boys broke into loud laughter, and Mr. Beale smiled and patted one of the laughing boys on the back as he walked to the blackboard.

Livio sometimes sat rubbing his knuckles, but then he thought about his father who was no longer a stonemason, only a bricklayer uprooted from a village that had died and been left behind, obsolete and empty, and now he was here laying bricks and working like a day labourer and never complaining. When Mr. Beale went by and tapped Livio on the shoulder, saying, "You do well Livio, you getta better every day," he sat locked in silence, confused and angry, remembering a little mute boy everyone in the village had made fun of, and his father had told him that there were voices inside the boy, deep inside, and all he had to do was open up the boy's mouth and put his ear as close as he could and he'd hear them, he'd hear strange old grandfathers whispering,

*"Come in,
come in, you're
among friends,"*

6

and one day Livio had pried the frightened boy's mouth open, staring down into the dark gaping hole that smelled so sour he had turned away, surprised as the boy broke into tears, his mouth hanging open, and Livio, sitting very straight in his seat, felt like crying, afraid that Mr. Beale might come and force open his mouth. Closing his eyes, Livio drifted off into a dream of village evenings and how he used to amuse his father and the men around the fountain with the little trick muscle in his wrist.

One afternoon Livio rolled up his sleeve and felt the two little cords that ran down his right wrist, and then he put a coin on the cords, clenching his fist, slowly turning his wrist. The cords tensed and then a small muscle popped up, the coin flipped over and landed perfectly on his wrist. Livio smiled. The boy sitting behind Livio poked him and said, "Hey, do that again." Livio shook his head. "Come on, I want to see that again."

Livio put the coin on the cords, clenched his fist and turned his wrist and the boy leaned forward. Livio, suddenly at ease, laughed with the boy as the coin flipped over.

"What's going on there?"

Livio slumped down in his seat, but the boy leaned into the aisle and said, "Livio has a trick, sir."

"Livio has a trick. What kind of trick?"

Mr. Beale, buttoning his suit coat, came to their seats.

"Let's see your trick, Livio."

Livio shook his head.

"Come on, we your friends, we gotta see everything you canna do." Mr. Beale turned to the class. "Don't we class?"

The boys shouted yes and the boy behind Livio pushed him. "Go on, show them."

Livio looked up and saw Mr. Beale, aloof, stroking his neck, the light on his narrow face from the big window, and Mr. Beale said, "You show us your little trick, eh, Livio."

Livio put the coin on his wrist. All the boys were watching him. The little muscle popped up and the coin flipped over. The class was silent and then someone called out, "Do it again."

Livio quickly put the coin back on his wrist, but Mr. Beale said no to Livio and then wheeled on the class with a wave of his arms. "We don't a turn thisa room into a circus." But there was no laughter. "We can't have this in the middle of class," he said sternly. "We've got work to do."

"But you said you wanted to see it," a boy cried.

Mr. Beale shrugged, as if what had happened was of no consequence because they were all friends and it was over, but Livio suddenly stood up and thrust the coin out at the teacher, who, startled, waved Livio aside, but Livio held out the coin to him again.

"You want me to try your little trick?"

"*You show us your little trick, eh, Livio.*"

Livio nodded and sat down.

"You think no one else can do your little trick?"

Mr. Beale rolled up his sleeve and put the coin on his wrist. Clenching his fist, he twisted his wrist back and forth, yet the coin stayed still. He flushed, staring, his long arm extended, his hand white. The class began to laugh. Humiliated by the laughter, he tossed the coin into Livio's lap and went back to his desk, picking up a book and then putting it down. He began to write all the dates of Caesar's conquests on the blackboard and he told them to memorize the dates.

When the class was over all the boys gathered around Livio. They smacked him on the back and asked him to do the trick again. Livio shuffled as if he were too shy. Mr. Beale, trying to be friendly and part of the good feeling, called out, "You don't want to forget the football game, boys," but no one paid any attention. Livio saw the teacher lift his arm as if to speak, but the boys were all laughing and Mr. Beale sat down. The room cleared and Livio and the teacher were alone.

With a loose smile on his face, Mr. Beale got up as if wanting to be bigger than Livio. Feeling awkward for a moment, Livio

finally looked up, smiling. "My English is a pretty good, eh?" he said helpfully. "I think I do pretty good."

"Very well, Livio, you've done very well."

"I think a so."

Livio didn't know what to do. There was a button missing on the teacher's suit-coat sleeve, and Mr. Beale stood twisting the loose nub of thread. He seemed to be waiting for some snide little swipe, sure that it was coming, but then Livio suddenly reached out and took Mr. Beale's hand. His own blue wide-open eyes had a vulnerable look, yet his grip on Mr. Beale's hand was firm. "I don't hold a no hard feelings, Mr. Teacher," he said. "You neither, I think, eh?"

"No, no. Of course not, Livio," he said stiffly, as if sure he was being mocked in some new way by a boy who deeply disliked him.

"Sir, it's only a trick," Livio said, fumbling for the right words. "I practise. You practise, too, sir, eh?" and he took the coin out of his pocket and put it in Mr. Beale's hand, the one he was holding. "Take it, sir. Friends now, eh?"

"Well, now, see here . . . " Mr. Beale began, his face suddenly flushing, and because of the way Mr. Beale was staring at him Livio felt uneasy. Mr. Beale now looked lonely and disappointed, a look Livio had seen in the eyes of men slouched around his father's fountain.

"Livio," Mr. Beale began, and then his hand tightened on Livio's, the grip suddenly so tight it was painful. "Thank you. Thank you very much," he said, his voice breaking a little. Looking at the coin he said quickly, "Yes Livio, I'll really hold on to this," as if he had hold of his self-respect again.

READING AND REACTING

1. With a partner, make a list of similarities and differences between Livio and Mr. Beale.

2. Write a character study of Livio and of Mr. Beale in which you evaluate the behaviour of each.

3. In a small group, discuss the following:

a) the ways in which Mr. Beale makes Livio feel like an outsider, and why he does this

b) the significance of the incident with the muscle trick for Livio and for Mr. Beale

4. Write a letter to Mr. Beale in which you explain how important it is for Livio to develop a sense of self-worth and how he should help.

REACHING OUT

1. In the voice of Mr. Beale, Livio, or one of the students, write a journal entry in which you describe your feelings about the muscle trick incident and what you learned from it.

2. a) In a small group, share experiences in which you or someone you know has had the experience of feeling like an outsider.

b) Write an account, a short story, or a poem based on the experience of someone who has had to come to terms with the need to
   (i) feel accepted
         or
   (ii) accept himself or herself

3. Rewrite the ending to "The Muscle" in a way that you feel is believable.

4. In a small group, discuss the relationship between learning and teaching. Consider the responsibilities that would be involved for the learner and for the teacher to make the relationship most fulfilling.

How to Harness That 'Missing' Brain Power

Frank Feather

Our education system has taught us all how not to think!

But there is no need to worry. With a little practice it is possible for us all to overcome that handicap and become both creative and opportunistic thinkers. Indeed, it is necessary for our future because already 75 percent of us are "knowledge workers" employed in Canada's new information economy.

The key to our future success, individually and collectively, is to develop our brain-power. The power of ideas is that they create wealth. Few economists, politicians, educators, or business managers understand this. But those who do are reaping the rewards. Shouldn't you?

Fortunately, creative thinking, or what I call opportunistic thinking, can be learned—just like riding a bicycle or driving a car. Yes, it's that easy.

Creativity results in a new idea when a breakthrough occurs in thinking, such as "when the penny drops." This is the so-called "Eureka effect" as when Archimedes sat in his bathtub and saw the level of the water rise, or when the apple fell on Newton's head.

The "Eureka!" breakthrough comes when we practise creative thinking. It usually occurs when the so-called "right-brain" clicks into action. The best example is the punch line in a joke. "Oh yes, I see!" (the point of the joke) is the precise moment when the right-brain is activated.

What is the "right-brain"? This refers to the right hemisphere of the brain. In an over-simplistic sense, brain research shows that creative attributes like imagination, response to patterns and pictures, emotional reactions, etc., are right-brain responses.

The left hemisphere of the brain looks after logical responses such as talking, walking, mathematical counting, and so on. Thus, when you are chatting on the telephone, your left-brain is doing the talking but your right-brain is doing the doodling on the telephone message pad.

The problem is that our right-brain functions have not been trained very well. Indeed, our education system has stressed linear, left-brain rote learning while creativity and innovation have been suppressed.

But creative problem solving and innovation can be learned by giving the right-brain some simple exercises that I call "The 20-Minute Brain Work-Out".

Here is one exercise called "Squeeze and Stretch". In this brain work-out you "stretch" a problem out to see just how much there is inside and how all of its parts relate to the whole. To stretch out a problem situation and discover its parts, you ask yourself a chain of questions beginning with "What . . . ?"

For example: What is the problem about? Answer: Judo. What is "Judo" all about? Answer: Physical efficiency. What is physical efficiency? Answer: Finding

11

optimal use of body movement.

The next step is to "squeeze" the problem down to its essential elements in order to view them in the correct proportional relationship to the overall environment. To squeeze a problem down to its essentials, ask a chain of questions beginning with "Why . . . ?" For example: Why am I doing this? Answer: I want to. Why do I want to? Answer: It makes me happy. Why will it make me happy? . . . and so on. There are dozens of similar exercises which people can practise in order to get their brains out of neutral and into better mental shape.

The massive problems we face today require innovative solutions because the old ways simply don't (won't) work any more.

Because creative thinking has not been taught in our educational system, Canada lags behind most of its competitors in the industrialized world in innovative research and development.

We must recognize that intellectual capital has become the most important asset of our economic growth and prosperity.

Every Canadian, from kindergartener to prime minister, should be doing two hours a week of creative thinking. If that can occur, then indeed the 21st century will belong to Canada.

Frank Feather is editor/publisher of *Executive Ideas* and *Canada Tomorrow* newsletters. Sample issues available from 22 College Street, Suite 107, Toronto, Ontario M5G 1K2.

R E A D I N G A N D R E A C T I N G

1. "Our education system has taught us all how not to think."

a) Explain to a classmate who has not read this article what the author means by his dramatic opening statement.

b) Have your classmate read the article. Together, decide whether the author has successfully supported his opening statement.

2. In a small group, choose a problem and do the "Squeeze and Stretch" exercise suggested by Frank Feather. Appoint a group member as leader of the session. The leader will ask the questions and try to keep the session focussed on the problem at hand.

R E A C H I N G O U T

1. With a partner, write a letter to the principal of a school that has an alternative education program, to request permission to visit one of the classes. Follow up the letter with a telephone call to the principal for his or her response, and to make arrangements for the visit. Observe the activities in class time, and try to talk to teachers and students afterwards to find out how they feel about the program. Make notes throughout your visit: list the classroom activities, materials used, classroom atmosphere, teaching style, and student reaction. After the visit, write a report in which

you evaluate the merits of the program, and compare it to the regular program. Include recommendations on what might be incorporated into the regular program. Revise and edit your report. Send a copy to your principal and the principal of the school you visited. Read your report to the class and ask for comments.

2. Creative thinking, by Archimedes in his bath, and by Newton when an apple fell on his head, led each man to a significant discovery.

a) Imagine that you are a journalist for a children's magazine and write a short article about the events surrounding either discovery. Explain Archimedes' Principle or Newton's Theory of Gravity as clearly as possible for your young readers. (Consult your science teacher if you need help.) Polish your writing with a partner's help. Arrange to read your article to an elementary school class. Be prepared to answer the children's questions.

or

b) With a partner, role-play a scene in which a reporter interviews either Archimedes or Newton about his "Eureka!" breakthrough.

3. "Our education system has stressed linear, left-brain rote learning while creativity and innovation have been suppressed."

a) In a small group, research the current theories on right-brain/left-brain thinking. Consult your school librarian for materials to read.

b) Evaluate your courses and try to decide whether the above quotation is true of your school. Support your view with examples. Follow up with suggestions for improvement.

c) Do an oral presentation for the class based on your evaluation. Invite your principal and other teachers to attend.

or

Stage a debate based on the above quotation.

4. In a group, ask for permission to plan and conduct a workshop in another class, in which you apply Frank Feather's techniques to a problem-solving activity.

▶ 'Soften' Is Password to Better Social Contact

Arthur C. Wassmer

The most frequently stated complaint of shy people is, "I never know what to say."

Forget your worry about what to say, and listen to what the other person is saying. Keeping your mouth shut and listening are two entirely different activities. It's true that you've been listening for a good part of your life, but what you've been listening to has been your own anxiety.

Non-shy people use ritual questions as a way of "breaking the ice" at the beginning of a conversation. Some common examples of ritual questions are, "Where are you from?" "What do you do?" and even "What's

your name?" The primary purpose of these questions is really to convey the message "I am interested in you" and "I think I would like to know you."

Since shy persons often say very little, their body language becomes an important means of communication—a way in which others can get some small idea of what they are thinking.

The most obvious way in which you signal people that you feel different or inferior is in the way you relate to space. We all behave as if the real boundaries of our bodies are not our skin but extend as much as three feet in every direction.

▼ 'Closed' Position

When you huddle in a corner or against a wall, you are saying, "Please don't come and make contact with me—I'm afraid you'll discover how different I am."

Your physical behaviour communicates much the same message. Trying to be as invisible as possible, you use as few gestures as you can because gestures attract attention. Your posture is generally "closed"—arms and/or legs crossed—and this signal discourages others from entering your space.

Eye movements are another important type of non-verbal communication. Shy people do not meet other people's eyes with any regularity.

Shy people also control their facial expressions carefully. If I am convinced of my inferiority or oddity, it makes real sense that I should provide you with as few clues as possible about what I am thinking or feeling. Maybe if I don't give any evidence to the contrary, you will think I'm normal even when I believe I'm not. I don't nod or otherwise indicate that I agree with you because you might be pulling my leg, and then think how foolish I'd look.

By avoiding physical closeness, by displaying closed and withdrawn physical postures, and by giving little or no facial indication of thoughts or feelings, the shy person creates an ambiguous situation for others, and they become anxious. Most shy people are not even aware that their behaviour makes others uncomfortable. Typically they are so preoccupied with their own fear that they fail even to notice what effect they have on others.

FIRST STEP

You can learn to use non-verbal signals to let others know that you're interested in them and in what they feel and think.

A first step in communicating that you are "open for contact" is to move toward the other person. A distance of three to six feet is necessary between people who are making initial contact.

If you find yourself more than six feet away from someone you wish to talk to, don't be afraid to get up and move toward that person. The person will receive this message at an almost subconscious level as meaning, "I want to be closer to you."

Most shy people, in their desire not to be discovered or to intrude on the space of another, tend to pull up or lean back. Unfortunately, the other person often interprets the backward lean as an indication of disapproval or disinterest. When you are sitting, lean forward toward the person you are talking to. When standing, simply

15

incline your head toward the person. When you alter your body position in this way, the message you're transmitting is, "I don't want to miss a word you're saying."

The average shy person tends to "cover up" physically by crossing arms or legs. He or she is imitating the turtle that pulls into its shell at the approach of danger. It may feel awkward at first to remain physically "open" for any period of time. Be assured, however, that your open posture presents a very strong, non-verbal message to others that says, "I am open to what you have to say. Please share yourself with me."

If you are like most shy people, you have actively avoided touching other people or being touched by them, because you have intuitively known that touch is a very powerful way of making contact.

Some kinds of touching convey specific meanings. An arm around the shoulders or waist indicates companionship. Using both hands to shake hands suggests warmth. Touching a seated person's knee with a finger serves to get his or her attention, while an open hand placed on the knee is a sign of affection.

A third group of non-verbal signals in-

volves your face. The first and most important signal is eye contact. The shy person avoids meeting the other person's gaze. To the other person your avoidance of eye contact presents an almost impassable barrier to communication.

A good way to train yourself to more consistent eye contact is to work into it by five-second intervals. At first, try to hold the eyes of another person for five seconds at a time. When you feel quite comfortable

with five seconds (as you will in a remarkably short time), try 10 seconds, then 15, and so on.

Another powerful non-verbal signal is smiling. When you smile while listening to someone, the message you are transmitting is, "I am enjoying being with you." Shy people are typically tense and anxious, so it's no wonder they don't have much experience in smiling. But as your anxiety level decreases, practise smiling as often as you can when in social situations, except when the other person's subject makes it inappropriate. As you convey your enjoyment at being with other persons, you'll find that they will relax, become less fearful of you and begin really to enjoy being with you.

POWERFUL SIGNALS

Finally, you can transmit very powerful signals of interest and acknowledgment by nodding your head. Head-nodding, as well as smiling and other facial expressions (frowning, concentrating, looking disgusted, raising the eyebrows in surprise), are ways of being responsive to the communications of another person.

When others observe you nodding, smiling, and otherwise being responsive to them, the signal is clear. They know that they are being carefully and attentively listened to. When you nod, you're not saying "I agree"; you are saying "Yes, I hear what you're saying and I think I understand."

Non-verbal signals are produced by internal thoughts and feelings. You can demonstrate this for yourself. Make a fist,

tighten the muscles of your arm, clench your teeth, and begin to breathe heavily. Within moments you will find yourself thinking something that makes you angry.

You can use the letters of the word SOFTEN as a way of jogging your memory to each one of the important non-verbal signals.

S mile
O pen posture
F orward lean
T ouch
E ye contact
N od

After a few weeks of practising the SOFTEN checklist, experiment with yourself to prove the power of these signals. Once, twice, or three times (enough to satisfy your curiosity), consistently do the opposite of every signal on the checklist. Don't smile. Close your posture. Lean back and away. Don't touch; look anywhere but at the person's eyes. Don't nod or give any signal that you are listening.

FUMBLE FOR WORDS

Now watch the effect that your old characteristic behaviours have on people. They become anxious and uneasy. They fumble for words. They ask questions. In a short period of time, they find a reason to break off the contact. When you try this, you will become very aware of the effect your non-verbal signalling has had on people for much of your life.

Reverse use of the SOFTEN checklist can play an occasional but highly useful role in discouraging people whom you are quite sure you don't want to talk to. You will find that reverse SOFTENing very successfully fends off unwanted approaches. These signals also discourage all but the most aggressive sales people.

READING AND REACTING

1. With a partner, read this article carefully and identify all the ways that people can use body positions and gestures to send non-verbal messages. List these messages in chart form under two headings:
   —Non-verbal messages that invite communication
   —Non-verbal messages that discourage communication
   Post the chart on the bulletin board.

2. Write a letter to a sibling or a friend who is very shy. Describe the techniques that Wassmer suggests for using body language to hide and overcome shyness. If possible, include in your letter personal anecdotes of how you overcame shyness at some point in your life.

REACHING OUT

1. Try the experiment described in the article: Hold a conversation with an acquaintance and use the SOFTEN techniques. Half-way through the conversation, switch your approach and do the opposite of what is recommended. Observe your listener's reactions in both cases. Before the experiment, you may wish to arrange for a partner to observe the whole scene and report his or her views to you later. Share your findings and those of your partner with others who have also carried out the experiment. Decide if the SOFTEN techniques were effective.

2. Role-play or mime a scene in which body language helps to get a message across. Replay the same scene using non-verbal gestures and body postures to obstruct the message. Have the audience make notes on the body language that is used and comment on its effectiveness.

3. Design a poster featuring the non-verbal signals represented in the acronym SOFTEN. Display the poster in the class.

Watch What You're Saying!

An estimated three-quarters of a manager's day is taken up in verbal communications. But the importance of the spoken word is often overlooked. People take their ability to say what they mean for granted. Making your point is not as easy as it seems . . .

It was December 19, 1942. Japanese forces were pushing the British, Indian, and Canadian defenders of Hong Kong back across the rocky spine of that island. The British general conducting the defence ordered his battle-torn brigades to withdraw and regroup for a counter-attack.

The order was duly passed by field telephone to an artillery battery to "get out of action." The battery commander took the message literally. He destroyed his guns, thus killing any hope of repelling the enemy assault.

This is a dramatic example of how faulty communications can be nothing less than disastrous in the conduct of an organization. It happened in the heat of battle, but the same type of destructive muddle can occur in any business or other organization in the course of an otherwise tranquil day.

The cause of the breakdown was careless wording. The order was ambiguous, having more than one possible meaning. Ambiguous instructions are only one of the ways in which language is misused in the workplace. And every time it is misused, it is capable of throwing sand in the gears.

Careless words cost needless effort, time, and money. If a message is misunderstood, things are done improperly; when the misunderstanding is discovered, they have to be done all over again. Because ideas are badly expressed, an organization may adopt the wrong policy. Verbal misunderstandings give rise to friction and resentment among co-workers, superiors, and subordinates, damaging corporate morale.

Every organization is at the mercy of language. The marvellous technical advances made lately in "communications systems" have done little to diminish the importance of the spoken and written word. The new electronic hardware is just that—hardware. It is like so many hammers and saws that are only as good as the material on which, and the skill with which, they are used.

Granted, much of the traffic that moves through the communications systems is in the form of figures. But even figures must be explained verbally if they are to make sense. In any case, it is remarkable that people in organizations do not try to be as exact with language as they are with numerical data. Men and women who will painstakingly double-check every calculation will take a hit-and-miss approach to what they say.

Similarly, people who take considerable care in composing a letter or memo will pay little attention to the words they speak while doing business. Most of the exchanges of information and ideas in the working world are oral, whether face to face, in meetings or over the telephone. A recent study of business communication practices found that the average manager spends roughly 30 percent of his or her time speaking and 45 percent listening. So a full three-quarters of a manager's working day is devoted to talking or hearing other people talk.

Yet the spoken word is the most neglected aspect of communications. Why? Apparently because people feel that oral language comes naturally. As training consultant Beverly Potter wrote, "Few understand the relationship between the specific words used and their effectiveness in supervising others. It is easy to believe that the basic message to be communicated is more important than the words themselves. It is assumed that once the idea is straight, the words will just fall into place."

The excuse for not striving for exactitude in the spoken word is that language is an inexact medium. Words mean different things to different people at different times. For example, a survey once turned up 164 different definitions of the word "culture." "Meaning is in people, not words," says communications lecturer Thomas E. Harris. "Words mean only what we assign them to mean."

That is debatable. Dictionaries do give explicit definitions of words, and people are taking a chance when they depart from them. For instance, it is said that in the constitution of New Jersey, the founding fathers of that state used the term "biannual" instead of "biennial," the former meaning twice a year and the latter meaning every two years. As a result of this slip, the legislature was obliged to sit every six months, not every two years as intended. All the legislators knew what they *meant* to say, but they had to abide by the definition of what they actually said.

"The difference between the almost right and the right word is really a very big matter—'tis the difference between the lightning bug and the lightning," as Mark Twain put it. The only true standard for the rightness of a word is in the dictionary—not in what one person or another might guess it means.

True, a language is a living organism that grows and changes as new and redefined terms enter the popular vocabulary. Nevertheless, if you used a term in a sense that is not spelt out in the dictionary, you can never be certain that your listener perceives it in that sense.

The precise dictionary definition of a word is sometimes superseded by common usage, so that using it in its "correct" sense also runs the risk of creating confusion. Though it is a pity to have to deprive ourselves of such "words in transition," it is best to avoid their use, in oral communication at least.

"It is important that the language medium should offer as little as possible resistance to the thought current, and this end is attained only when the symbols of language are ones that convey precisely the same meaning to all who use the language," Eric Partridge wrote in his *Standard English*. Without the broad and basic standards contained in the dictionary, our society would be a Tower of Babel. It would be as if it were left to each individual to decide the length of a metre or the weight of a kilogram.

▼

It Sounds Impressive, but What Does It Mean?

It would, of course, simply be silly to expect the majority of people to exercise a high degree of verbal precision in casual conversation. We all use verbal shorthand, and we all think at the same time as we talk. Our word formation sometimes lags behind our thought formation, and we skip over the intervals. Among people who know us well, this is of no great consequence.

Their familiarity with our speech habits and "body language" enables them to bridge the shortcomings in what we say.

But when we are doing business, it is not too much for our employers and associates to ask that we think out the best way of saying something before we say it. In conveying the instructions, information, and judgments that make an organization run, there should be a firm grasp of the meaning of the words used among all concerned.

This calls for precision. Many people seem to shrink from attempting to be precise, presumably because they feel that if they use "big words," others will not understand them. In fact, precision can be achieved with the plain words that are in almost everyone's vocabulary. With a little forethought, people with a solid stock of standard language can adjust their speech to the hearer's ability to comprehend.

Those who ignore precision may also fear being thought of as pompous. They evidently believe that to be precise is to use a great many words in refining what they have to say. On the contrary, being precise is the opposite of being long-winded. Precision demands that you use one exact word in the place of many inexact ones. True, lawyers will speak repetitively in an apparently long-winded fashion in efforts to avoid any possible misunderstanding. While this may be effective in the courtroom, it usually defeats clarity anywhere else.

We all know people who regale their listeners with big words and long phrases in the hope that it will make them seem learned and intelligent. In business these days, they are likely to indulge in "buzzword" phrases like "interactive parameters" and "integrated criteria." It sounds impressive, but what does it mean?

In fact, people who indulge in buzzwords might not be sure themselves of what they mean. Verbal smoke-screens are often thrown up to cover up defective thinking or a lack of knowledge. They may also serve as a cover for someone's true opinions or intentions. It is a standard tactic of politics for speakers to cloud over their meaning when the truth does them no good.

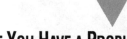

IF YOU HAVE A PROBLEM, LOOK FIRST TO YOURSELF

Buzzwords fall under the general heading of jargon, which, in standard usage, is the "inside" language current among experts on a subject. Jargon is a useful verbal shorthand in its place. When two mathematicians talk about parameters, for instance, they are referring to something definite. When two laypeople toss the word about, they are talking about something obscure.

There are those who inject jargon into their speech because they feel that it is up-to-date or "with it." They should be informed that jargon and the practice of flaunting it for effect is anything but new. Almost 300 years ago John Locke wrote: "Vague and insignificant forms of speech, and abuse of language, have so often passed for the mysteries of science; and hard or misplaced words with little or no meaning have, by prescription, such a right to be mistaken for deep learning and the height of speculation, that it will not be easy to persuade either those who speak or those who hear them, that they are but the covers of ignorance and the hindrance of knowledge."

The misapplication of jargon and similar abuses of the spoken word defy the rule that the sender of a message is responsible for its reception. When communications are fouled, we often hear people complain: "The stupid so-and-so didn't listen to what I said." If you have a communication problem with a person, look first to yourself for the solution. In most cases, the speaker, not the hearer, is to blame when a message is confused.

WARNING: SLOPPY LANGUAGE MAY LEAD TO SLOPPY THINKING

Words are symbols for thoughts, so that when language is distorted, it distorts reason and reality. Joseph Joubert likened language to glass, which "darkens everything it does not help us see." Some figures of speech are like frosted glass to begin with. These include slang, profanity, and *clichés*, which are delivered so automatically that they fail to focus on the ideas and sentiments a person wants to express.

"The cliché is the greatest labour-saving device ever invented by man; it eliminates

the necessity of thought," quipped Richard Tobin. True enough; but the link between the way people talk and the way they think is not as direct as it might appear. Some intelligent people are naturally inarticulate, while others litter their speech with slang, clichés and jargon. The danger is that sloppy language may lead to the habit of sloppy thinking. For most of us (visual artists, mathematicians and musicians excepted) language is the raw material of our mental processes. If the words that form our thoughts are imprecise, then those thoughts are liable to be imprecise, too.

In any case, it is logical to conclude that someone who talks like a fool really is a fool. If such a person represents an organization to the outside world, the organization looks foolish by association. When it comes to personal advancement, the person most likely to succeed is the one who communicates clearly. This is because skill with words is likely to be reflected in a person's record. "He who can explain himself can command what he wants," said G. H. Palmer. "He who cannot is left to the poverty of individual resource; for men will do what we desire only when persuaded."

So, as Shakespeare urged in *Othello*, "mend your speech a little, lest it mar your fortunes." Unfortunately, this will not be easy for some. Their schooling has left them with little grounding in English usage, and with inferior standards to live up to. A whole generation has come to adulthood under the misapprehension that language is a matter of "doing your own thing"—and, like, they're sort of tongue-tied, you know?

▼

THRIFT WITH WORDS HELPS TO FIGHT VERBAL INFLATION

Not that the shoddy standards are confined to the younger generation. In recent years society at large has been suffering from verbal inflation, which stems from much the same reasons as the economic kind. The reckless spending of some words has subtracted from their value. In the hands of the media, a problem has become a "crisis," a change, a "revolution," and an outstanding performer, a "superstar." Sportscasters are probably the leading contributors to the inflationary process. One reported that a team was on a "two-game losing streak."

In economics, a general dedication to thrift is the strongest shield against inflation. In the fight against verbal inflation, we can all do our bit by spending words with greater care. There is a certain cost-efficiency in language which depends on how quickly and carefully it carries its message to the listener. Now is the time for people—especially management people—to examine the effectiveness of their speech with productivity in mind.

Effective speech entails avoiding vague and clumsy words that are capable of misinterpretation. Among those common in business and the bureaucracy these days are "implement" (which could mean *do*, *start*, *carry out*, or *execute*); "finalize" (which could mean *finish*, *stop*, *conclude*, or *complete*); and "factor" (which could mean *element*, *part*, *circumstance*, or *consideration*). When a word is susceptible to so many differing meanings, it in itself comes to mean nothing. An effective vocabulary has no room for meaningless words.

IT'S NOT THE WORDS SO MUCH AS HOW THEY'RE PUT TOGETHER

There are few among us whose vocabularies could not be improved by occasionally browsing through a dictionary. Improving your vocabulary does not necessarily mean adding words to it; it may mean learning the exact meanings of the simple, recognizable words that make up the bulk of the English language, and using them in their fullest sense.

Communication problems often arise not from a lack of adequate words, but from putting them in the wrong places. This has to do with syntax, which is the way phrases and sentences are formed. In spite of the differences between writing and speaking, you can gather a fair idea of how words are put together to their best effect by observing the syntax of good writers. You will find that the most readable and informative of them avoid complex constructions, setting forth their thoughts in straightforward sentences. In the same manner, the easiest speakers to understand are those who express themselves in simple sentences and do not digress from their point.

Why should people bother about such things? First of all, if they learn to express themselves better, they will get along better with others. Second, clarity in communications helps to get things done. It follows that a good communicator will have better career prospects than a poor one. So it is in your own interest—as well as the economy's and the society's—to "mend your speech."

R E A D I N G A N D R E A C T I N G

1. "In most cases, the speaker, not the hearer, is to blame when a message is confused." In a small group, identify the factors mentioned in the article that contribute to, and hinder, effective oral communication. State each idea in one clear sentence and present all the statements in a two-column chart like the following:

For Effective Communication	
Do	Do Not

2. a) List the words that are important to the meaning of "Watch What You're Saying!" Consult a dictionary and write beside each word the precise meaning for the word as it is used in the passage. Exchange words with your classmate and test your ability to define the word correctly.

b) Explain the following phrases in the context of the sentence in which each is used. Rewrite the sentences omitting the phrases, but make sure that the same meaning is communicated. Exchange sentences with a partner and decide whether the original or the rewritten sentences are clearer.

    i) throwing sand in the gears

    ii) hit-and-miss approach

    iii) Tower of Babel

R E A C H I N G   O U T

1. In a small group, exchange stories of times when an unclear message you gave or received was misunderstood. Suggest why the misunderstanding occurred and how it could have been avoided. Present the most interesting story to the class.

or

Write a short story based on the problems that arise when an important message is not made clear.

2. a) In a small group, list the buzzwords, clichés, and expressions currently used by your friends. These words may be slang or the kinds of expressions that are "in" for the moment. After each group member writes a brief definition for each word or phrase, compare definitions. Ask adults to define some of the items on your list, and compare their definitions with yours. Present several examples of your findings to the class and assess the implication of using language that does not have a commonly-held meaning.

b) Each specialized area of business develops its own "in-talk" that includes buzzwords or jargon. Frequently, no one knows precisely what these words mean. Collect one such word used in education from a teacher, and one from a person in business (indicate the kind of business the word came from.) Pool your words with other classmates on a board list. As a class, discuss what the words might mean. Point out the problems with using buzzwords, and suggest precise words to take their place.

3. a) With a partner, select an editorial from your local newspaper.

b) Script the casual conversation that might have taken place between the reporter who covered the story and the editor who wrote the opinion piece.

c) Write a radio news story that covers the events dealt with in the editorial.

d) Compare the two versions of the story in terms of word choice and style.

▶ A LITTLE ENGLISH IS A DANGEROUS THING

Bill Bryson

Any language in which the unassuming word 'fly' can signify an annoying insect, a means of travel, or a critical part of a gentleman's apparel is bound to be full of booby traps for the unwary foreigner.

Some diligent scholar once sat down and worked out that there are more than 5,000 languages in the world, but it appears that he overlooked one of the more splendid ones—fractured English. About 360 million people around the world speak English and the rest, it seems, try to. Putting it mildly, the results are often a trifle irregular.

Consider, for example, this sign in a hotel lift in Belgrade: "To move the cabin, push button for wishing floor. If the cabin should enter more persons, each one should press number of wishing floor. Driving is then going alphabetically by natural order."

Or this warning to motorists in Tokyo: "When a passenger of the foot heave in sight, tootle the horn. Trumpet at him melodiously at first, but if he still obstacles your passage then tootle him with vigour."

The following instructions graced a packet of convenience food from Italy: "Besmear a backing pan, previously buttered with a good tomato sauce and after, dispose the cannelloni, lightly distanced between them in a only couch".

Clearly the writer of this message was not about to let a little ignorance of English stand in the way of a good meal. In fact, it would appear that one of the beauties of the English language is that, even with the most tenuous grasp, you can speak volumes if you show enough enthusiasm—a willingness to tootle with vigour, as it were.

Take this hearty announcement in a Yugoslavian hotel: "The flattening of underwear with pleasure is the job of the chambermaid. Turn to her straight away." Or this polite request in a Tokyo establishment: "Is forbitten to steal the hotel towels please. If you are not person to do such thing is please not to read notis." The syntax may not be entirely faultless, but how could any two messages be more brimming over with discretion and goodwill?

To be fair, English is full of booby traps for the unwary foreigner. Any language where the unassuming word "fly" signifies an annoying insect, a means of travel, and a critical part of a gentleman's apparel is, it should be obvious, asking to be mangled.

Consider for a moment the plight of the poor foreigner who has to learn that in the English-speaking world one writes down a name but lights up a cigarette; that one can slow up or slow down but can only speed up and not speed down; that the simple word "set" has 58 uses as a noun, 126 as a verb and 10 as a participial adjective.

With such baffling complexities to contend with, it is perhaps little wonder that the traveller to Hong Kong can see a dentist's sign announcing: "Teeth extracted by the latest methodists." Or even this exhortation outside a tailor's in Jordan: "Order now your summer suit. Because is big rush we will execute customers in strict rotation." Another notice, this time in a Bangkok dry-cleaning establishment, suggests: "Drop your trousers here for best results."

The vagaries of the English language are such that even native speakers cannot always communicate effectively—as almost every Briton learns on the first day in America. Indeed, Robert Burchfield, editor of the *Oxford English Dictionary*, not long ago created a stir in linguistic circles on both sides of the Atlantic when he announced his belief that American English and English English are drifting apart so rapidly that within 200 years the two nations won't be able to understand each other at all.

That may be. But if the Briton and American of the twenty-second century baffle each other, it seems possible that they won't confuse many others—not, at least, if the rest of the world continues expropriating words and phrases at its present rate.

Already Germans speak of "die Teen-agers" and "das Walkout" and German politicians snarl "No comment" at German journalists. Italian women coat their faces with "col-cream," Romanians ride the "trolleybus" and Spaniards, when they're chilly, put on "sueters." Almost everyone in the world speaks on the telephone or the "telefoon" or even (in China) the "tel le fung." And almost everywhere you can find hamburgers, nightclubs, and television.

The French have always viewed this creeping polyglotism with a touch of disdain, and in 1977 introduced legislation outlawing all foreign words in advertisements. Instantly exiled were "le week-end," "le hot dog," "le brainstorm," and "les refuelling stops," among many others. "Flash-back" became "restrospectif," "hit

27

parade" became "palmares," and "chewing gum" became "pâte à macher."

To be sure, all too many French advertisers had latched on to "le snobisme" appeal of English, but as one French advertising executive moaned: "The problem is that English is a crisp selling language and French is not. Saying a thing in French takes more words and sounds dull."

Elsewhere, however, English continues to be a growth industry, even if it is sometimes adopted in a rather striking manner. The Serbo-Croats, for instance, picked up the English word "nylon" but took it to mean a kind of shabby and disreputable variation, so that a nylon hotel is a brothel, while a nylon beach is where nudists frolic.

Other nations have left the words largely intact but given the spelling a novel twist. Thus the Ukrainian "herkot" might seem wholly foreign until you realize that that a "herkot" is what a Ukrainian goes to the barber for. Similarly, unless you heard them spoken, you might not instantly recognize "ajskrym," "muving pikceris" and "peda" as the Polish for ice-cream, the Lithuanian for moving pictures and the Yugoslavian for pay-day.

The Japanese in particular are masters at the art of seizing a foreign word and alternately beating it and aerating it until it sounds something like a native product.

Thus the "sumato" (smart) Japanese person seasons his or her conversation with "upatodatu" expressions like "gurama foto" (glamour photo), "hi-kurasu" (high class) and "kyapitaru gein" (capital gain). Awkward words are simply and brusquely truncated—"modern girl" becomes "moga" and "commercial" ends up merely a short, sharp "cm."

Whatever the motivation for fracturing the English language, it certainly is not a new phenomenon. More than a century ago Mark Twain passed on to the world this hypothetical conversation he came across in a genuine Portuguese-English phrase book:

"How is that gentleman who you did speak by and by?"

"Is a German."

"I did think him Englishman."

"He is of the Saxony side."

"He speaks the French very well."

"Though he is German, he speak so much well that among the Italyans they believe him Italyan; he speak the French as the Frenchies himselves. The Spanishmen believe him Spanishing, and the Englishes, Englishman."

"It is difficult to so much well enjoy several languages."

With educational standards around the world constantly rising, it is perhaps inevitable that fractured English, like Cornish and Sanskrit, will one day become a dead language. But it is hoped that at least for a few years yet English-speaking travellers abroad can still expect to tootle with vigour and have their underwear pleasurably flattened. There are a good many of· us who so much well enjoy it.

READING AND REACTING

1. "English is full of booby traps for the unwary . . . ." With a partner, find all the examples of fractured English in the article. Rewrite each example in clear, concise English. Be sure to maintain the tone and intention of the original writer. Share your re-writes with the class.

2. With a partner, define "polyglotism." Make a two-column list of examples of polyglotism which shows the word(s) borrowed from English and the language which has adopted them. If you can think of other examples, add them to your list.

REACHING OUT

1. With a partner, go on a fractured English hunt. Search newspaper personal columns, and hand-written advertisements for examples. Ask teachers, employers, family, and friends if they know of any instances where words have been misused with an unexpected outcome. Write a brief report based on your findings and share it with a small group.

2. Take one example of fractured English from the selection. Write a short story based on a misinterpretation of the statement.

3. Imagine that you are the marketing manager for a multi-national company. Write a memo that will be read by your sales force in many countries. Explain the importance of communicating clearly in their dealings with foreign business associates and customers. Recommend procedures for avoiding problems with fractured English. Share your ideas with a small group.

4. Consult the magazine index in your resource centre for articles that discuss the implications of language and cultural differences on international trade and commerce. Summarize the article in a brief written report and present your report to the class.

5. Interview a business person from another culture. Inquire about difficulties with the English language that this person has experienced. Ask for information about the differences between this person's homeland and Canada and how such differences have resulted in communication problems. Write a short report on the material you gather during your interview. Present your report to the class.

▶ Now Listen Here!

A poor listener lives in an incomplete world and doesn't even know it. How well do **you** *listen?*

Robyn Peterson

Most of us have the ability to hear. We're born with it. Sounds occur and our brains detect those sounds through our ears. All of us know that. It really seems so simple. But this seeming simplicity can be deceptive.

The gift of hearing is truly a precious one. Just ask people who suffer from hearing impairment or loss. They can tell you of the countless important sounds great and small that they cannot hear properly or cannot hear at all.

The word "hearing" relates closely to the word "listening." But do they mean the same thing? If you can hear well can you listen well? Basically the answer is "yes." But a key term in this question is *"can you?"*

Let's try another question. If you can hear well, *do* you listen well? This becomes a bit more interesting. If you belong to the majority of people and answer honestly, your answer will be "no."

When we really stop to think about it, we know that listening and hearing are not necessarily the same thing.

Try a little experiment. Stop reading for a minute or so. During this time write down a list of all the sounds you can hear. Listen for sounds you might not normally be aware of. Listen . . . !

After a minute or two you will likely have put a good list together. The sounds you become conscious of during this experiment were likely all occurring before you stopped to listen for them. But were you really hearing them before? The answer is "yes." But you may not have been *conscious* of hearing them.

Just think of it. Each day we hear all sorts of things without consciously realizing it. Good listening is really a skill of self-activation.

Now, if we're not conscious of hearing some things, do those things matter? The answer may well be "yes."

People may grow accustomed to the weirdest of noises, especially if those noises follow an identifiable pattern. So you find Jane saying about her husband, George, "He can sleep through anything!"

In fact, of course, even if you do sleep through loud or irritating noises, those noises may still be getting through to you. But you may register them in your dreams or in changes in your brain wave patterns. In other words, you may hear those things at non-conscious levels of brain activity.

Our bodies respond autonomically at times to outside noises. Did you know, for instance, that your finger swells measurably when you hear a loud sound?[1]

Theoretically, an ultra sonic sound generator can be rigged up that could produce sound that could kill you, or at least cause a lot of cell destruction. And you wouldn't hear a thing!

We all hear all sorts of things all the time. And yet, most of us don't register what we hear in our conscious minds.

In his book *The Natural History of the Mind*, Gordon Rattray Taylor points out

that the brain's central problem is "how to cope with too much information." We're all being bombarded with incredible amounts of information these days. Members of our families, friends, associates at work, the general public, radio and television, and just the general hustle and bustle of our electro-mechanical civilization seem to crowd in on us. Often we may find ourselves saying, "I can't cope, I just can't cope. It's too much!"

This is what Marshall McLuhan meant when he referred to the "implosion effect" of our electronic media.[2] These media, whether in the form of telephones, radios, public address systems, television networks, or holographic transmission devices, are all accelerating our information bombardment.

The only way we survive all of this is by developing our own 'screens' for in-coming information. Our brains have literally been programmed to screen out certain types of information and only to let through those types of information that we consider important.

This has to be. We have to do this type of screening just to survive. But the screening you now possess is a construct of your life experience and education. It's a form of programming based on past events that you often had no awareness of. Your brain screens may no longer be serving you well.

You can test your own screening activity

the next time you're at a party. You may be deep in conversation with someone else, oblivious to a conversation others may be having across the room. At one point, however, someone in that other conversation speaks your name. Do you hear it? More than likely you do.

You'll feel your ears perk up just like the family dog, when it hears something new. Your brain's non-conscious sound monitoring system picked up the sound of your name. This sound has special significance for you, so it registered at the conscious level.

A trained mechanic does the same sort of thing when he listens to your car's engine. So does the skilled doctor when she applies her stethoscope to your bare chest. And the experienced sailor does the same when he hears the sound of the wind in the sails and the water against the hull.

We say that people with these kinds of hearing skills "know what to listen for." In other words, part of their training has been in selective forms of listening. In the course of doing your job you must apply selective forms of listening as well.

Perhaps you listen for key words. You may listen for different emotional tones. Or you might listen for contexts. In your life you've developed all sorts of things that you personally listen for. And your sound monitoring system, or listening pattern, is unique to you. You may well hear things that others do not hear—at least at the conscious level.

We don't just listen passively to those chunks of in-coming information that do penetrate our consciousness. As A.Z. Young says in his book, *Programs of the Brain*:

"Recognizing speech, like seeing and other perceptual acts is an active process of 'reconstruction,' not a mere passive reception."[3]

We reconstruct what we hear in terms of our own inner values, knowledge, and desires. And our brain screens provide the bulk of the reconstructing activity at the non-conscious level. So we do tend to hear what we want to hear and, in the main, we do this quite honestly!

Listening is very much an active part of the way we deal with the world. We listen in a way that we've developed over many years of life. And most of us never pause to take stock of our listening.

When was the last time you examined the way you really listened? Chances are it's been quite some time, if ever.

We all know some people who never take stock of their listening habits. They blithely assume that their listening is automatically effective. But they are the very people who are most likely to hear things that weren't said, or to miss important things that were said.

A poor listener really suffers from a form of deafness. She or he lives in an incomplete world and doesn't even know it. A poor listener can be a real hazard at work. Instructions may not be followed correctly, heated arguments may flare up, or organizational decisions with disastrous consequences may occur.

If you can improve your listening you will automatically improve your ability to function effectively at work and at home.

You can begin to improve your listening ability simply by taking stock of your listening habits from time to time. Realize that you may inadvertently have fallen into certain habits of exclusion, inclusion, or interpretation that are giving you a distorted version of what you're hearing. Ask yourself, "Am I listening as effectively as I should in business and home situations?" Pay attention to the comments others may make about your listening habits.

If you're honest with yourself, you will find specific things that you can deal with to improve your listening.

Try the questionnaire provided here. It may help you to identify some specific things right away.

		Yes	No
1.	When someone else is talking, I tend to keep track of external sights and noises.	—	—
2.	If I think what the other person is saying is starting to sound too difficult, I stop listening.	—	—
3.	Any time a speaker says something I don't understand or I disagree with, I interrupt.	—	—
4.	The other person's general appearance and way of talking let me know whether he's got something to say that's really worth listening to.	—	—
5.	When someone else is talking and says something that annoys me or that I disagree with, I will immediately show my annoyance or impatience.	—	—
6.	It is possible for me to "hear" something said by someone else that wasn't actually said.	—	—
7.	When someone else is speaking, I tend to concentrate on what I'm going to say when I get my chance to speak.	—	—
8.	When someone else is speaking I can easily be thinking of other things as well as listening to what's being said.	—	—

If you answered "yes" to any of those questions, then you've got some work to do on your listening skills. Re-examine your way of dealing with each situation high-lighted by your "yes" answers. This will provide you with an important first step in improving your listening.

In addition, try to keep these points about effective listening firmly in mind.

1. Try to deal with what the other person is saying at all your levels of mental awareness.

2. Pick up on "message reinforcers" used by the speaker (e.g., sketches, diagrams, or slides) and relate them to the associated words used by the speaker.

3. When something isn't immediately clear to you, try to clarify it for yourself by listening for the contexts the speaker uses for it.

4. Avoid, if you can, making judgments about what the speaker has said while she or he is still speaking.

5. Avoid making or receiving side comments to or from someone else while the speaker is still talking.

6. Remember, most speakers have at least a few worthwhile things to say.

7. At the end of the speaker's talking try to summarize in your own mind what he or she just said in terms of: central argument or theme; key facts used; conclusions made.

8. Prepare yourself to ask questions at an appropriate time to clarify or expand on points made by the speaker.

9. At all times try to listen to others in the way you would want to be listened to by others.

You can become a better listener than you are right now. It just takes a bit of conscious effort on your part. You will find the rewards that inevitably follow well worth the effort.

REFERENCES

1. Taylor, Gordon Rattray. *The Natural History of the Mind*. New York: E.P. Dutton, a Division of Else-vier-Dutton Publishing Co. Inc., 1979. Page 319.

2. McLuhan, Marshall, *Understanding Media*: The Extensions of Man. New York and Scarborough, Ontario: New American Library, 1964. Page 102.

3. Young, J.Z. *Programs of the Brain*. Oxford: Oxford University Press, 1978. Page 183.

▼

READING AND REACTING

1. In a small group, discuss the difference between listening and hearing. Write a definition of each term and share it with the class.

2. Make a list of all the sounds you hear during a two-minute time interval that you might not normally be aware of. Compile a class list of the sounds heard. Suggest reasons why these sounds might have gone unnoticed.

3. a) With a partner, identify three people who "know what to listen for." Justify your choices.

   b) Discuss with your partner the cost of not listening well. Summarize these ideas in a point-form note.

4. Try the quiz on listening habits. Compare your answers to a partner's. If possible, give your partner specific examples of when you have experienced one or two such situations.

5. Read the nine points about effective listening. Reduce the points to a list of nine key words or phrases. Cover your list, and outline to a partner the nine points.

6. In a small group, make a list of all the sources from which you receive information in a day. Brainstorm the listening techniques which would be most effective for each source.

REACHING OUT

1. a) In a small group, create a form that could be used to assess the listening skills of your classmates when oral presentations are given. Make a copy of your evaluation form for each student in your class.

   b) Co-operate with a partner to assess each other's listening skills during an oral presentation or a class discussion. Share your assessment with each other.

2. Script a scene that shows the consequences—comic or tragic—of a person's inability to listen. Dramatize the scene for the class.

3. In your journal, write about a time when you had something important to say and no one would listen to you. Describe how the experience made you feel.

4. a) Listen to a radio broadcast of a sports event. Write down all the expressions that the announcer uses to describe the action. In a small group, combine your lists and examine the phrases. Are the words themselves accurate descriptions of what took place?

   or

   b) Choose a television show to listen to. As you listen, select key words and phrases that will identify the program. Do not pick any proper names. In a small group, read your list and ask your group members to identify the show.

5. Take the list of words or phrases that you collected in 4 a) or b). Script a short passage using the words and read it to the class so that it sounds like a portion of the radio or television show.

6. Prepare a set of questions based on a tape of your favourite singer, speaker, poet, writer, story-teller, or stand-up comic. Play the tape for your class and determine how well they listened by asking them your questions.

Homemaker's, October 1985

▶ WORKING IN THE FIELD

A fresh look at solving the youth unemployment crisis

Rona Maynard

There is no better bridge between school and work than co-operative education—it combines classroom learning with hands-on experience and students emerge infinitely more employable.

Lydia Duarte seemed amply qualified for a career in community work when she sent out more than 200 résumés. She had two BAs from McMaster University (one in political science, the other in sociology), and strong credentials as a volunteer. But all she could find were temporary jobs—researching here, typing there. And many paid less than the summer jobs she had held as a student.

"It's so disheartening," says the 25-year-old Hamilton, Ontario woman. "The worst part is getting your hopes up when you see an opening you really want in the newspaper. You rush to put your résumé together, then you wait for the phone to ring—but it never does. At first the tension is terrible, but after awhile you just don't care anymore."

Young adulthood, once an age of hope, is fast becoming an age of despair as men and women like Duarte bear the brunt of the worst economic slump since the Great Depression. With plant closings and corporate cutbacks forcing experienced workers down the work-force ladder, many novices can't gain a foothold on the bottom rung. Fifteen-to-24-year-olds face a 16.2 percent unemployment rate, compared to 10.5 percent for all Canadians. In Newfoundland, the hardest-hit province, 34.1 percent of youth can't find jobs. Nationwide, 488,000 are waiting out layoffs. "Unemployment is a clear message to youth that they aren't valued," comments Lynn Eakin, executive director of Toronto's J.D. Griffin Adolescent Centre.

Jobless youth face a cruel irony: The longer they wait, the less appealing employers find them. And with high unemployment predicted to last until the turn of the century or longer, the least-skilled risk spending much of their lives out of work.

What's holding youth back? Hit-and-miss guidance counselling in high schools, inadequate apprenticeship programs, too few government incentives for employers hiring the young—all these and more play a role. But generally speaking, two causes stand out: a stagnant economy and young people's poor preparation for the nine-to-five realities of working life.

Listen to Brien Gray, vice-president and general manager of the Toronto-based Canadian Federation of Independent Business (CFIB): "I constantly hear employers complain that young people want to do too little, too soon and for too much pay." A 1983 CFIB survey bears him out. Asked what conditions would spur them to hire more young workers, employers put a

healthier economy at the top of the list—but "better work attitudes" are next in line and "better skills" close behind.

The youth crisis has inspired no end of sound and fury, with the educational system and the government bearing most of the blame. But neither can act alone. Consider the schools' limitations. The pace of technological change has become so dizzying that no degree can guarantee a meal ticket. In an era of cutbacks and computerization educators predict five or six career changes for young Canadians—often interspersed with periods of retraining or even unemployment. More than ever before, the schools' role is to teach the problem-solving skills that students will need in a volatile workplace.

The limitations of government bureaucracy are already plain, despite more than $1 billion of federal money spent on youth employment in 1986. A confusing welter of federal and provincial programs spring up and vanish so quickly that youth workers are hard-pressed to stay current. Most rely on short-term funding—three years or less. But, as Eakin cautions, "It takes three years just to get a program up and running, with staff trained and the bugs out."

Besides, each community grapples with its own employment demons—Nanaimo, B.C., with a floundering forestry industry and Sault Ste. Marie, Ontario, with a glut of jobless steelworkers. Each region faces its own fluctuating skill shortages—sales personnel in P.E.I., construction workers in Saskatchewan. Can anyone in Ottawa see the whole picture? Not likely.

That's why youth employment is a grassroots issue facing business, school boards, service clubs, unions, even concerned individuals. With no shortage of examples to follow, our challenge is to multiply them countrywide.

We can start by joining forces—the idea behind the Youth Employment Opportunity Initiative, launched in 1985 by The

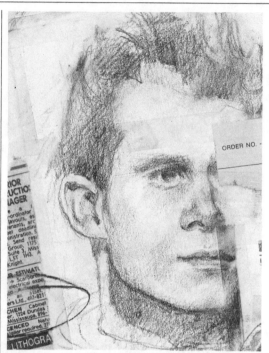

Canadian Chamber of Commerce. To date, this pilot project involves some 35 cities and towns, at least one in every province. All raise their own funds. "The local chamber acts as a catalyst," explains Executive Director Elie Thimot from his Ottawa office. "Our goal is to unite all the leaders in a community, including young people themselves, and mobilize the available resources."

Information heads the list. It's not unusual for four or five community groups to attack the same problem in isolation. The result: wasted energy and money. "A city government might spend months researching unemployed youth," says Thimot, "when the facts it needs are already available at the local Canada Employment and Immigration Commission office."

Government money is the next key resource. Why not decide jointly how to raise and spend it? And finally, there is the creativity and commitment of the citizens. Some communities enlist retired managers to coordinate their efforts full time; others persuade a local business to donate an executive (Thimot himself was seconded to the cause by his employer, Bell Canada).

We can build new bridges between the separate worlds of school and work. Trained primarily in educational theory and personal counselling, most guidance counsellors know little about the bottom-line concerns of business. Meanwhile, employers, frustrated by the inadequacies of young job-seekers, often lambaste the schools without considering their own responsibility to show the next generation what makes commerce hum. Project Business, a nationwide venture run by the U.S.-based nonprofit association Junior Achievement, is helping to close the gap. Since 1981, it has been taking volunteer executives into Grade 8 and 9 classrooms. A group might role-play labour negotiations or conduct job interviews with each other. During the 12-to-15-week program, they also discuss marketing, finance, and other topics seldom explored by the average classroom teacher.

There is no better bridge between school and work than co-operative education. Sometimes known as "work study" or "work experience," it combines classroom learning with hands-on experience in the office or workshop. Virtually unheard of a decade ago, this approach is best established in Ontario, where a supportive ministry of education lets roughly 25,000 students earn academic credits for co-op courses that meet its requirements. But momentum should grow nationwide now that the federal government has earmarked $3 million to help local boards of education start and expand co-op programs.

Why all the interest? For starters, co-op education can bring any subject alive, at any level of academic difficulty. A business student can practise word-processing in an office tower, while an aspiring scientist heads for a hospital laboratory. Using state-of-the-art equipment no high school could afford, students learn that while 50 percent may be a passing grade in high school, employers expect 100 percent—letter-perfect correspondence and thoughtfully prepared work orders. Meanwhile, they compare youthful fantasies to workaday realities.

"Co-op clarifies objectives for the ones who change their career goals from week to week," says Jim O'Connor, Co-operative Education Co-ordinator for the Hamilton Board of Education and president of the Co-operative Career Work Education Association of Canada. "It's good for the morale, too—the average or below-average student may blossom as a salesman and get an A for the first time in his life."

Thanks to the allure of job preparation, the young rebel who cuts class daily will seldom be late for work. The implications aren't lost on the Scarborough, Ontario, Board of Education, which runs Canada's largest co-op program, involving some 2,000 students. In 1984, the board rallied community support for a unique co-op project designed to keep potential dropouts in school. A year later, 35 teenagers spend weekday afternoons at unpaid jobs learning administrative skills, stocking shelves, or waiting on customers for merchants at Cedarbrae Mall. Mornings, they work with a teacher on independent study courses such as math and English and "work and employability skills" (everything from interview etiquette to resolving disputes at work). Cadillac Fairview, which owns the mall, donated the classroom space, while Allstate Insurance, a longtime supporter of co-op education, donated $2,000 worth of blazers for the students to wear at work.

Many of the students have made obvious progress. His confidence bolstered by helping customers at a local store, 16-year-old Rick Nicholson has decided to aim at a more challenging career in market research. He hopes to enter community college sometime within the next five years. "At my old school I thought I'd be a big hotshot businessman driving around in a limousine," he remembers, "but that's not reality; that's dreaming. This place has really changed my thinking."

What about young people who have already left school—the ones most at risk for the welfare rolls? There are lots of them hitting the streets. Approximately 40 percent of Ontario's Grade 9 students leave before obtaining a diploma. And to judge from a 1984 Newfoundland study, half of that province's students do not graduate from high school.

Schools must change to motivate the disaffected, warned the study, which offered no blueprint. The good news is that communities can mobilize to guide the very youth who appear unemployable.

So Winnipeg has found with its Youth Business Learning and Development Centre Inc., a nonprofit company owned by 58 of the city's major employers, including Boeing of Canada, C.P. Rail, and Esso Canada Resources. Since the centre opened over a decade ago, it has helped more than 500 people to target job goals, earn the equivalent of a high-school diploma, and hone practical skills, whether word-processing or drafting. The average entering student dropped out of school five years previously—with a Grade 8 or 9 education—and has worked for less than one of those years. Even so, at least 75 percent now hold jobs in their chosen field.

Each corporate owner contributes $2,300 toward a student's six-month course in either industrial or clerical skills (the federal General Industrial Training Program pays the $4,400 balance). In addition, the companies provide a total of 255 hours of work experience for every student. Although there's no requirement to hire the graduates, many have gladly done so. "We're in tune with local employers' needs," says executive director Warren Gander, "and we have people in almost every office in town. There's a lot of community pride in our track record."

▼

JOBLESS YOUTH MAY NOT KNOW HOW TO APPLY THEIR TALENTS TO ONE OF THE 7,000 EXISTING OCCUPATIONS. HOW CAN WE HELP?

Indeed. Even the city government backs the cause by engaging the centre's teachers to train welfare recipients in word-processing and other job-related skills. Profits from this service, now being marketed to local businesses, should gradually reduce Ottawa's contribution to the program until it becomes self-sustaining. The message is clear. With grassroots support, putting youth to work need not entail massive expense year after year.

Winnipeg is neither the first nor the only community to help disadvantaged job-seekers. Loosely modelled on a Montreal project founded during the '60's, the centre also has a close counterpart in Halifax. And across the country, concerned volunteers are combatting functional illiteracy. This invisible obstacle—less than 10 years of schooling—condemns about 4.5 million Canadians, 70 percent of them native born, to here-and-gone jobs or no jobs at all.

Nobody knows how many illiterates are under 25. But Toronto-based Frontier College, Canada's oldest literacy-training centre, reports an increasing number of young students whose inability to read phone books and application forms has driven them from the job market. Where are the openings that don't require reading? These days, the cook in a pizza parlour could well receive orders on a computer printout—not shouted over a counter.

The answer is one-on-one tutoring, says John O'Leary, Frontier College's director of development. And any concerned person can do it. With adult tutoring programs underway across Canada, the College has found that one or two full-time staff can train and supervise 75 to 100 students. Its federal funding—a modest $175,000—stretches far, yet cannot accommodate all the would-be tutors and students. More government support could build on already successful community efforts. Insists O'Leary: "We don't need a huge, expensive bureaucracy to solve this problem."

Most jobless youth have fewer strikes against them than illiterates do. But they may not know where their talents lie, or how to apply them in one of the 7,000 occupations that exist in Canada. What can we do? North York, Ontario, has found a solution. At the Vocational Career Centre, visitors can test their aptitudes at 16 "work stations"—simulations of skilled jobs. They can install a pipe under the sink at the plumbing station, or complete a diagram at the drafting table. Meanwhile, a counsellor assesses speed, accuracy, and work behaviour.

Funded by the North York Board of Education, the centre is free to North York students referred by their schools. Several other boards offer a similar service, but only North York welcomes the entire community. A $225 fee, subsidized by the board, covers an assessment that takes as long as 59 hours. Together, counsellor and visitor explore the big questions: they consider not only performance at the work stations, but past experience and scores on aptitude and interest tests (while the average high-school guidance department has at most one or two of these tests, the centre boasts a dozen).

Once visitors have targeted a list of occupations to explore, they narrow it down in the centre's career library. There are videos, college and university calendars, binders packed with details on specific occupations, and even a computer program, Choices, that aids in focussing goals. According to supervisor Marilynn Burke, the entire process can be particularly exciting for young women raised to view them-selves as teachers or homemakers. Some, unexpectedly pleased by the hands-on tinkering, leave the centre determined to investigate a skilled trade.

No matter how effective such programs are, the fact remains that there is not enough work to go around. "Almost as fast as we can produce results, just as many people lose their jobs or enter the work force," argues Al Hatton of the YWCA's Montreal-based Job Generation Program, which trains disadvantaged youth in 10 cities from St. John's to Vancouver. "If we train our youth to be smarter unemployed people, we're in big trouble." The program works to meet community needs. Take St. Catharines, Ontario, where employers need more trained staff for a $50-billion-a-year horticulture industry. The Job Generation Program will open a greenhouse and offer life-skills counselling to the people who staff it. And working closely with local educators, politicians, and Chambers of Commerce, the Y will soon begin setting up businesses staffed by youth, perhaps using local managers as mentors.

The community's job-creation clout has already been proven in towns like Nanaimo, B.C., which suffered massive layoffs in the mid-70s after all its major employers fell victim to declining international demand for Canadian forest products. What Nanaimo needed was not temporary government-run make-work projects, but something to process and sell besides trees.

Enter Colville Investments Corporation, a community-based organization that helps aspiring entrepreneurs to start new businesses and expand existing ones. Founded in 1980 with a $500,000 federal grant, it lends money to people who can't qualify for bank loans, but have a bright idea and the know-how to make it fly. Every loan must be secured, however modestly; every proposal must pass muster with the board of directors. But no bank offers a service like this. "A bank manager won't run around town doing a feasibility survey," explains manager Keith Hodgson. "We will."

This isn't charity: of money lent out, only 1.5 percent has been lost as bad debts. Accumulated interest, plus venture capital from the federal Local Employment Assistance and Development Program, keep Colville a going concern. Today, 60-odd new businesses, from roofing companies to day-care centres, collectively employ more than 400 people. And well over half of those people are under 25.

So are a few of the entrepreneurs. When 20-year-old Mark Woodhouse couldn't find a job as an apprentice car mechanic, he turned his high-school vocational courses and lifelong passion for tinkering to a more creative use: a portable car cleaning, painting, and touch-up service that tends local residents' cars in their driveways or on workplace parking lots. A $4,000 loan from Colville Investments recently helped Woodhouse and a friend buy a van and the necessary equipment. As he says, "When there's no work around, you have to make your own."

▼

READING AND REACTING

1. With a partner, prepare a line graph that shows the percentage unemployment rate for Canadians on average, for the age group 16 to 24 years, and for Newfoundland. Share your concerns about these statistics in a small group. Make a list of suggestions which will help you to avoid becoming one of these statistics.

2. In a small group, identify the reasons given in "Working in the Field" for high youth unemployment. Individually, react in your journal to one or more of the reasons identified by your group.

3. In a group of three, summarize the information given in the Youth Unemployment Opportunity Initiative, Project Business, and co-operative education. Add information on any other youth employment programs that you are familiar with.

REACHING OUT

1. a) Imagine that you are employed by Canada Employment and your job is to publicize employment programs that provide job training and job creation opportunities for young, unskilled workers. On your own, prepare a set of speaking notes based on the information given in the selection "Working in the Field." Be brief, but thorough. Set up your notes so that the key programs and points that you would want to cover stand out clearly.

b) Present your talk to a small group. Be prepared to answer any questions.

2. With two partners, investigate the government agencies and private organizations that provide work experience to help you get your first job. Present your information in a brief, oral report to the class. Your investigation should include direct contact with the agencies. Employment Canada, the Chamber of Commerce, and your guidance office will provide information.

3. In a group, investigate what is offered by apprenticeship programs. A guidance counsellor, a teacher of technological subjects, an apprenticeship employer, and an apprenticing student are all possible sources of information. Organize your information and present it to the class.

4. Individually, or with a small group, research the opportunities available in your school through a co-operative education program. Seek help from the director or teachers in charge of co-operative supervision. Interview students and employers who are enrolled in a co-operative education program.

a) Design a brochure that explains the concept of co-operative education.

b) Write one or more feature articles on employers and students who are involved in co-operative education, and publish it/them in a booklet to be distributed, with the permission of the appropriate authority, to students and employers.

c) Form a panel with several co-operative students and employers. Present an overview of the program to your class or to students who are considering opting for credits in this way. Plan to receive questions and comments from the audience. Offer your services to the co-operative supervisor or guidance director.

5. Suppose that you now hold a job and see changes ahead that will threaten your security. Investigate the programs available from your Canada Employment Centre. Write a memo to your fictional employer, outlining the changes you foresee and proposing that you make arrangements for company employees to take advantage of government sponsored training and re-training courses. Restrict your research to either the National Training Program or The Industrial Training Program.

6. Collect information from the Canadian Armed Forces recruiting office in your area. Prepare a display for your classroom or school that shows opportunities available through the armed forces.

▶ FOR ADULTS, SCHOOLING NEVER STOPS

Theresa Tedesco

At least three times a week, Gabriella Caravaggio puts aside her household chores for a couple of hours in a laboratory classroom at a downtown Toronto campus.

The 43-year-old mother of three has been attending school for the past eight years and is 26 credits short of obtaining a degree in food and nutrition at Ryerson Polytechnical Institute.

Her children were not enthusiastic about their mother trekking off to high school every day five years ago but have since warmed to the idea.

"My husband and my mother-in-law don't understand why I would want to go to school and that's why they don't agree with what I'm doing," she said. "I don't mind if I don't get my degree but to think that I can't have a good education is to feel that I am really losing out on something."

A large number of Canadians, like Mrs. Caravaggio, are tackling high school and university courses in order to improve their opportunities in the job market, hone their physical skills, and sharpen their minds.

About 19 percent of Canada's population aged 17 and over (about 3.2 million people) took an adult education course in 1983. This means one in every five Canadians 17 years of age and older was enrolled in educational activities—ranging from job-related training to hobby classes—taken outside a full-time program.

A total of 5.2 million courses were taken in 1983; close to two-thirds of those enrolled took only one course while another 21 percent participated in two. Ontario's participation rate was 20 percent, slightly above the national average of 19 percent.

"The part-time degree programs and continuing education non-credit courses are very healthy," said Alex Waugh, vice-president and registrar at Woodsworth College at the University of Toronto. There are about 20,000 students enrolled at the university's School of Continuing Studies.

Business-related courses, such as accounting and computer programming, continue to draw the most applicants, while the humanities and social sciences are gaining ground.

Academic courses are taken at high schools, colleges and universities for credits toward a diploma, certificate, or degree. Also included are job-related courses which provide skills applicable either to a person's current job or one for which they wish to qualify, such as word processing, auto mechanics, and computer programming.

"There is a trend away from professional areas to the humanities and social sciences," Mr. Waugh said, adding that general interest courses are also making headway.

"An extraordinary percentage of the population is engaged in continued education," he said, and the movement away from professional courses may be the result of increasing numbers of women enrolling in adult education programs.

Nearly 70 percent of the 10,000 people registered in part-time courses at Woodsworth College are women "who discovered they are missing something, not with a specific goal in mind but just for the sake of going," he said.

A study by Statistics Canada in 1983 showed that women were more likely than men to enrol in adult education. Of the 92,000 people surveyed across the country, 56 percent of those participating in adult education were women.

Brock University in St. Catharines, Ont., boasts one of the highest proportions of part-time enrolments in the province. The university had 3,142 part-time students of a total of 8,091.

"Students take whatever courses are

Graham Cunningham, a chartered accountant, teaches a management consulting course at Toronto's York University.

available," said Ainsley Towe, registrar at Brock. "They usually do a general studies program toward a degree only in a shorter time because the part-time course allows them to do it by taking less administrative courses."

Mr. Towe said the university's most popular programs always include computer programming, stock market training, and small-business seminars but added that wine appreciation and physical education courses are packing in students as well.

The province's 22 community colleges are also benefitting from the surge in part-time education. Last year there were 100,000 full-time students compared with 600,000 who were registered on a part-time basis.

"The game is very much toward getting a job," said Robert LaRose, executive director of the Association of Canadian Community Colleges. "People want to make themselves more valuable in the workplace, particularly those whose jobs have become redundant."

Mr. LaRose said there has been "a falling out" of interest in hobby-related courses because people have become more sensitive about losing their jobs and increasing their marketability.

Courses offered by provincial school boards show no signs of a decreased interest in leisure-type activities. Although area schools and community centres provide credit courses, such as English, Mathematics, Science, and History, hobby/craft/recreational courses continue to be the big attractions.

Other training, which does not fit into one of the groups, for example, marriage preparation, prenatal instruction, driver-training, and first-aid, are also high in demand.

But of the three groups of part-time, adult courses offered, job-related courses rank first in Ontario followed by personal development instruction and hobby classes.

Toronto's Board of Education offers about 1,600 part-time credit and non-credit adult courses a year for over 55,000 students across 20 secondary schools spread across the city, including the Adult Learning Centre which provides daily classes for people who want to upgrade their skills during the day.

Bert D'Antini, department co-ordinator, said traditional job-related and business courses such as word processing, typing, and computers "are usually booked solid within the first few days of registration because they improve people's chances for a job."

He said credit courses are usually taken "depending on the gap in people's educational background," but credit and non-credit prefixes are less important than what the course will actually teach the individual.

For example, Mr. D'Antini said enrolment in physical fitness courses, such as aerobics, yoga, and break dancing, have reached incredible heights in recent years because of the health kick of the 1980s. "People are getting a lot out of those courses and they really enjoy them."

Barbara Rowe of York Region School Board said people take credit courses for a specific purpose while interest courses are offered for personal enrichment. Last year, York Region provided more than 400 courses in 13 schools for 7,600.

Walter Ward, principal of the continued education program in Peel Region, said part-time studies are also the result of people feeling they have left something incomplete. "They discover when they go back that taking one or two courses is enriching. People are more serious-minded because they are mature, and our high success rates prove this."

Peel Region has experienced a 5 to 10 percent growth rate in part-time studies and the number of courses offered has increased to 200.

READING AND REACTING

1. a) In a small group, discuss Mrs. Caravaggio's motivation for taking further courses, and identify the problems she had to overcome to achieve her goals.

b) Script a scene in which Mrs. Caravaggio, her husband, her mother-in-law, and her children discuss her wish to go back to school. Show how Mrs. Caravaggio overcomes their objections.

c) Rehearse the scene and act it out for the class. Ask the audience for comments.

2. a) On a line graph, show the popularity trend for business-related courses, the humanities and social sciences, and professional courses.

b) On a pie chart, indicate the percentage of men and women enrolled in continuing education courses across Canada.

3. You are an aide to your local member of parliament and you have completed a research task on your community's requirements for continuing education courses. Write a report to your M.P. to inform him or her of the reasons why people want and need to take further education. Recommend the courses that should be offered in your community and suggest the physical and human resources that would be required. Base your report on the information contained in the article "For Adults, Schooling Never Stops." Give your report a title and include a memo that briefly explains the purpose of the report.

REACHING OUT

1. Visit an adult education centre and talk to some of the students and a staff member. Find out the students' reasons for being there and what motivates them. Ask if they have any problems finding the time to attend classes and whether they are satisfied with what they are getting out of the classes. Share findings in a small group discussion.

2. Compile a brochure of courses available through Continuing Education Services sponsored by your school board, or by private groups in your community. Distribute your brochures within the school, to parents, to neighbours, and to local businesses. Be sure to get authorization before you publish your information.

1. As you approach graduation from high school, it is time to decide what further education you will pursue. Because technology and economic and social conditions are changing so rapidly, it will be necessary to seek education on a continuing basis throughout your life.

   Compile a detailed educational plan that spans the next five years of your life. Assess your present accomplishments, your future goals, and your present skills, and determine which skills you will need to develop. Plan the formal education you will take. Investigate the institutions that offer programs you require, and state the entrance requirements, the nature of the courses, and the predicted benefits. Estimate the cost of undertaking further education and prepare a detailed projection of your expenses. Include your personal attitude on the value of education.

   The following resources may be helpful:

   a) a guidance counsellor

   b) SGIS and CHOICES computer programs

   c) community college and university calendars

   d) business people in your community

   e) family members

   f) former students

   g) government agencies

   h) published predictions of economic trends

   i) newspaper and magazine articles

2. Research your family history. Here are some suggestions to help you with your task.

   a) Talk to as many relatives as possible as you collect your data.

   b) Tape your conversations and keep copies of the questions you ask.

   c) Write letters to relatives and friends of the family and ask them to contribute information and anecdotes about your history. Keep copies of your letters and the responses you receive.

   d) Cameo portraits of your most colourful ancestors would make interesting reading.

e) Old letters, photographs, birth records and documents would be an addition to your project, and appropriate material for your appendix.

f) If your family has a homestead or a piece of property that has been in the family for more than one generation, search the registry office for records of transactions.

Prepare a detailed family biography. Use a published family biography from your resource centre as a model. Ask a history teacher to make suggestions about the proper format for your project. Present copies of your family biography to relatives.

3. Most school jurisdictions have implemented special programs for students as an alternative to the traditional school program. The educational approach used by these programs has implications for all students. Research the special programs offered for students in your area. Provide a description of the program, the criteria for measuring achievement, the administration of the program, and the curriculum, as well as an evaluation of the program by participants, teachers, parents, community members, and school administrators. Special education for gifted, trainable mentally retarded, and French Immersion students are examples of such programs.
   You may find the following resources helpful.

a) in your resource centre—books, magazine and newspaper articles, material from educational journals

b) in your school—principal, vice-principal, teachers with special expertise in special education, students who have taken the program

c) at your education centre—a consultant who has organized a special program

d) in your community—parents who have researched the subject and have children enrolled in special programs

4. In a small group, or as a whole class, prepare a style manual for effective writing.

a) Study several documents for an idea of what your manual will look like and what it will include.

b) Most large companies have a style manual. Consider appointing one person to write to one or more companies to request a copy of their publication. Place these manuals in your classroom library. Keep copies of the requests on file in your classroom so that they are not duplicated from year to year. Be sure to send a thank-you letter for any material that you receive.

c) Prepare a blueprint of your manual. Make decisions about the content and the format so that your work is designed with a consistent pattern.

d) Assign sections of the workload to the participants in the project.

e) You might make arrangements with students in a typing class to produce your final copy.

f) Keep your manual as an authority on style for classroom work. It should remain in the classroom at the end of the school year to serve as a model for future projects.

g) Consider offering your manual as a guide to students in other classes at your school or at an elementary school. A presentation by a group explaining the contents and how to use the manual would be useful to potential users outside your classroom.

▶Tracking the Right Job

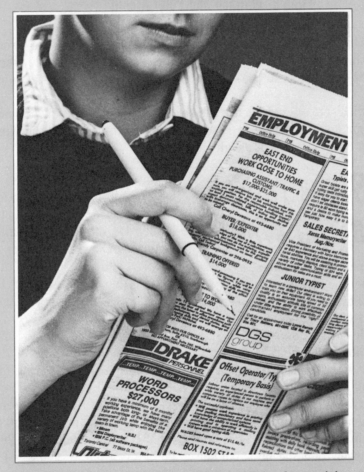

Several times in your life you may be in the position of looking for a new job. This unit aims at developing a systematic approach for locating and getting the job you want.

► ARE YOU LOOKING FOR A JOB?

Your first one, or a better one? Here's help.

Ellen J. Wallach and Peter Arnold

Many people are—but they're going about their search in the wrong way. Finding the position you want requires more than luck. It takes knowledge, insight, and persistence—it takes good strategy and the ability to stick with it.

In the following section, you'll learn the best way to organize your job search, including how to set your goals and how to reach them. Read on to learn the winning formula that helps you find the job that's right for you.

EIGHT STEPS TO GET THE JOB YOU WANT

Certain aspects of the job-search process cause people more trouble than others. The following eight steps were designed to help you use your time and energy more efficiently.

1. Have a job-search goal. As much as you can, know what you're looking for before you begin.

2. Set weekly objectives, follow through on them, and evaluate your progress. Plan the job search week by week and keep yourself on target, building on small successes. At the end of each week, review your work, focussing on what went well and what didn't. Then determine how to improve your performance. This helps you maintain control over the job-search process.

3. Develop and use contacts. When a job is advertised, sometimes hundreds of people mail in résumés. Even when a job isn't advertised, the personnel people can hardly keep their heads above the mountains of paper that arrive each morning. Face it: the competition for jobs is stiff. But if you use your contacts to develop the hidden job market, the number of people against whom you are competing is much smaller, and your chances of securing the job are that much greater. Don't be hesitant about asking others to get involved in your job search.

4. Be prepared. Spend time every week researching organizations, developing job information and preparing for interviews. As a football coach at Indiana University once said, "Luck is when preparation meets opportunity." You should understand that all of the opportunities in the world won't be of any value to you at all unless you're prepared to use them.

5. Keep accurate, up-to-date records. Don't even try to remember what you did last week, whom you spoke with, what was said, or someone's telephone number. Write it down, and use a system for recording and retrieving it.

6. Get help when you need it. It may be emotional support, additional knowledge, or added skills. If you're stuck, confused, or want to be part of a job-search group, get assistance. It will help maintain your emotional equilibrium.

7. Evaluate job options before accepting a new position. The adage "Marry in haste, repent at leisure" can easily apply to the person who accepts a job too quickly. Never accept an offer on the spot; instead, take time to weigh every job offer against your ideal job.

8. After getting a job, evaluate your search. Review your efforts. What worked and what didn't? What have you learned for the future? According to the U.S. Department of Labour, people change jobs every three years on the average. So when you find a job, keep in mind that you're really just between job searches!

READING AND REACTING

1. a) In a small group, evaluate the usefulness and/or effectiveness of each of the eight steps described in the article.

b) If you have used other "steps" to find a job, share your tips with the group.

c) Rank the steps from the article and those suggested by group members in order of importance. Compile a chart, titled "____ Steps to Get the Job You Want," that lists all the steps from the most important to the least important. Each step should be described in one clear sentence.

REACHING OUT

1. In a small group, talk about your long-term career goals. Explain how you are preparing to achieve your goals.

2. Keep a directory of contacts who might be helpful to you in a job search. Record the individual's name, the company she or he works for, his or her telephone number, address, and any other important information. You could include in your directory the names of contacts that you make during your job search.

3. The technological change we see today will result in an expansion of certain industries and a decline in others. With the help of your guidance counsellor and local employment office, find out how these changes will affect your career opportunities. Research the predictions for high growth and low growth industries. Show on a chart the number of jobs (both existing and new) that analysts forecast will be available in the next decade.

HOW TO FIGURE OUT WHAT YOU WANT

What is the first question job-seekers ask? It's "Where are the jobs?" or, to say it another way, "What's out there? What are my options?"

These questions reflect a common wish for a "menu" from which to choose a job. The job-hunters are really saying, "Tell me what you have, and I'll take the one I want."

There's no book to tell you what jobs are available. And if anyone tried to write it, the information would be out of date before it was published. On any day of the year there are millions of jobs available and they're constantly changing.

So instead of looking at the market, look carefully at yourself. Knowing where you're going will make it much easier for you to plan the most efficient and effective way to get yourself there.

Before we set a goal for your future, let's evaluate your past. Organize your work history by evaluating your last job or jobs. These may have been full-time, part-time, or volunteer.

Use a different "Where Have You Been?" worksheet for each job, beginning with your current or most recent one. Consider your likes and dislikes for each job. Think hard and be specific. Answer these questions.

Responsibilities: Which responsibilities do you most enjoy? Most dislike?

Knowledge and skills: Which knowledge and skills do you most enjoy using? Least enjoy?

The organization: What do you like and dislike about the organization you work for? Consider its corporate philosophy and culture, work environment, and the product or service it sells. If you like privacy, for example, you probably value having your own office; if you find meetings a waste of time, you're probably frustrated working in an organization that schedules many of them.

The people: What do you like and dislike about the people you work with? Be specific about the personalities and work styles of your peers, superiors and subordinates. Name names. You might, for example, appreciate Mary's attention to detail but dislike her inability to see the big picture. Jeff might be a great boss who delegates, allows others to be creative, and provides constructive feedback, but who drives you crazy by changing his mind daily.

Location and travel: What do you like and dislike about the location of your job? Is commuting a problem? Is parking expensive? Is there too much or too little work-related travel? Is weekend travel required? Is your organization located far from people you'd like to see more often? You may have mixed emotions on this subject.

Compensation: What do you like and dislike about your total compensation package—your salary and benefits? Benefits might include health and insurance programs, educational reimbursements, seminar and workshop opportunities, stock purchase plans, equity in the company, a company car and gasoline credit cards, relocation and mortgage assistance, a credit union, and so on. You might, for example, like the fact that your company has its own private golf club, but that may not count for much compared with the very low pay increases you've received over the past three years.

Non-tangible benefits: What else does your job offer or lack that's important to you—the non-tangible benefits? Put the ones you get and value in the "likes" column and those you miss in the "dislikes" column. Are there chances to learn and grow, for example, as well as opportunities for promotion? Does your work offer variety? Does it give you a sense of achievement? Job security? Management responsibilities? Friendship with co-workers? Recognition?

Flexibility? Creative freedom? Take the time to figure out what's important to you, and does your organization offer it?

After evaluating your past and current work experience, consider what you've learned. Of the items that you've listed, which are more important than others? Underline the ones that are most critical to your job satisfaction. The goal of your job search now becomes clearer: to build the factors that you like into your next job and avoid those that you don't like. Life is full of compromises, but the clearer you are now about what you want, the better trade-offs you're apt to make later.

If you are working now, be careful not to burn your bridges too fast. Take a look at your dislikes. Is there any way at all that you could remain in the same company and convert the dislikes that you have into likes? Are they minor irritations that have piled up to the point of frustration? Before moving on to the next job, consider the possibility of improving your present position or of moving up or "sideways." You may be able to negotiate some changes in what you do, where you do it, whom you do it for, or with whom you do it.

▼

R E A D I N G   A N D   R E A C T I N G

1. With your class, define the terms *compensation* and *non-tangible benefits*. Make a list of examples of the types of compensation and benefits that are offered to employees. Research and list examples of jobs where the various benefits are found.

2. a) In a small group, brainstorm to come up with a list of all the jobs that you have held to date. Interpret "job" in its widest sense. Volunteer work, part-time work, such as babysitting, positions of responsibility in a club or organization—all contribute experience that can be considered in a job.

   b) Your teacher will provide you with copies of the chart, "Where Have You Been?" Follow the instructions in "How to Figure Out What You Want," and evaluate your last job or jobs if you have had more than one.

   c) In a small group, discuss what you have learned about yourself and what you would look for in a job. State how the exercise will help you find your ideal job. If you did not think the exercise was helpful, explain why.

WHERE HAVE YOU BEEN?

Job Title		
Organization		
	Likes *Be Specific*	**Dislikes**
Responsibilities		
Knowledge and skills		
The organization		
The people		
Location and travel		
Compensation package		
Non-tangible benefits		

REACHING OUT

1. Appoint members of your class to go to people holding each of the following jobs to collect information on compensation and benefits. You may want to add to the list jobs in which you are particularly interested.
   —a caretaker
   —a teacher
   —a secretary
   —a storekeeper
   —a manager
   —a waiter
   —a mechanic

   You might ask these questions:
   (i) "If it is not too confidential, will you tell me the salary range for workers in your occupation?"
   (ii) "In addition to your salary, what tangible benefits are offered to you?"
   (iii) "What are the non-tangible benefits in your job?"

   Share the information with the class.

WHERE ARE YOU GOING?

N ow let's look at your future. People do their best at the work they most enjoy. What would you most enjoy doing and where?

You'll undoubtedly have to make compromises, but for now, try to visualize the ideal job so that you can:

Focus your job search by knowing what you're looking for.

Make trade-offs to ensure that your next job meets your most important priorities while giving up only those that mean less to you.

Make better decisions. Most people have difficulty making up their minds because they lack information about what they really want and about their chances for getting it.

What do you want from your next job? You'll find key answers in your "Where Have You Been?" worksheet. Review them carefully. What have you learned from past work experiences that will be important considerations in finding your next job? Remember though that you may have changed over the years, so some things that used to be important to you may not

be now. You may not want to duplicate skills and responsibilities of former jobs. Instead, use clues from the past to make some major changes now.

1. When you think about your job-search goal, list the important issues to be considered. You need to weigh what's most important to your job satisfaction, what you truly enjoy doing, and where you really want to do it. All these factors are key to your giving your best job performance. Think about the following specific issues:
a) What responsibilities do you want?
b) What knowledge and skills are required?
c) What kind of organization?
d) With what kinds of colleagues?
e) With what type of manager?
f) Job location—commuting and travel requirements?
g) What must the compensation package include?
h) Most important non-tangible benefits you want.

2. What factors are so important that they're non-negotiable? For some people, what they do is all that matters; for others, where they do it is critical. What trade-offs are you willing to make, however reluctantly? There is no right or wrong in making these choices. All that counts is what's important to you. Grapple with these issues now and you'll have an easier time later weighing job offers.

3. What is your job-search goal? You don't need to worry if you feel you can't be precise. As you think about it, understand that job-search can be general ("I want to work for a small, rapidly growing company in a field with great growth prospects") or they can be far more specific ("I want a senior-level marketing position in a large consumer-product manufacturing company within an hour of Chicago").

Your goal will take on a clearer form as you gather more information during the job search. You'll also find that your goal may change as your search progresses.

"... DO IN LIFE ??"
DEPENDS WHICH YEAR
IN MY CAREER PLAN
YOU'RE REFERRING TO !!

COULD YOU BE MORE SPECIFIC?

READING AND REACTING

1. Your teacher will provide you with copies of the chart "Where Are You Going?" Carefully consider each of the questions in the article and enter your answers on the chart.

WHERE ARE YOU GOING?

Job Title		
Organization		
	Likes *Be Specific* Dislikes	
Responsibilities		
Knowledge and skills		
The organization		
The people		
Location and travel		
Compensation package		
Non-tangible benefits		

REACHING OUT

1. a) Write a job description (see Student Guide, page 315) for your dream job. Include information on the tasks and responsibilities involved, the skills required, the location, the working environment, and the benefits and compensation package.

b) Imagine that you are a Personnel Manager and write an advertisement for your dream job. Read the Employment Available columns of your local newspaper for ideas on how to set up your advertisement.

c) Ask your partner to write a letter recommending you for your dream job. In the letter, your partner should describe the skills and characteristics that make you a suitable applicant.

▶ *CHOICES* PUTS THE WORLD OF WORK AT YOUR FINGERTIPS

hoices is the most flexible, user-friendly, computer-assisted career information and exploration system available. It is an innovative and cost-effective tool for counsellors in addressing the occupational and educational information needs of clients of all ages. *Choices* has already been used by over one million people in secondary and post-secondary schools, vocational rehabilitation offices, and other career counselling centres throughout Canada and the United States.

Counsellors and clients do not need any special knowledge of computers in order to benefit from *Choices*. The computer uses simple instructions, in everyday language, displayed on the computer screen. It even addresses clients by their first names. Indeed, clients report that talking with *Choices* is "just like talking to a friend."

Choices was created by Employment and Immigration Canada and is distributed worldwide under federal licence by the Canada Systems Group.

READING AND REACTING

1. Ask your guidance counsellor for help in arranging for the class to use *Choices*, the computer-assisted information system to explore career interests. Afterwards, in a small group, discuss the insights you gained into possible careers.

REACHING OUT

1. Arrange with a guidance counsellor to use the Student Guidance Information Service. You may choose to do an Exploration of Career Interests, a search of specific Occupational Information, and/or a survey of Programs and Courses for your chosen career. Discuss the print-outs with several classmates.

2. Invite a person employed in a field that interests you to speak to the class about his or her job. Ask the speaker to cover educational requirements, a job description, predictions for future opportunities and changes in the occupation, skill requirements, personal characteristics needed, rewards of the work, and advice to students about to seek employment. As part of the exercise, include a letter confirming the invitation and a follow-up letter of appreciation.

3. a) Visit the resource centre in your school and compile a film catalogue on careers and job search information.

   b) Arrange to show one or more of the videos or films. Conduct a class discussion after the viewing.

4. Visit the guidance office. Compile an annotated bibliography of materials that give career information. Give a copy to each classmate and supply your guidance office with several bound copies of the bibliography.

5. Identify a career that interests you. Research in the guidance office the institutions offering courses leading to the career.

   a) Write a report giving the name of the schools that offer the courses, the address and location, a description of the course, and the admission requirements.

   and/or

   b) Make an oral report to the class giving the above information.

   and/or

   c) Supply the guidance office with a bound copy of your report for other students to use.

► THE APPLICATION FORM

SAMPLE APPLICATION FOR EMPLOYMENT

Position being applied for	Date available to begin work

PERSONAL DATA

Last name	Given name(s)	Social Insurance Number
					—				—			

Address	Street	Apt. No.	Home Telephone Number

City	Province	Postal Code	Business Telephone No.

Please indicate how you want to be addressed in any correspondence. ☐ As above ☐ Mr ☐ Mrs ☐ Miss ☐ Ms

Are you legally eligible to work in Canada? ☐ Yes ☐ No

Are you between 18 and 65 years of age? ☐ Yes ☐ No

Are you willing to re-locate? ☐ Yes ☐ No	Preferred location

To determine your qualification for employment, please provide below and on the reverse, information related to your academic and other achievements including voluntary work, as well as employment history. Additional information may be attached on a separate sheet.

EDUCATION

SECONDARY SCHOOL	BUSINESS, TRADE OR TECHNICAL SCHOOL	
Highest grade or level completed	Name of course	Length of course
Type of certificate or diploma received	Licence, certificate or diploma awarded? ☐ Yes ☐ No	

COMMUNITY COLLEGE		UNIVERSITY		
Name of Program	Length of Program	Length of course	Degree awarded ☐ Yes ☐No	☐ Pass ☐ Honours
Diploma received? ☐ Yes ☐ No		Major subject		
Other courses, workshops, seminars		Licences, Certificates, Degrees		

Work related skills

Describe any of your work related skills, experience, or training that relate to the position being applied for.

EMPLOYMENT

Name and Address of present last employer.	Present Last job title	
	Period of employment From To	Present Last salary
	Name of Supervisor	Telephone
Type of Business	Reason for leaving	

Duties Responsibilities

Name and Address of previous employer	Previous job title	
	Period of employment From To	Final salary
	Name of Supervisor	Telephone
Type of Business	Reason for leaving	

Duties Responsibilities

Name and Address of previous employer	Previous job title	
	Period of employment From To	Final salary
	Name of Supervisor	Telephone
Type of Business	Reason for leaving	

Duties Responsibilities

For employment references, may we approach:

Your present/last employer?   ☐ Yes   ☐ No
Your former employer(s)?   ☐ Yes   ☐ No

List references if different than above on a separate sheet.

Activities (civic, athletic, etc.)

I hereby declare that the foregoing information is true and complete to my knowledge. I understand that a false statement may disqualify me from employment, or cause my dismissal.	Have you attached an additional sheet? ☐ Yes ☐ No
	Signature Date

READING AND REACTING

1. Your teacher will give you copies of application forms.

a) In a small group, read each form carefully and define the terms in the forms. If you are not sure of the meanings of some of the terms, look them up in a dictionary.

b) Fill in the forms as neatly as possible. Exchange completed forms with a friend and check each other's work carefully.

c) You may wish to use your completed form to apply for your driver's licence, your age-of-majority card, or a job.

REACHING OUT

1. a) Write a letter to the personnel manager of a company requesting that he or she send you copies of the company's job application forms. Be sure to coordinate your letters with your classmates so that each company receives only one request. Company addresses may be obtained from telephone directories, annual reports, or from the *Fortune 500* directory.

b) As a class, examine all the forms received, and note the similarities and differences. Choose one of the forms, put it on an overhead transparency, and together fill it out.

c) Practise filling in several application forms on your own, choosing a different job for each one.

2. With a partner, research the Human Rights Code or contact a Human Rights Officer to discover what information an employer is not allowed to ask for in an application form. Share your findings with the class and discuss the significance of the Human Rights Code in giving everyone equal opportunity in a job application.

How to Write a Sure-Hire Résumé

Jeffrey G. Allen

A résumé should be a clearly written, organized representation of yourself. Since the first step in an employer's weeding-out process is usually an evaluation of a stack of résumés, the better your résumé, the greater your chances are for landing the job of your dreams. Follow these step-by-step guidelines to writing the résumé that will convince potential employers they must see you.

Before You Begin

Keep in mind that an employer wants one of two things from a prospective employee: to help the organization make more money, or to help make someone else's job easier. Your résumé should reflect your proven abilities in these areas. Don't clutter it with extraneous information either. Less is often better.

Your Rough Draft

A professionally organized résumé consists of five parts.

Part 1: Address. Centre your name, address, and telephone number at the top. Do not use any abbreviations (except for a middle initial).

Part 2: Personal Data. Although it is illegal for an employer to consider factors such as marital status, age, or health in the hiring process, it is perfectly acceptable for

you to include this information on your résumé. However, disclosing this personal information has both advantages and disadvantages, depending on the type of job you seek. For example, an employer looking to fill a position that requires someone who is good with children may be impressed by the fact that you have two children. On the other hand, an employer who wants someone to work long hours and possibly even weekends may be deterred from hiring someone who has family commitments. Only you can decide if disclosing this information makes sense. Remember, it's not necessary.

Part 3: Education. Always include this information somewhere on your résumé. List your most recent education first and continue in reverse order. Almost every job opening has minimum educational requirements. Do not include a list of irrelevant education courses.

Part 4: Affiliations. In this section, list any job-related affiliations and volunteer work. Again, the key is to be selective. If you have ever held a title of office, such as treasurer, secretary, or president of any organization, list that first. This demonstrates leadership qualities and shows that you're motivated and can handle a variety of duties simultaneously—home, family, career, and volunteer work. Omit affiliations with religious or fraternal organizations—they could prejudice a prospective employer.

Part 5: Experience. There are two ways to present this information, depending upon your experience and past employment record.

A chronological résumé lists your previous employment, starting with the most recent job. You should include your title or position in that company and then list three or four of your most significant duties and achievements. Start each sentence with a positive action verb (see "Action Verbs" below). This type of résumé is preferred by most personnel departments because it presents factual information in a clear and orderly manner. If there are any major gaps between jobs you've held, give an explanation. For example, if you left a job to return to school or to raise a family, include that information in this section.

A functional résumé is organized to highlight skills and qualifications, rather than the time or place of employment. This type of résumé is best if you have been with only one company for a number of years or if your past employment record is sporadic. For example, if you've been working as a seamstress/designer from your home, you might want to divide this section with headings such as:

Creative: designed patterns for customers

Innovative: created new pattern designs

Motivated: expanded business to accommodate 20 steady customers, clearing over $200 weekly

This type of résumé also allows you to highlight skills and experiences you are not currently using. Perhaps you are a salesclerk, but are taking computer programming courses in the hopes of getting a job in the computer field. Highlight your proficiency in computers in this section, rather than focussing simply on your sales experience.

30 Action Verbs for a Winning Résumé

Analysed
Managed
Conceived
Motivated
Controlled
Negotiated
Designed
Participated
Developed
Performed
Directed
Prepared
Effected
Produced
Initiated

Established
Researched
Evaluated
Solved
Expanded
Streamlined
Expedited
Strengthened
Generated
Supervised
Implemented
Trained
Improved
Eliminated
Reorganized

THE FINISHED RÉSUMÉ

Once you've completed a satisfactory rough draft of your résumé ask several people to read it and tell you how the résumé makes them perceive you. Incorporate any of their helpful ideas and suggestions. Check your spelling, and be neat. The résumé should be typed with black or dark blue ink and centred on white or off-white paper with a one-inch border all around. If necessary, use a typing or type-setting service. Copies should be clean and clear. If you don't have access to a good copier, invest in a copy service or have your résumés printed professionally.

One more tip: If you're away from the house a lot, consider investing in an inexpensive telephone answering device. This will ensure you are receiving all your messages and also allow you the advantage of returning calls when you are prepared.

READING AND REACTING

1. a) In a small group, examine the suggestions offered in "How to Write a Sure-Hire Résumé." Evaluate each point for its importance.

b) Brainstorm other steps that can be taken to write an impressive résumé.

c) Incorporate the above information into a point-form report on how to write the most effective résumé. Share your report with the class.

2. The author lists verbs that you can use in a résumé to emphasize the things you have done. Take each word in the list and follow it with a phrase that describes something that you have done. Check off the accomplishments you are most proud of. In a group, compare phrases and ask group members for suggestions to add to your list.

REACHING OUT

1. a) Discuss with a partner the personal information that you would give on a résumé. Give your reasons for including or excluding specific statistics. To evaluate your decisions, your partner will need to know something about the job you would be applying for.

b) List the educational achievements, hobbies, or volunteer work that you will include on a résumé.

c) With a specific job in mind, follow Jeffrey G. Allen's outline and prepare a rough draft of the material that you will put in your résumé. Include the phrases that you wrote in Reading and Reacting, #2.

d) In groups, examine the rough drafts. Are there ways to improve the appearance of your résumé? Could the information be organized more efficiently or uniquely? Consider the job that you are applying for and tailor your résumé to emphasize the skills, qualities, education, and experience you have that qualify you for the job. Bear in mind who will read your résumé. What will appeal to that reader?

e) Revise your résumé until you are satisfied that you have presented yourself in the best possible way. Remember to seek reactions to your developing drafts and to have your final copy proofread.

1) Take your résumé to a Canada Employment Centre. Ask a counsellor to give you feedback on its strengths and to make suggestions for improvements. Share the critique with your class.

2. Conduct a library search in the resource centre for texts that give instructions and samples of résumé writing. Make an annotated bibliography of the books that you locate.

3. Make contact with any business people that you know, or with your principal, and ask them what attracts them to some résumés, and what detracts from a résumé. It would be very helpful if your business contact could remove identifying details from actual applications and discuss with you their strengths and weaknesses. If you collect some samples of real résumés, make transparencies and analyse them with the class. Maintain confidentiality by removing any information that would identify the applicant.

4. Read the poem "Want Ads" below. Look through the classified ads in your local newspaper and choose a job listing that appeals to you. Compose a résumé that presents the ideal candidate for the job, based on the five parts referred to in "How to Write a Sure-Hire Résumé."

WANTADS

EMPLOYMENT OPPORTUNITIES

Looking through the paper there's sure a lot of jobs I don't want.

By: ROBERT GARRISON

► THE RIGHT WAY TO WRITE A COVER LETTER

Jeffrey G. Allen

With every résumé you send out, include a personally typed (not reproduced) cover letter. Think of this letter as your personal sales pitch. Use it to highlight or emphasize those skills you think would most impress the employer you want to work for. Make the letter brief—one typed page, consisting of four steps that contain the following information.

1. Get to the right source. Address your cover letter to the person who will be conducting the job interview. A phone call to the company's information operator or personnel department can help you ensure that your résumé gets to the right person. Make certain you get the correct spelling of his or her name and the proper title. Always precede the employer's name with Mr. or Ms.

2. State the job you're after. The first paragraph should specifically state what job you are applying for. If you were referred to the employer by someone, mention that person in this paragraph. It will give the prospective employer an immediate frame of reference for you and will single your résumé out from the others.

3. Sell yourself. The second paragraph should emphasize the skills that will be most attractive to that employer. You should include some tidbit of information that you did not include on your résumé. For example, let's say that through research you've discovered that XYZ Company has recently acquired a new computer system to update its bookkeeping department. You can then mention in your cover letter that you are currently taking a computer course, or that you have a home computer which you've programmed to handle the family's finances. Once again, how well you've done your homework and how well you use the information you've uncovered can make or break your cover letter and chances for a job interview.

4. Be positive. Close your cover letter with a request for an interview. State that you will be calling within the week to arrange a time and date for your meeting, and then be sure to make that follow-up call. Keep a copy of every letter you send out and then refer to it when making the follow-up phone call. Take notes on the copy of the letter so you won't forget what was discussed. If an employer does not wish to meet with you, don't be afraid to ask for feedback. Why weren't you selected? Does he or she have any suggestions/improvement or know of any other job openings for which you might be qualified? The answers may help you uncover hidden job opportunities and, possibly, get you a job referral.

January 20, 1983

C F O S Broadcasting Station
270   9 Street East
Owen Sound, Ontario
N4K 1N7

Dear Sir or Madam:

"UNPAID LABOUR FOR ONE WHOLE WEEK!"

Yes, if you act now, YOU have the opportunity to receive UNPAID labour, for one whole week, from an enthusiastic student who is asking for the chance to "gain some experience"!

My name is Tilla Seh. I am a grade 12 student from Grey Highlands Secondary School in Flesherton. Our school is sponsoring a "work-week," and I would just love to work for YOU!

I hope to pursue a career as a television news anchor woman and I plan to attend Ryerson in Toronto. As the president of my school's Students' Council, I have gained a variety of communication skills. Working at a radio station would really top it off.

I am capable of doing *anything* I am trained to do. My secretarial skills are excellent and I would not mind an office job at all. (I even do windows!) The point is that I would like to start at the bottom just like that famous Canadian broadcaster did—Gordon Sinclair. Being able to see exactly what goes on within a radio station and meeting new people is experience enough for a student such as myself.

If your response is favourable towards this letter, I could come in any week that is convenient for you. I am willing to come in during my holidays in March or even during the exam week—(but I'm sure my teachers will miss me!!)

Thank you for reading this letter. Remember, you were young and seeking the chance for some *experience* once too, and because of that chance here you are today! So won't you lend a helping hand??

Sincerely yours,

Tilla Seh

READING AND REACTING

1. a) In a small group, decide if Tilla's letter follows the steps suggested by Jeffrey G. Allen. Do you recommend any changes? Are there things that Allen identifies as important that Tilla did particularly well?

   b) Identify display techniques that Tilla used to make her letter attractive and attention getting, and then evaluate whether they were effective. Would you recommend changes in the format of her letter, in the choice of content, or in the wording? Identify how Tilla attempted to persuade her reader to accept her application.

   c) Rewrite Tilla's letter, making any improvements that you wish. Incorporate the suggestions that were raised by the group.

2. a) In a small group, read Tilla's letter of application and try to imagine what Tilla is like.

   b) Describe the person you imagine Tilla thought she was writing to. What position at the radio station do you suppose Tilla thought her reader would hold? Did she expect the person to be male or female, young or old, old-fashioned, or up-to-date? Compare your group's description with that of other groups.

REACHING OUT

1. a) In preparation for writing a cover letter, make an outline with the following information: job objective; complete name and address of the prospective employer; relevant skills.

   b) Follow the suggestions in "The Right Way to Write a Cover Letter" and prepare your own letter for a real job that you would like to obtain. You might apply for a part-time job, a work experience position, a co-operative job, a summer job, or a permanent job. If you have prepared a résumé in a previous assignment, design your letter to go with it.

   or

   Clip an advertisement from a newspaper for a job that appeals to you. Prepare a covering letter in response to this advertisement.

2. Imagine that you are the person to whom Tilla wrote. Reply to her letter, either offering her a job or rejecting her application. Give reasons for your decision.

► How to Sell Yourself

in the first four minutes of meeting someone new

Janet Elsea

Janet Elsea believes that when you first meet someone, the impressions that you make in the first four minutes of meeting are the most important ones.

You never get a second chance to make a first good impression. And you make first impressions every day. They begin with what others see in you and you in them—and it takes only two to four minutes to make that impression positive or negative (on the telephone it takes just seconds).

First impressions are made of things people notice about you during those crucial first minutes—your appearance, facial expressions, movement, tone of voice, as well as the words you say. If that first impression is positive, it's like putting money in a skyrocketing stock: your investment will pay big dividends. But a negative impression may be difficult—even impossible—to change.

In order to control the impression you want to make, whether on the job or on a date, you need to ask yourself these questions: "What do I look like?" "What do I sound like?" Once you know the answers, you'll have a great deal of valuable information about how effectively you communicate.

When you meet someone for the first time, the other person tends to focus first on what he or she can see. While social scientists disagree on the precise sequence of factors by which people make judgments about you, their order of importance generally appears to be: appearance, facial expressions, eye contact, movement, personal space, and touch.

So much meaning is conveyed by these five factors that many communication experts believe that "what you look like" constitutes more than half the total message: fifty-five percent of the meaning is conveyed by facial expressions and body language alone. Next, people focus on what they can hear. When you speak, your voice is characterized by its speed, loudness, pitch, tone, and articulation. Your voice—not including your actual words—may transmit as much as 38 percent of the meaning in face-to-face conversations. (It conveys a great deal more information about you on the telephone, of course.)

Finally, the other person gets around to your words, which contribute a mere 7 percent to the meaning. It's not that your words are unimportant, but if others don't like what they see in your appearance or hear in your voice, they may not care at all about what you said. Their minds already may be made up; their first impression formed.

Here's what you should know to ensure that you really sell yourself in those vital first few minutes:

Study photos, and note which ones you look best in and why. Is it your clothes? Hairstyle? Accessories? Weight? Look at

EYE CONTACT

FACIAL EXPRESSION

APPEARANCE

PERSONAL SPACE

MOVEMENT (POSTURE, GESTURES)

TOUCH

Above are the key areas people focus on when they size you up.

What you look like constitutes more than half the total message: 55 percent of the meaning is conveyed by facial expressions and body language alone.

It's not that your words are unimportant, but if others don't like what they see in your appearance or hear in your voice, they may not care what you say. Their minds are made up.

the clothes in your closet (including shoes). Study your image in a full-length mirror; note your posture, the tilt of your head.

Do you feel more confident when wearing a certain colour or style? Do people compliment you when you wear certain clothing? You may be pleasantly surprised at what a difference these simple aspects of your appearance can make.

● **Face your face**

Your facial expressions are the next cue; they're the teleprompter by which others read your mood and personality. The face is easily controlled, however, which makes it notoriously inaccurate as a source of information about what's going on inside its owner's mind. What might your face say to someone you are meeting for the first time? That you are angry because of your perpetual frown? That you aren't interested because your face looks blank? That you're nervous and anxious because you have a tight little smile?

What is critical is that facial expressions be consistent with the tone of voice and the words being spoken.

● **Making the right moves**

Movement is a critical way to present a confident, assured impression, because walk and posture are closely tied to emotional state. A wealth of information is available on how someone sits, gestures, and stands; the individual's level of confidence, degree of anxiety, and efforts to deceive are evident to those who know what to look for.

Poor posture is a typical problem. Keep your torso erect, not rigid, your shoulders even, and both feet on the ground (not planted, but weight evenly distributed).

People tend to forget they have hands until they are about to give a presentation—and then they don't know what to do with them. To avoid awkward gestures, it's best to hold your hands where they can be seen and where you can move them naturally to illustrate what you're saying.

Nodding can indicate agreement or encourage further discussion. It can be a sign that you're listening, but it also can mean that you're passively trying to keep a dialogue going, and that may be a sign of nonassertiveness. Nodding also can be an unconscious habit signalling agreement to others when you don't mean that at all.

If you haven't thought about such movements, you may be missing some of the most revealing facts about yourself. By moving with confidence and energy, you're more likely to be perceived that way.

● **Your personal space**

Study a photograph of yourself with friends as you talk or relax. Note the distance

How Men and Women See Things Differently

There are gender-based differences in eye contact. Women engage in more direct eye contact than men, especially when men are talking. But women tend to avert their eyes more frequently than men when it's their turn to speak.

Is It Smart to Put on a Happy Face?

Not always. Smiling is the most important facial expression for communicating, but it can create a double bind for women. While studies show that people who smile are considered more attractive, they also show that women who smile a lot are perceived as less effective managers. Therefore, the key is to keep your expression consistent with your message. If the context and message call for a pleasant expression, then by all means smile. If not, don't.

between you and the others. It's probably a matter of inches, with one or more participants leaning in toward the others, perhaps touching someone. Compare that with the amount of space you maintained when a repair person came, when you met a new colleague, when you greeted a former client. Then recall instances when your new boss stood over you while you sat at your desk. In each case, your "bubble of privacy" depended on your size, height, and weight; your cultural background; whom you were with and how well you liked each other; how much power was being wielded and by whom; and whether you're male or female.

How you guard your personal space and how big it is at any one instance is something you respond to unconsciously, often in reaction to someone else's movement. You expand or contract your personal space according to how intimate you want that encounter to be.

During initial interactions with someone who doesn't know you, you may give an impression of personal power if you simply occupy more space when you stand or sit and if you do not move out of the way for people attempting to dominate you.

● **Touching experiences**
Touching behaviour can be fraught with misunderstanding. A firm handshake may signal acknowledgment or equality, a limp one, lack of interest or timidity. A pat on the head or face can signal liking, but easily can be constructed as condescension. A one-finger thrust can indicate dislike or anger, while a soft touch with an open hand may reveal positive feelings.

One of the difficulties of touch, especially with people who don't know each other, is exactly what to construe from it. The best advice is to take all areas of body language into consideration when you're making, or receiving, an impression.

● **Speak up**
You can regulate your voice to make the impression you want, but to do this you must first increase your knowledge of vocal sounds, using your own voice as the model for analysis and improvement.

Try tape-recording three samples of your voice—either in conversation or reading aloud—two or three minutes each, at different times: first thing in the morning, when your voice is relaxed and fresh; early afternoon, when stress and exhaustion tend to be high, and late evening, when you're relaxed but tired. Breathe calmly and slowly as you speak. As you analyse your voice on tape, check for the characteristics and problems described.

Rate. Listen first to how fast you speak. Count the number of words per minute (you can do this easily by counting the number of words for fifteen seconds and multiplying by four). You're an average talker if it's between 120 and 160 words per minute. How fast should you talk? It depends upon several factors: the physical environment (a small room vs a conference hall), noise levels, the nature of the material and your emotional involvement with it, and the medium used (on the telephone a rapid rate is difficult to understand because there are no nonverbal cues to help the listener understand). A good rule of thumb, however, is to vary your rate of speech. When you're meeting someone who has never heard you, start slower than usual if you're a fast talker and build to your normal rate. Remember, in those first few moments the other person has to digest all of that nonverbal information about you before getting to your voice.

Loudness. As you listen to your taped voice, recollect for a moment: Do people ask you frequently to speak up or repeat things? Conversely, if they lean back or step away when you talk, they may be giving you nonverbal cues that you're talking too loudly. The best guideline for volume is to turn your "dial" up or down as the material, competing noise, and other factors dictate.

Pitch. Knowing the highness or lowness of your voice can give you greater control over the impressions you make because listeners form all sorts of judgments about you—often with startling accuracy—based on your tone of voice.

Listen for these typical problems.

A rising or upward inflection at the end of sentences. Your tone should come down at the end of most sentences to signal completion and certainty. Improper inflection gives the impression of tentativeness.

A singsong quality to the pitch. Vary tones for the sake of meaning, not variety. Remember your kindergarten teacher's singsong instructions? That sort of voice in a businessperson gives an immediate impression of immaturity or passivity.

Monotony. Avoid a lack of variation in pitch levels, the flipside of "singsong." You may hear that in a bored employee. People may interpret your own monotonous voice as a lack of caring.

Vocal Quality. Also called "timbre," this distinguishes your voice from anyone else's. Be alert to the negative features that detract from tonal quality.

Nasality. "Talking through your nose" is a common and annoying problem. Some nasality is important, but only for the sounds *n*, *m*, and *ng*. To find out if you're a nasal speaker, pinch your nose closed and say aloud, "Whoa, oh horse of mine." There should be no vibrations in your nose except for the word *"mine."* The other sounds should come entirely from your mouth. To correct nasality, simply open your mouth more to get those vowel sounds out. You may need to speak more loudly and articulate more actively.

Breathiness. Breathy speaking creates a first impression of bewilderment, delicacy, or conspiracy. To correct this, simply project your voice toward your listeners.

Thinness. This refers to a voice that seems to be childish, lacking in depth and resonance. It's difficult to convey authority if your voice has a weak reed-like sound. As with breathiness, thinness is easily cured by speaking with more resonance and openness of tone.

Stridency. Nothing turns people off more quickly than a shrill voice which broadcasts tension and nervousness. Caused by hypertension and insufficient breathing, a strident quality is a sharp, metallic sound with a high and squeaky pitch. Because stridency can lead to unpleasant side effects (such as a sore throat and laryngitis), try these relaxation exercises: yawn, roll your neck, massage your jaw.

Harshness. When you are angry or feeling irritable, your voice may take on a rough, hard quality, often low-pitched. The first impression on strangers may be that you are unsympathetic, sarcastic, or overbearing. If relaxation and breathing don't get rid of this problem, see a throat specialist.

Articulation. Articulation refers to the distinctness of the individual sounds you make. (It is often confused with "pronunciation," which is your choice of sounds to emphasize.) Listen to yourself on tape. Do you hear words like "gonna," "didchwannta," or "Warshington"? Do your words run together? Are important sounds muffled? Are unimportant ones stressed? If so, you're afflicted with "lazy lips." Being clear doesn't mean being artificial. It means making sounds appropriate to your meaning and conveying the impression that you know what you're doing and that you're in control.

Seeing yourself as others see and hear you is critical if you're trying to create the best first impression. Once you assess what needs to be done to make you look better, do it. Whether it involves practising facial expressions in the mirror, walking with more confidence, making more direct eye contact or improving your use of effective language, the key is to practise. It will pay off—and you'll see the results in seconds!

READING AND REACTING

1. As you read "How to Sell Yourself," jot down the things that, according to Elsea, people notice when they meet someone for the first time. In a small group, discuss how these factors influence your first impressions of others.

2. Janet Elsea suggests ways that you can control the impression you make by your facial expressions, body posture, gestures, and use of space. With a small group, list a set of impressions that you might wish to create in your business life. Identify from the article the things you have to do to convey messages that are appropriate in the situations you have named.

3. Follow Elsea's instructions and tape three samples of your voice. With a partner, design a scale, based on the suggestions in the article, to assess the qualities of your voice. As you listen to the tape, analyse your voice and make notations on the things you wish to change.

REACHING OUT

1. a) Choose a favourite picture of yourself or a picture from magazines, and design a photo layout of how you would like to present yourself in an interview situation. Indicate what you will wear— stick a photo of your face above a picture of your favourite outfit.

   b) With captions or notes, write a script to go with the picture. Indicate all the points you would try to remember about creating a favourable impression with your facial expressions, posture, gestures, and voice.

▶ A Successful Interview

Joyce Denebrink

Dos and Don'ts

When your job search results in an interview, make the best impression possible by considering these pointers from career consultant and *Glamour* "Job Strategies" columnist Marilyn Moats Kennedy.

DON'T wear something brand-new to the interview. Choose an outfit, including shoes, you've worn before. If you're comfortable in your clothes you will confidently forget about them and concentrate on what you're saying.

DO speak clearly and slowly, in a normal tone of voice. In their nervousness, many job applicants rush through sentences, making it difficult for the interviewer to hear or understand them. And speak up—this isn't the time to appear either shy or withdrawn.

DO carry a nice leather briefcase. Borrow one if you have to. It looks bad if you pull a crumpled résumé from the depths of your handbag—and invariably you'll be asked for another copy. Be able to produce an immaculate one from your briefcase.

DON'T attach samples of your work (drawings, sales reports, story clips, etc.) to your résumé. Instead, "feed" them one or two at a time to the interviewer to illustrate points you are making. Nothing speaks for itself—so explain why the sample is important.

DO sit slightly forward in your chair when you answer questions—it makes you appear eager and animated, and more interested in the job.

DON'T ask if the job involves overtime or whether you'll be paid for it. Leave that for the negotiations after they've made you an offer.

DON'T lose your cool or good manners regardless of the interviewer's behaviour. If he or she snaps, "I just don't see how you think you'd fit in here!" don't reply rudely, "I just told you how," say, "Perhaps I didn't mention my experience in . . . ." Don't ever allow yourself to become irritated.

The Best Answers to the Most Common Questions

Tell me about yourself. You'll seldom have a better opportunity to sell yourself. So begin with the phrase, "One of the things I'm proud of is . . . ." Mention your skills and background and why they make you an ideal candidate for the job. Measure your accomplishments in facts, dollars, and numbers.

• **What type of position are you interested in?** If you don't have your heart set on a specific position, then tell the interviewer what you do best: "I'm good at keeping track of supplies. I work well with people and would like a position relating to office management." If you have a specific job opening in mind, say so, but add that you would consider other openings that offer future promotion opportunities.

• **Where do you want to be five years from now?** Three good responses, "Where could I be?" "What programs do you have?" "In the same company, but with more responsibility."

• **Are you willing to transfer?** You cannot predict the future. Always say "Yes, I'm open to transfer opportunities."

• **What are your strengths?** Think up at least three examples. They should be job-related, such as "I'm flexible. I worked 18 hours a day for 10 days during the Girl Scout fair." (Employers fear you'll always have to go home on time.) "I'm well organized. I'm good at following through on all my family's and PTA projects." And, "I'm a good letter writer and speller. My friends are always asking for help with correspondence and reports."

• **What are your weaknesses?** Again, formulate at least three examples ahead of time. These should not be job-related, and never volunteer anything truly negative. Instead name strengths disguised as weaknesses, such as, "I tend to get really involved in work and think about it at home. I'm too hard on myself when I make mistakes. I have trouble delegating—so I tend to do all the work myself."

• **What would you do if . . . ?** Your solution to whatever problem posed by the interviewer is not nearly as important as maintaining a positive attitude. Be inventive enough to have several possible choices.

• **Why do you want to work for our company?** Respond with one or two personal statements related to the company, such as, "I like working with creative people," and, "I have a commitment to the arts."

You probably won't be asked about your age, marital status, number of dependants, or religion. Interviewers know they shouldn't ask discriminatory questions. But they are only human and sometimes say whatever pops into their heads. So if you are asked a tough question, take your time to think, and keep the following tips in mind:

• **The best response to a discriminatory question:** "Is that a prerequisite for this position?" Chances are the interviewer will back down, and you'll both come out of the situation gracefully.

• **The best way to deal with child-care doubts.** If you feel there is a subject the interviewer can't bring up because it's illegal to do so—like who will take care of your kids—bring it up yourself to quell any doubts. For instance, you might volunteer, "I have a very reliable babysitter and excellent backup babysitters—my son's grandmothers."

• **The best way to talk salary.** It's a good idea to try to find out beforehand the salary range for the job for which you're being interviewed. The company's personnel department can tell you. Let the interviewer bring up the subject of money. If the interviewer mentions a salary that is lower than you want, you might then ask, "Is that a firm figure or is it negotiable?" The interviewer may go higher, but remember, there are other benefits to consider. Ask about advancement opportunities and employee benefits.

▼

READING AND REACTING

1. With a partner, list in order of importance the tips offered in "Dos and Don'ts." Compare your list with that of another pair. Be prepared to support your ranking order.

2. In a small group, read "The Best Answers to the Most Common Questions."

a) Evaluate the effectiveness of the answers provided. Suggest ways in which the answers can be strengthened.

b) Share with the group other questions that are asked frequently at interviews. Try to arrive at the best way to answer these questions.

3. Create a display that illustrates the most important points to consider when preparing for a job interview. Incorporate the suggestions from these two articles.

REACHING OUT

1. a) Set up a panel discussion on the interview. Appoint a moderator and choose as panel members classmates who have been interviewed for a job. Each panelist will prepare a brief description of her or his interview experience. Tell about the job, the employer, your age at the time, and any other details that you think relevant. Describe specific questions that you remember being asked.

   b) Invite your audience of classmates to contribute their experiences with interviews after each panelist has made his or her presentation.

   c) Ask the audience to analyse any problems that occurred and to suggest ways of handling the situation.

   d) Make a bulletin board display of questions asked at interviews.

2. a) With a partner, role-play an interview that results in a job offer. Identify the context and characters clearly for your audience. Try to incorporate the suggestions from "Dos and Don'ts."

   b) With a partner, role-play an interview that goes badly. Have the audience identify what went wrong and suggest how things should have been done.

3. Interview an adult who has had experience conducting interviews. Make a record of his or her favourite questions, pet peeves, and helpful hints. Report back to the class.

   or

   Interview an adult who has had extensive working experience. Record his or her advice about how to prepare for the interview, how to handle difficult questions, and how to follow up the interview. Many applicants will have an amusing or embarrassing incident that they will be willing to share with you. When you report back to the class, be sure to respect confidentiality where it is required.

4. During an interview, the applicant is often asked, "Do you have any questions?" In a small group, brainstorm a list of questions you could ask the interviewer the next time you are faced with that question. Compare questions with those from other groups and compile a master list of the ten most appropriate questions to ask the interviewer. Share the list with the class.

▶ A Thank-You Letter

Joyce Denebrink

Believe it or not, only one percent of job applicants send a thank-you note to follow up on an interview, according to corporate personnel directors. Often, they are the ones who end up getting the job, because that simple courtesy makes them stand out from all the other job applicants with similar credentials.

Send a handwritten thank-you note the same day or the day after the interview. It's more personal than a typed note. Use the letter to restate any positive points you want to make about yourself (or to include any important information you may have forgotten to emphasize).

What exactly should you write? Here's a good format to follow.

Dear _____

I just wanted to express my thanks and tell you how much I enjoyed our conversation today. The _____ job sounds very interesting. I believe my _____ skills and experience make me well qualified for this position. I am even more enthusiastic about it after meeting you and hearing about your company. I will call in a few days, hoping that you will have reached a favourable decision for both of us at that time.

Joyce Denebrink

▼

R E A D I N G A N D R E A C T I N G

1. List the main points covered in Joyce Denebrink's sample letter. Write a thank-you letter to someone (real or imagined) who interviewed you recently, which follows Joyce Denebrink's format.

R E A C H I N G O U T

1. Have friends or family done you a special favour recently? Has the Students' Council organized a special activity? Has a teacher or fellow student given you help? Is there a public person or a group of people to whom you would like to show your appreciation? Write a letter of thanks to submit to your school or local newspaper.

► EMPLOYER LOOKS FOR ATTITUDE, APPEARANCE

non-politic...
, while maintaining
mpete on an interna-
Foreign policies are
create harmony be-
s on all fronts (al-
not always achieved),
d, it is in the interests
see that a Canadian...
ours...
um,
nselve...
event...
usion
he re...
ealth
on tw
ting t
black
for the
uth Afr
value
in build

boycott has be...

spiring confidence. So, in future, I
will scoff at the suggestion of Third
World "disunity and impotence."

letes
corp...
other
e
v

We felt impelled to write about the youth unemployment problem. We are a company that is hiring 24 students for this summer's painting season. We have filled almost 20 of those positions in just over three months. It has been a surprisingly arduous task.

We are unquestionably looking for experience in those we hire. However, the prerequisites are a responsible attitude and appearance, because they are the cornerstone of our business. A focus on presentation, service and treatment of customers has borne us success. To ensure this we look foremost for employees who will be responsible and who reflect well on the company.

In looking for such employees, we found that four of the first six applicants on a single day did not show up, without calling to cancel or explain. There were two more no-shows later in the day and two latecomers among 20 applicants. Some had the gall to call several days later, requesting another interview, at their convenience, with no apology or explanation for their missed interviews.

Getting a job with us is no problem for those who come neatly dressed with a responsible and enthusiastic attitude. We are eager to hire such persons. Such persons unfortunately appear to be in short supply. Most of those we offered jobs to had several others to choose from. Most of the applicants we did not hire will probably have a hard time finding jobs.

It is all up to you. You do not have to be part of the unemployment problem. Be positive with yourself and your desire to work. If you have a responsible attitude and neat presentation of self, it will place you in a category of personnel for which employers are always looking. Good luck this summer!

RENE JANSEN in de WAL
STEVEN DONALDSON
BRIAN BURGESS
Scarborough

ining
ing fo

on: In th...
olitical scene, what is worse
e hypocritical attitude of
nadian and other Western
ments in singling out South
as a violator of human
...the more horren-

...and personal signature, address
and phone number of sender;
street names and phone numbers
will not be published. The Star
reserves the right to edit all
contributions but will take every
precaution to preserve the core of
...dent's argument.

▶ 20 REASONS WHY PEOPLE DON'T GET HIRED

To find out exactly what mistakes people make when applying for a job, Northwestern University's placement director, F.S. Endicott, surveyed personnel directors at 153 companies. The following, listed in order of importance, are the most common errors job applicants make.

- Poor personal appearance
- Overaggressive
- Inability to express information clearly
- Lack of interest and enthusiasm
- Lack of planning for career; no purpose and no goals
- Nervous, lack of confidence and poise
- Overemphasis on money
- Unwilling to start at the bottom
- Makes excuses
- Lack of tact and courtesy
- Lack of maturity
- Condemns past employers
- No genuine interest in company or job
- Fails to look interviewer in the eye
- Sloppy application form
- Little sense of humour
- Arrives late at interview
- Fails to express appreciation for interviewer's time
- Fails to ask questions about the job
- Vague responses to questions

R E A D I N G   A N D   R E A C T I N G

1. From the list "20 Reasons Why People Don't Get Hired," identify the six characteristics that you find most annoying. In a small group, share your peeves and give an account of a time when you encountered such behaviour and how you handled the situation.

2. a) Make a point-form list of the complaints the letter-writers have about applicants to their job advertisement. Compare your list with "20 Reasons Why People Don't Get Hired." Identify those errors made by applicants that appear on both lists.

   b) Using positive advice from the letter and your own opinion, make a list of ways to impress a prospective employer. Post the list on the bulletin board.

R E A C H I N G   O U T

1. With a partner, interview an employer. Ask what he or she looks for in a person seeking employment. Share the ideas you collect with the class.

2. Write a letter to a young person who will be seeking summer employment. Give advice on how to land a job.

3. Write a letter to the editor in response to Jansen, Donaldson, and Burgess's letter. Express your point of view about the difficulties that young people encounter in looking for a job.

from
▶ A MORTAL FLOWER

Han Suyin

EVERY DAY I WALKED FROM HOME TO THE AMERICAN nuns' temporary college, behind the North Sea Park, and back again. It was the mule track I trudged, the one in front of our house, and the white dust came up to my ankles, filling my tennis shoes. Passing over the great marble bridge in front of the park I would linger to see the white thirteenth-century pagoda, crowned with gold, commanding the mirror lake. The willows become green-swathed and supple in the patchy spring, and my parents debated where I could apply for a job: to the Belgian bank? or the French bank? But my job was decided, not by them, nor me, but by my friend Hilda Kuo.

Hilda takes an enormous amount of space, though so little time, in my adolescence. Even today, her memory stirs me; I long to see her again. She was three years older than I, and for a short while all I wanted to look like, sound like, dress like. She was the only girl I knew who told me I wrote excellent letters. She made a plaster cast of my face. She had opinions on everything. She took a picture of me, at sixteen, which I have still. She and I were nearly killed, falling off a hillside road in her small car. Hilda was so full of life, I cannot believe her dead.

and my parents debated where I could apply for a job

I met her in the street, I walking, she riding a Mongolian pony on the pavement, and that was Hilda all over. She stopped the pony and we talked. I told her I needed a job. "Why don't you apply where I work, at the P.U.M.C.?"

I said: "What is that?"

"It's that big hospital there, you goof." She pointed with her riding-whip to the green-tiled roofs that rose high above the low grey houses and shops. "The Yu Wang Fu," I said, giving it the Chinese name. "Rockefeller Foundation." I was awed.

The massive marble and pillared palace had been the residence of the Emperor's uncle, now acquired by the Rockefeller Foundation, and turned into a hospital and teaching school called the Peking Union Medical College. When anyone said "Rockefeller Foundation" there was even more reverence in their voice than when they said "Generalissimo Chiang Kaishek".

The day after meeting Hilda I wrote a letter to the

Rockefeller Foundation, applying for a job.

Neither Father nor Mother thought I would get in. "You have to have pull. It's an American thing, Rockefeller Foundation. You must have pull."

Mother said; "That's where they do all those experiments on dogs and people." All the Big Shots of the Nanking government also came here to have medical treatment, and sometimes took away a nurse to become "a new wife."

It made sense to me, typing in a hospital; I would learn about medicine, since I wanted to study medicine. And as there was no money at home for me to study, I would earn money, and prepare myself to enter medical school. I had already discovered that a convent-school education was not at all adequate, and that it would take me at least three more years of hard study before being able to enter any college at all. Science, mathematics, Chinese literature and the classics . . . with the poor schooling given to me, it would take me years to get ready for a university.

"I will do it." But clenched teeth, decision tearing my bowels, were not enough; there was no money, no money, my mother said it, said it until I felt as if every morsel of food I ate was wrenched off my father's body.

"No one is going to feed you doing nothing at home." Of course, one who does not work must not eat unless one can get married, which is called: "being settled at last." But with my looks I would never get married, I was too thin, too sharp, too ugly. Mother said it, Elder Brother said it. Everyone agreed that I should work, because marriage would be difficult for me.

Within a week a reply came. The morning postman brought it, and I choked over my milk and coffee. "I'm to go for an interview. At the Peking Union Medical College. To the Comptroller's office."

Father and Mother were pleased. Mother put the coffee-pot down and took the letter. "What good paper, so thick." But how could we disguise the fact that I was not fifteen years old? I had claimed to be sixteen in the letter. In fact, said Papa, it was not a lie since Chinese are a year old when born, and if one added the New Year as an extra year, as do the Cantonese and the Hakkas, who become two years old when they reach their first New Year (so that a baby born on December 31st would be reckoned two years old on the following January 2nd), I could claim to being sixteen.

"You *look* sixteen," said Mama, "all you have to do is to stop hopping and picking your pimples. And lengthen your skirt."

"What dress should I wear?" I had two school uniforms, a green dress, a brown dress, and one dress with three rows of frills for Sunday, too dressy for an interview. I had no shoes except flat-heeled school shoes, and tennis shoes. There was no time to make a dress and in those years no ready-made clothes existed. Mother

"No one is going to feed you doing nothing at home."

lengthened the green dress, and added her voile scarf. I squeezed two pimples on my forehead, then went to the East market and bought some face powder, Butterfly brand, pink, made in Shanghai by a Japanese firm.

The next morning, straw-hatted, with powder on my nose, I went with my father to the gates of the hospital.

"It's not this gate, this is for the sick. It's the other gate, round the corner," said the porter.

The Yu Wang Fu Palace occupied a whole city block. We walked along its high grey outer wall, hearing the dogs scream in the kennels, and came to its other gate which was the Administration building gate. It had two large stone lions, one male, one female. We crossed the marble courtyard, walked up the steps with their carved dragons coiling in the middle, into an entrance hall, with painted beams and intricate painted ceiling, red lacquered pillars, huge lamps. There was cork matting on the stone floor.

"I'll leave you," said Papa. "Try to make a good impression." And he was gone.

I found the Comptroller's office easily, there was a messenger in the hall directing visitors. An open door, a room, two typewriters clattering and two women making them clatter.

I stood at the door and one of the women came to me. She had the new style of hair, all upstanding curls, which I admired, a dress with print round the hem; she was very pregnant, so that her belly seemed to be coming at me first. She smiled. "Hello, what can I do for you?"

"I have an interview."

She took the letter from my hand. "Glad you could come. Now just sit you down. No, sit down *there*. I'll tell Mr. Harned you've come."

The office had two other doors besides the one to the corridor, on one was "Comptroller", on the other "Assistant Comptroller." That was the one she went through and returned from.

"Mr. Harned will see you now."

Mr. Harned was very tall, thin, a small bald head, a long chin, enormous glasses. I immediately began to quiver with fright. His head was like a temple on top of a mountain, like the white pagoda on the hill in the North Sea Park. I could not hear a word of what he said. A paper and a pencil were in my hand, however, and Mr. Harned was dictating to me, giving me a speed test in shorthand.

I went out of his office and the pregnant secretary sat me in front of her own typewriter. I turned a stricken face to her. "I couldn't hear. I couldn't hear what he said . . . "

"Wait, I'll tell him." She bustled off. At the other desk was a blonde, thin girl, who had thrown one look at me and then gone back to clattering. The pregnant one reappeared, a pink sheet in hand: "Now just copy this on the typewriter, best you can."

I hit the keys, swiftly; the typewriter was the same make as mine, a Royal.

"My, you are fast. I'll tell Mr. Harned."

And Mr. Harned came out, benign behind those enormous goggle glasses. "Well, Miss Chou, we've decided to take you on as a typist, at thirty-five local dollars a month. To start Monday. Is that all right?"

I nodded, unable to speak. Had he said ten dollars I would have accepted.

The kind secretary said: "Now take your time, and wipe your face. How old are you, by the way?"

"Sixteen, nearly."

"Is that all? Why my eldest is bigger than you, and she isn't through school yet. I told Mr. Harned you were shy and upset,

and that's why you couldn't take dictation. He's all right, just takes getting used to, that's all."

"I couldn't understand his English."

"Oh, you'll get used to it. Now, I won't be around on Monday, I'm going to have a baby. It's your letter that got them interested in you, you wrote such good English, better than all the other letters we've had. Mr. Harned will give you a try." She whispered. "I put in a good word for you."

"Thanks, thanks a lot . . . I need the money, I . . ."

"Yes, dear, we know." Obviously she wanted her typewriter back, and her chair. I was still sitting on it. "Well, toodle-doo for now, hope you enjoy yourself in this job. I've been here six months and I've enjoyed *every minute*. Don't let Mr. Harned worry you, he's really great, once you get used to him."

I had a job, had a job, had a job . . . I walked home treading on air, I could not have sat in a rickshaw. Outside our house was

*I had a job,
had a job,
had a job . . .*

the mule track, and opposite the house was the well, a well which nestled under a tree. All the creaky squeaky water-carts of the quarter come here to fill their barrels from this well. The well winch was turning, clear water, the beautiful clear spring underground water of Peking gushed out, one by one the water carts lined up, the men naked to the waist, wiping their sweat, and spitting. While her husband drew the well water, the well woman sat as usual by the stone margin, breasts exposed, feeding her last baby.

Oh, how wonderful life, happy like this water, gushing out so clean and so cold, ice-cold in the June heat! I smiled at the well woman, who had wonderful teeth, and though she was so filthy her skin was always clear and smooth; she never combed her hair, she was a real northern woman, slovenly, unkempt, though she and her husband owned that beautiful well. Mother hated her, and the well woman laughed at Mother, laughed deliberately, standing well back on her planted hips and legs, carrying her large baby across her stomach, breasts hanging like two melons on either side of her open jacket; rippled with well-water laughter.

The more Mama shouted at the well woman, the more she laughed, and her husband who turned the handle of the well-beam and made the water gush stared at Mama, and in his drawling Peking blurr said: "Now what is she angry about on this beautiful day?" And the water-carriers chuckled. I smiled at them now. I had a job, a job, gushing money like water from a well . . . .

READING AND REACTING

1. Although this story is set in China in the 1930s, it could easily have been about a teenager in Canada today. In a group, identify those elements in the story that make this possible.

2. With a partner, identify the different steps of the narrator's job search process. Analyse her handling of each stage of the process and note the factors that worked in her favour.

3. a) The author relates to and is influenced by several people. In a small group, discuss each relationship and evaluate its importance to the author at this stage in her life.

   b) In the voice of the author, write a journal entry in which you explore your feelings about someone who is important to you.

4. Imagine that you are the narrator's classmate. Twenty years after this story takes place, she has become a famous doctor and author

and you are a well-known journalist. In your column write about your friendship with the narrator. Describe the qualities that she reveals in this story and relate them to her achievements.

R E A C H I N G O U T

1. Imagine that you are the narrator and write a letter of application for a job at the Rockefeller Foundation. Include a résumé.

2. The narrator makes a very mature assessment of her present circumstances and her future needs in the paragraph beginning, "It made sense to me, typing in a hospital . . . " (p. 86). Think of a time when you had to make an important decision in your life. In a paragraph similar to the author's, state the decision and then go on to explain the reasoning process that led to your decision.

3. Write a short story about a person's first successful job search.

   or

   Describe in a personal narrative the events that led to your first job.

   Compile the class writing in a booklet titled, "I Have a Job!" Design a cover for the booklet.

4. Think of a person who has been as important to you as Hilda was to the narrator. In a journal entry, describe this person and how he or she has influenced your life.

5. You have decided on a career for which you feel you are suited. Your parents/friends/relatives are sceptical and try to dissuade you. With one or two friends, tape or role-play a scene in which you give reasons for your choice and your parents/friends/relatives try to convince you that you've made a mistake.

6. Interview a person who has immigrated to Canada. If possible, tape the interview. Write an account of the immigrant's job search experience here in Canada. Share your account with the class. Play the tape of the interview.

COMMUNICATION PROJECTS

1. Prepare a visually appealing job-finder's kit for young people who are looking for a job.

a) Provide instructions and information for seeking work through the channels listed below:
   —employment agencies
   —job advertisements
   —personal contacts
   —cold calls
   —Canada Employment job entry programs

b) Interview three people—one who is looking for a job, one who is participating in a government-sponsored job entry program, and one who has recently got a permanent job. Ask each person the following:
   —What education do you have?
   —What kind of work are you looking for?
   —What job training have you received?
   —What frustrations and disappointments have you experienced?
   —What job-search strategies have you tried? What worked? What didn't?
   —What advice do you have for young people looking for a job?
   Write a brief profile of each person interviewed and follow it with a transcript of the interview.

c) Conclude with some positive commentary from people who have found fulfilling jobs.
   Present your kit to the guidance counsellor for display.

2. Identify and view five videotapes or films that deal with the job-search process.

a) Prepare an annotated filmography that includes
   —title
   —source
   —length
   —summary

b) Develop questions and activities on the films, suitable for small group work; a quiz; and a viewer evaluation form.
   Present your package to the class and to students in career awareness courses.

▶ ALL IN A DAY'S WORK

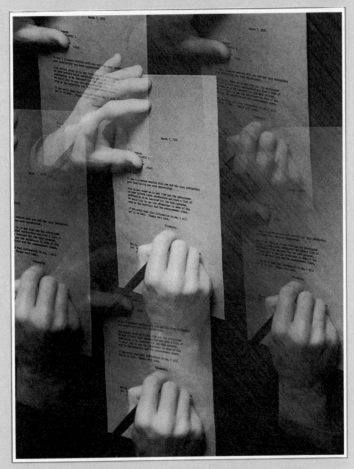

This unit examines some of the issues that you may face at work. Understanding how you are affected by the conditions in which you work is the first step toward gaining control over your work environment.

► FIRST JOB

Howard White

Two weeks ago he knew it was a snap
smart college boy like him deadheads like them
a week ago he'd given up all hope
today he thinks he has a chance
if he can only learn to beat
the sense of blindness backing up
steering one way in the mirror
Euc going the other way on the grade
but it's not to be today: first load
the fill gives truck shifts
like the bottom falling out of the world
all he can do is clench with terror
only goes halfway over but road is blocked
seriousness of it mounts in his brain
as the other trucks roar up one by one
stop in a line drivers gather
get out their thermos jugs and ask nothing
mentally calculates lost earnings in the
thousands someone mutters looks up
foreman charging toward them
grimace under an orange hardhat
guts swimming around thinking
what a relief it would be to only be fired
hat goes by shouting orders comes back
"Alright get in there and be more careful!"
mouth works without words feet find the way
winchline tightens truck shudders wallows
slips back heaves up onto the road
like a walrus onto an ice floe
                              foreman gone

next day shovel cable breaks
trucks line up again coffee comes out
any excuse to take one away from the boss
the kid gets out his greasegun and rag
"Hey you, it's coffee time!"
"Aw, my truck needs greasing . . ."
keeps working

                              and that mistake

he must live much longer

                          to live down

▶ RELIEF LOCATIONS MANAGER

Herbert Scott

Relief is everywhere
at once. He's on his way
up. When he works the front,
the register jumps
under his fingers,
groceries flashing past
like landscape,
his arms almost
screaming with motion.
If he comes to help you
in your section, you know
you're moving too slow.
You go home ashamed
of your thick, clumsy hands.
Relief's bucking for manager
in a new store. You hope
he'll make it.

READING AND REACTING

1. The poet has written "First Job" with almost no punctuation. With a partner, take turns reading the poem aloud. Together, add punctuation to the poem so that the meaning is obvious. Compare your punctuated poem with your classmates. Be prepared to justify your choice of punctuation.

2. In the voice of the "smart college boy," write a letter to a friend to tell him or her of your first two weeks on the job. Your letter should include all the events described in the poem and reveal your feelings about your mistakes.

3. In a small group, discuss the meaning of the following lines:

a) from "First Job":
> "and that mistake
> he must live much longer
> to live down"

b) from "Relief Locations Manager":
> "Relief is everywhere
> at once. He's on his way
> up." . . .

> "Relief's bucking for manager
> in a new store. You hope
> he'll make it."

On your own, explain each set of lines in one or two sentences.

4. In a small group, compare the "smart college boy" with the "relief locations manager." You might wish to focus on their personalities and their attitudes toward work.

or

With a partner, script a meeting between the "smart college boy" and the "relief locations manager" in which they compare notes on their job situations and their colleagues. Role-play the scene for the class and ask for their comments.

REACHING OUT

1. a) In a small group, exchange anecdotes of mistakes you made when you were on a job. (If you have never worked, relate a story from a parent or a friend). Describe how you felt about your errors and how your supervisor and colleagues reacted.

   b) Choose your favourite anecdote (not your own) and write a one-page story around it. Have the person who related the anecdote help you polish the story.

   c) Post all the stories on the bulletin board.

2. In a small group, compose a set of guidelines to help young people settle into new jobs with a minimum of awkwardness and embarrassment. Show your guidelines to the guidance counsellor in your school. He or she may wish to post the guidelines in the guidance office.

3. a) In a small group, discuss why an enthusiastic worker like "relief locations manager" can antagonize his or her co-workers.

   b) Brainstorm ways to make working with such a person a pleasant experience.

4. Write a memoir of your first two weeks on a job or in high school. Describe the most stressful and the most pleasant situation.

You Can Make "That Damn Job" Better If You Try

Wade Roberts

Does this sound familiar? You loathe 8 a.m.; you anticipate 5 p.m. The high point of your workday is lunch. Mondays are the end of the world; you live for the weekend.

But as much as you look forward to your time away from the office, you can't enjoy it. You don't have the inclination, let alone the energy, to do anything but watch television. Maybe you drink. Maybe you take drugs. You have trouble sleeping. Or you get plenty of sleep, perhaps even too much, and yet you're always tired.

You can't get interested in anything. All you can do—day in and day out, at the office, in the car, at home—is think about how unsatisfied you are. And that damn job.

"That job," more than likely, is the root of your problems.

Okay, so you're unhappy at work. Isn't everyone?

You're certainly in company. Not necessarily good company, but you definitely aren't alone. At any given moment, 11.5 percent of the workers in the North American marketplace can be described as "troubled," estimates the National Personnel Association, a Washington research institute.

"I'd go further than that," said Robert Bell, former head of the management department at Fordham University's graduate school of business in New York. "I'd say most workers today are troubled."

California Survey

And a recent survey of 1,509 workers in the California computer industry's Silicon Valley yielded some statistics that illustrate a few of the results of employee unhappiness. Of those surveyed, 65 percent admitted coming into work late or leaving early; 29 percent said they used illicit drugs at work; 34 percent said they worked under the influence of alcohol.

Obviously, not exactly the picture of contentment on the job.

The effects of job-related malcontentment? From the employer's point of view: Decreased productivity and revenues; increased absenteeism and insurance costs. No small potatoes, those. But for an employee, job unhappiness can be devastating.

"It can drive him or her to drink or consume drugs," said Mary Houlihan, a regional marketing manager for Milpitas, California-based Psychological Management Systems. "It can manifest itself in compulsive behaviour, like gambling. It can lead to depression, attacks of anxiety, insomnia, sleeping, and eating disorders."

But that's life at the grindstone, right?

Wrong. No matter how discontented you are at work, no matter how menial or routine the task, no matter how unappreciated or underpaid you are, there are ways to boost your working morale.

"It's a mistake to think that an employer is completely responsible for the happiness of employees," said Denis Waitley, a San Diego management consultant. "Actually, it's a shared responsibility. The employer can't do it all. People make their own happiness."

How? There's no single, sure-fire method. "What works? For different people, different approaches," said Houlihan.

But there are some general rules of thumb:

• **Rest**: Don't short-change your time with the sandman. "A rule that's often overlooked," said Waitley. "How can you be contented at work if you're rundown?"

• **Good nutrition**: That means three well-balanced meals a day, especially breakfast.

• **Exercise**: Very important, especially for office workers. "You build up a lot of adrenalin at work, even if you're just sitting. You need to work it off on a daily basis," said Waitley. Houlihan suggests running, racquetball, tennis, "something that allows you to work off steam," she said.

• **Recognize your talents**. Take stock of your strong points, then emphasize them. "Realize that you make a real contribution at work, no matter what your job is," says Waitley. Take pleasure in the unique things that only you can bring to the job.

▼

EYE ON SUCCESS

• **Self-assessment**: Learn from your successes. But don't overlook your mistakes; learn from them, too. Take stock of your weaknesses. Make a commitment to remedy them. "Often, a former weakness, once corrected, can become your biggest asset," Waitley said.

• **Avoid routine**: Boredom begets unhappiness. If your tasks are routine, find new ways of accomplishing them. "As long as you're green, you're growing," said Waitley. "Once you ripen, you start to rot." If you can't escape the routine of work, vary your life away from work. Drive different routes to and from the office; stop off every evening at the grocery store; go window-shopping.

• **Seek challenges**: Even success can become boring, so reach for a higher pinnacle. Take a risk. "Successful people can find themselves in a comfort zone they may not want to be in," said Waitley. "They find themselves in the centre lane going nowhere." Ask for new tasks, greater responsibilities. "Those who rest on their laurels," he said, "often find themselves knocked on their rears."

• **Expand your horizons**: Consider

enrolling in continuing-education classes. Classes related to your job can improve your chances of advancement. Even non-job-related study can be beneficial. "You're sure to learn things that you can bring to bear at work," said Houlihan.

- **Hobbies**: Don't let yourself stagnate at home. A hobby can take your mind off a minor work annoyance and leave you fresh and untroubled for the next day. Don't fall into the television rut. "Watch television one night, read the next, go to a movie the next," said Waitley. "Try for an enriching life away from work."
- **On-the-job breaks**: Take them and use them. Don't stay at your desk. Don't go from sitting at your desk to sitting in the cafeteria. Go for a walk. Engage in an activity completely unlike your work activity. "If you have to use your eyes on detailed paperwork, listen to music," Waitley said. "If you have to use your ears, like in a sales job, read on your breaks."
- **Office politics**: Roundly decried, but widely practised. "It's pointless to say it's bad when it's not going away," said Bell. But there's a right way to play and a wrong way. "Play defensively. Don't knife others. Promote yourself," he said. "Want a promotion? First, figure out what the boss wants. Then emphasize those qualities in yourself. Show that you have what he/she needs."
- **Shun alcohol and drugs**: They won't help, but they will harm. "You do want to keep your job," Waitley said. "They're destructive escapes."

AIR COMPLAINTS

- **Air your gripes**: Don't smoulder in private. "Don't be a grudge collector," said Waitley. If you feel you can't talk to your boss, confide in friends, co-workers, your family. "Share your frustrations," said Houlihan. "Don't let them build until they explode or drag you down." Gripe, and then forget it.
- **Counselling**: Sometimes, confiding in those you know just isn't enough. "There are times when you need a detached listener," said Houlihan. Don't resist the idea of seeking professional help. It's nothing to be ashamed of.

Those are some ways to go about it, but why try? Why should you be happy at work? Because it's worth it. "Look at it this way," said Waitley. "You're at work five out of seven days. Can you really be happy with life if you're dissatisfied with five-sevenths of it? You're left with two-sevenths. And a person simply can't lead a full life that way."

READING AND REACTING

1. "People make their own happiness."

a) In a small group, discuss the above statement in the context of the article.

b) On your own, either support or argue against the statement in a one-page essay. Exchange essays with someone who took the opposite stand and see if you can be convinced to change your mind.

2. Show on a two-column chart the effects of job dissatisfaction on the employer and on the employee.

3. Reduce each of Waitley's 14 "rules of thumb" to one clear statement. Design a flyer based on the statements. Distribute the flyer to schoolmates who have jobs and ask for their comments.

or

Rewrite Waitley's 14 "rules of thumb" so that they apply specifically to school work. Design a poster featuring your school-related "rules" and display it in the class. Ask your classmates to comment on your "rules."

REACHING OUT

1. In a journal entry, describe a situation you were involved in recently (either at work or at school) in which some of Waitley's advice might have been useful.

2. Script and act out two scenes which show different approaches to the same working environment. In one scene, show an employee who feels that "that's life at the grindstone" and in the other, an employee who feels that there are ways to make the best of a situation.

3. Write an essay in which you evaluate your attitude to work—school or job related—on the basis of the 14 rules listed in the article. Include any other rules you feel are appropriate.

4. In a small group, compile a list of work-related problems from people you know. Brainstorm ways in which the worker can solve each problem. Consider situations in which you feel solutions to the problem are beyond the worker's control and find out whether the class agrees.

▶ Time Flies By in a Muddle If You Don't Learn to Manage It

Helen Bullock

Every batch of mail that comes in contains something about time management. Entire consulting companies are devoted to time management concepts and corporations pay large sums of money to put the time of both employees and managers to better use.

My personal resolution this year was not to waste any more time reading about managing time.

How difficult can it be?

I am willing to admit I often mismanage a few hours here and there, fritter, procrastinate, blame the nature of the work, and insist that I don't have the type of job that fits into those hourly planning diaries so beloved by some time managers. It's just the nature of life, to get into a muddle.

But a conversation with American time guru Merrill Douglass, who runs the Time Management Centre in Grandville, Michigan, and made Who's Who by telling people what's what, has somewhat changed my attitude.

Douglass says 90 percent of people manage time poorly and it's no wonder. Time management is really a collection of habits and patterns and we learn to be ineffective time managers from the cradle.

Many of our patterns are developed in the first 20 years of life, through childhood,

adolescence, and early adulthood when nothing is really critical. There isn't a heck of a lot we want to accomplish during those years, Douglass says.

Don't Know How

"Then, by the time we reach our 30s and need to be organized, efficient, and accomplished to get ahead in our careers, we don't know how. The bad habits are ingrained. About 10 percent of the population are naturally better managers and they zoom ahead. The rest of us have to learn new habits to replace the old."

Douglass has created a Time Profile kit, a self-diagnostic pamphlet with 60 questions. The first 48 apply to anyone; the last 12 to supervisors and managers.

Individuals can work through it themselves, but more importantly, it's a way for managers to motivate staff to handle time productively.

"A manager can sit down and say 'let's do this together,' Douglass says. "It pinpoints not only weaknesses, but strengths and that's a positive place to start improving from."

Business and industry are desperate to

improve the time skills (read productivity) of workers.

"The last four or five national surveys in the U.S. have shown that workers are productive 55 percent of the time. That means they're unproductive 45 percent of the time. If you calculate 45 percent of the gross salaries across the nation, that's how much it costs industry. The figure is so staggering you can hardly take it in."

BEHAVIOURAL PROBLEM

What makes it difficult, says Douglass, is that handling time is a behavioural problem. If an employee doesn't care how his or her time is spent and is not motivated to improve, there's little a manager can do.

"About 25 percent of the working population is hard-driving, ambitious, willing to improve for the sake of the job," he says. "The rest is less excited about work, period. They're not lazy *per se* but their interests are elsewhere."

One of the problems in learning new time techniques is that people operate on a set of assumptions about time, oft-repeated and all false, says Douglass. For example:

"No one ever has enough time."

"Delay will enable you to improve the quality of your decisions."

"Most people can solve their time problems by working harder."

"Most day-to-day activities don't need to be planned and most people couldn't plan for them anyway."

"If you really managed your time, you'd be a robot."

"Busy, active people who work the hardest are the ones who get the best results."

Douglass maintains that none of these common assumptions is true.

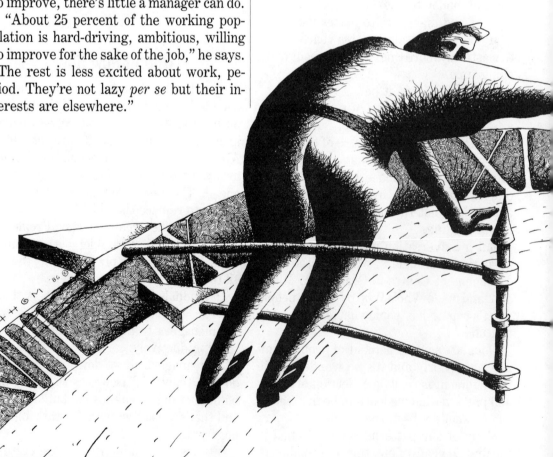

It's not the nature of the job, it's the nature of the person that causes overwork. And from time to time everyone is overworked, usually as a result of failing to delegate, inability to say no, not establishing priorities, or spending too much time on trivial details.

Saying you don't have enough time is nonsensical. The problem, says Douglass, is not the amount of time you have but how you spend it.

People rarely spend any time thinking about who they are, where they're going, and how best to get there.

"Most are too action-oriented to spend much time in thoughtful analysis," he says. "They prefer to be doing rather than thinking. It can be counterproductive."

He dislikes the notion that delays make for sounder decisions. Often they're another word for procrastination, especially if you habitually delay decisions out of fear of making a mistake or lack of confidence that your decision will be the right one in the company's eyes.

The excuse that dealing with people makes it impossible to establish priorities is nonsense, too. All people may be important, but all the events, projects, pressures, and problems they want to involve you in aren't. It's easy to prioritize them.

Furthermore, working smarter always beats working harder, says Douglass. From childhood we're told if we try harder, we'll be rewarded. It isn't always so. Doing the wrong thing harder doesn't accomplish anything. The key is to analyse the work and demands and restructure if necessary to work more efficiently and effectively.

Douglass says ordinary day-to-day activities are just the ones that need to be planned out if you want to control time.

There is a great fear of becoming "robotized" by overplanning that Douglass claims is unfounded.

When the have-to, mundane areas are organized, you have freedom from both tasks and pressures to seek out pleasurable activities or give your full attention to challenging ones.

Nor is it true that busy, active types are the achievers. Teachers and parents started early admonishing us to "keep busy," he says, but busy doing what except keeping busy? Few of us think and plan before we act. A lot of energy and time is wasted on accomplishing very little.

Time management is not dull, Douglass insists, because if you control time and can finish what has to be done in half the time, you're free to go on to really dynamic accomplishments.

He stresses that time is personal and no one can manage it for you. But much of what we believe we can or can't do is tied to our assumptions and these are tied to our behaviour. Change the assumptions, says Douglass, and the behaviour will change, too.

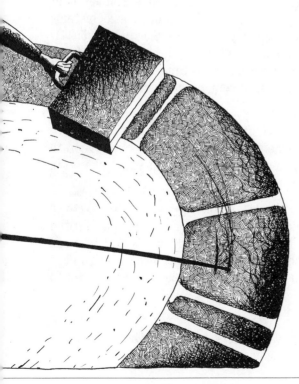

1. According to Merrill Douglass, people don't use time management techniques because they hold wrong assumptions about time. In a small group, examine the six statements (beginning with "No one ever has enough time") listed as examples of common misconceptions, and decide whether they are indeed "all false." Give reasons for your decision.

2. a) With a partner, read through the article carefully, and identify and list
   (i) the obstacles that prevent people from working efficiently;
   (ii) the tips for good time management.

   b) Assume the role of a manager or supervisor and, in a memo to your staff, outline ways in which they can achieve effective time management.

R E A C H I N G   O U T

1. Appoint one member of your class to write to the Time Management Centre for the Time Management Profile questionnaire. Answer the questionnaire. Then discuss your profile with a partner. (The questionnaire is available through time management consultants. A list of these is available from Performax Systems International, 12755 State Highway 55, Minneapolis, Minn. 55441) Have your partner write an assessment of your profile that identifies your strengths and weaknesses in time management. Do the same for your partner. Share your profiles with your teacher if you wish.

2. You are the manager of a company and would like to improve productivity. Devise a scheme to motivate your employees to improve their time management skills. Explain your scheme in an oral presentation to your staff.

3. a) Make a list of all the school work you have been assigned to cover during the next four-week period. Devise a master plan, in the form of a calendar, to illustrate how your time would be used most efficiently. Show how you would approach each assignment and how much time you would devote to each. Be prepared to justify your decisions.

   b) One month later, follow-up your master plan with a written assessment of how closely you stuck to your plan and how you might have improved your time management.

▶ WHO CALLED THIS MEETING?

When you are in the chairperson's seat, you must take charge. Here's how.

Rosa Harris-Adler

She pulls herself up to full height, jowls quivering, and issues a diatribe that is one part vitriol and three parts ramble. In a 15-minute monologue she manages to stab her colleagues in the back while patting her own, all the while making little or no relevant point.

Every meeting harbours one such personality—the derailer, the pompous windbag, the giant bore or the well-meaning meanderer, and they can make the difference between a meeting that works and one that doesn't. Unfortunately, there is only one person who can control them: the chairperson.

As people rise through the ranks of commerce, politics, and the professions, they increasingly find themselves in this role. Even the most articulate and creative chairpersons had better learn the ropes— and when to pull them—or they will find their meeting bogged down in rhetoric and confusion. A sound knowledge of meeting protocol is a must.

"I've found the more democratic you are, the more a meeting drags on," says Marnie Fortier, who, as director of the Eastern Canadian region of the International Association of Business Communications, presides over a 16-member board. "It's hard to cut people off, to bring them back to the agenda, without being accused of being undemocratic. So you have to use the rules to your advantage. Set up a speaker's list before each meeting and allot a specific time for each subject. Often you don't stick to the list, but you have to try. At the least, participants are aware that the structure is there. Besides, it's a lot easier to say 'We're running 15 minutes over schedule' than it is to say 'You're talking too much.' "

The first step is becoming familiar with meeting methodology. In formal meetings, like it or not, what was good for General Henry Robert in 1876 remains (for want of a choice) good for us today. Robert was responsible for *Robert's Rules of Order*— and a humourless, intimidating reference work on parliamentary procedure it is. Sample paragraph: "This division of a question is really an amendment, and subject to the same rules. Instead of moving a division of the question, the same result can be usually attained by moving some other form of an amendment. When the question is divided, each separate question must be a proper one for the assembly to act upon, even if none of the others were adopted." Got that? Move to the head of the class.

Inevitably, the only people who seem to have committed every word of *Robert's* to memory are the very same bores and blowhards who are the bane of every meeting; perhaps they were born with a *Robert's* gene. Because they follow the rules to the letter, it's hard to reproach them when they disrupt an otherwise productive session; the solution is to fight on their turf. However, most sane individuals have what psychologists call an approach avoidance

relationship with the general. They hate him yet they need him. Says Carol Ann Fried, a time-management instructor at the McGill University Management Institute in Montreal, who runs workshops on meeting management: "*Robert's Rules* are outmoded. Stuffy. Complicated. For the birds. They add time to meetings. But I've been to appalling meetings in which everyone talks at the same time and there is no agenda. I believe meetings need form."

Structure keeps the lid on and participants' interest perking. The person who chairs the meeting creates the structure and keeps it on track—and a distilled version of *Robert's* is ultimately the most effective way of doing that. There is a method in its maddening obsession with vocabulary: when you use formal terms, it's harder for a meeting to be sidetracked. The terms define the methodology: what follows is the essential meeting terminology.

A *quorum*: the number of people—usually a majority—it has been decided is the minimum needed to hold an official meeting. If a quorum is present, the meeting begins. The members then take each item on the agenda and discuss it. Discussion at this point is informal—and ideally just long enough for the members to feel ready to act. When a member wishes to propose action, he or she does so in the form of a *motion*, which must in most cases be *seconded* by another member of the group before the more formal discussion begins. The mover has the right to open the formal discussion and to speak last on the subject before a vote is called; all other members may speak twice on each issue. The chairperson may participate in the discussion only by temporarily relinquishing the chair to someone else, and he or she may only vote on motions to break a tie.

Only one motion can be considered at a time, although some motions take precedence over the one being debated. A motion to adjourn takes precedence over any other motion on the floor, but the mover must have a good reason (the washroom is ablaze and leaving the building seems the path of least resistance).

A motion to *call the previous question*, wherein a member and seconder move to end debate on the original motion under consideration, also takes precedence. There is no discussion permitted on a move to call the question—if the assembly votes in favour, the original motion must then be put to a vote.

A motion may also be *amended* before voting if, in the course of discussion, changes or additions appear necessary—and even amendments can be amended. If further information seems called for or a pressing matter intercedes, a motion may be *tabled*—postponed—until later in the meeting or a future meeting.

The chair rules, and like a good traffic cop can interrupt the flow when necessary to redirect it elsewhere. But other board members may only interrupt a speaker on a *point of order* or a *point of information*. The first is an excellent tool for controlling pomposity and windbaggery. When the speaker's comments are irrelevant or he or she doesn't follow procedure, protesting on a point of order is legitimate. The chair determines whether the protest is valid. A point of information is simply a method of asking the speaker or the chairperson a question.

That, in a nutshell, is all you really need to know about meeting terminology and formal methodology. But veterans of smoky boardrooms know there's more to running a successful meeting. It's a little like being a diplomat in a hotseat: you must sit carefully and stay alert if you don't want to be burned. Some advice on meeting management from Fried and Fortier:

1. Determine what the meeting should cover long before it takes place.

2. Alert colleagues that you are planning the agenda and ask them to submit their items by a specific date.

3. Allot specific times for each item, giving priority to the most important, and include times on the agenda.

4. Circulate the agenda a minimum of three days in advance.

5. Start and end the meeting on time.

6. Lead. Preside. Interrupt when people carry on. Keep them on track.

7. Don't be drawn into personality squabbles. Keep discussions objective and impersonal.

8. During long meetings, schedule breaks—fresh minds mean fresh insights.

9. Listen carefully and solicit the opinions of participants who don't contribute on their own.

10. After the meeting, circulate a report stating when action will be taken on the decisions reached, and who is responsible for carrying it out.

The derailers are a tenacious lot and deserve, as usual, a last comment. "Put their concerns last, or towards the end of the agenda," Fortier recommends. "That way, if you're strapped for time, they can't go on. Even if they do, the important things are behind you. But you have to be patient, to handle them with magnanimity. Different people have different viewpoints and your job is to bring them all together."

One last word. Your meeting has gathered to get work done. But as you, the chairperson and traffic cop, cajole, listen, judge, and guide the meeting down the rocky road of procedure and protocol, it's easy to forget that you're there to effect change, to take a quantum leap forward. Don't lose sight of your goal.

▼

READING AND REACTING

1. Find the terminology in the article "Who Called This Meeting?" that relates to meetings. List the terms and their definitions. Compare your list with others and compile one consolidated list of "meeting" terminology. Provide a copy of the list for each classmate.

2. Individually, or with a partner, design a cartoon style representation of the derailer, the pompous windbag, the giant bore, and the well-meaning meanderer. Display your art work in the classroom. If you think of other disruptive personalities to represent, add them to the ones suggested.

3. Prepare a questionnaire that asks respondents to rate their experience with attending and conducting meetings with the 10 points of advice given by Fried and Fortier in the article, "Who Called This Meeting?" Circulate your questionnaire to those who regularly attend meetings and to those who are executive officers of organizations; for example, teachers, principals, secretaries, union and federation members, and student council members. Discuss the results with your class, and plot a graph that will indicate what areas need most improvement.

REACHING OUT

1. a) Consult an office procedures textbook or a secretarial handbook to find the duties of the executive officers of an organization. Your school constitution will give the duties of council members.

b) Make a list with a brief description of each of the items known as the order of business at a meeting, and file this for future reference.

2. Attend a meeting. You may choose to go, for example, to a club meeting, a municipal council meeting, or a meeting of the students' council. Take notes and prepare your own set of minutes. A tape recorder would help with your note-making. (Be sure to ask permission before you record.) Issue minutes from the meeting that you attended and report to the class on the business that was conducted. Comment on the efficiency of the meeting.

3. Poll the class for an issue to raise with the students' council. Prepare a motion and present it on behalf of the class at the next meeting. Be sure to notify the secretary ahead of time that you have an item for the agenda. Provide the secretary with a written copy of the motion.

4. Interview the executive officers of any club or organization to find out their duties, their frustrations, and tips on how to run successful meetings.

5. In a small group, issue an agenda and hold a class meeting on some topic of interest to the class. Appoint some classmates as observers to comment on how the meeting was conducted. Appoint a group member to take and issue minutes of the meeting.

▶ THE NEUTRAL ENEMY

Don Bailey

"You may have management training but you've got no instinct for the work."

DAVID RENKIN IS IN A RAGE. THE AIR CONDITIONER has been turned on. What was the point in spending a fortune on a suit that was guaranteed to breathe and remain cool in holocaust heat when some fool had adjusted the temperature so low that his office has the stinging chill of a root cellar. No one had consulted him. He was the manager of this bank, wasn't he? Yes, the weather was hot. Boiling. July and August in Winnipeg were tropical. In the three years he had lived here, he had become convinced that the population suffered nine months of the year from snow blindness and were feverish the other three months with sun stroke.

He lights a cigarette, sucking the smoke and using it as a kind of blanket to smother the anger. Soon he would be transferred. Maybe back to Toronto where he had started. But his phone calls and letters to the head office seemed to have been deflected into some bureaucratic limbo. He lives in terror that his employment will be terminated. His reasonable request to his superiors as to what they have in mind for his future has been met with silence. He has lost weight and a recent medical check-up revealed that his blood pressure is dangerously high.

He hears the laughter. It is a familiar sound. Almost a welcome noise to fill the void of his isolation. The rumble of mirth fills the room with a physical presence. David settles back in his chair to await the speaking voice that always follows the laughter. At the same time he tries to reason with himself that what he is hearing is really the hum of the air conditioner. What he needs to do is take a vacation. But last year he flew to Mexico for three weeks of grand fun and frolic. He got into a fight with the tour bus driver the fourth day. A shouting match but he had wanted to hit the man. He caught a plane home that night and stayed in his apartment, almost hiding for the remainder of his holiday time.

The voice speaks. The words are distinct and familiar.

"Renkin, you should've stayed a teller. You may have management training but you've got no instinct for the work."

David remembers the man's foul breath and the swollen nose that seemed afflicted with terminal varicose veins. His name was

Hartley Harland. He was David's supervisor. He might have been harmless except he wielded enormous power with his spirit of meanness. But he knew the banking business as well as some men know their families. Hartley had no family. His most intimate relationship was with the bank. He taught David what he knew with an attitude of reluctance as though it was a waste of his time. Information had to be pried from him and often his responses were belligerent. David attributed this to the man's drinking. His supervisor was a drunk. A lush. Maybe even an alcoholic. David understood the condition. His father had been a drinker. But a silent one. Hartley was nasty and said out loud all the things to David that his father might have said if he had had more nerve. Or as Hartley would have said, guts.

"But I fixed you," David mutters to the empty room.

After two months Hartley had vented his frustration with David by calling him a spineless failure who would never advance in the business because contrary to popular belief, banking was fraught with risk. And he, David Renkin was incapable, unwilling and probably paralysed by the prospect of taking a chance on anything. David was hurt by Hartley's attack but it made him angry too. More angry even than when his father's kidneys had suddenly failed in the middle of a meatloaf supper and he had died before the ambulance arrived without offering one word of explanation for the silent fear that had controlled his life.

David reported Hartley for drinking liquor on the job. He said he had seen his supervisor sneaking drinks in the vault. Out of a silver flask. The story was a complete fabrication but everyone was aware of Hartley's weakness and when he didn't defend himself, he was fired. David was confused when the man did not dispute the story he had made up. It seemed out of character, but then David decided that Hartley had really wanted to retire. The bank was paying him a good pension. Maybe he had done the man a favour. For a while, David enjoyed the reputation of being a ruthless young man on his way up the banking ladder. And then, less than a month after his forced retirement, Hartley died. Choked to death on something in the middle of the night. Alone and drunk.

David felt badly about Hartley's fate but he had no time to dwell on it because he was suddenly ordered to Winnipeg, as one of the youngest branch managers in the country. At twenty-six he was on the move.

The elation and excitement of the promotion didn't last long though. He was in a city that might as well have been a foreign land. He knew no one that he could call in the middle of the night to come to his small apartment and share a pizza that he had heated in the fancy microwave oven. The branch he had been sent to was tiny. Only nine employees, including himself.

His most intimate relationship was with the bank.

And the place was haunted. By Hartley Harland.

One day after everyone else had left, David wandered the bank reluctant to leave the familiar surroundings for his dreaded apartment. The bank had a harmonious feel to it while his own place was like a vacuum that sucked at him. He was enjoying the quiet when it was interrupted by a series of gulping, gasping, gurgling sounds. At first he thought it was a toilet backing up but before he could check, he heard the voice. A voice speaking clearly and directed at him. It was Hartley Harland's voice.

"So Renkin, you're the big shot here."

David ran from the bank and was not free of the mocking laughter until he had securely locked the door behind him.

The voice remained within the confines of the bank. It never followed him home or visited him in a restaurant while he was having a solitary meal. And the voice was formless. No putrid body from the grave appeared to support David's fear that he was going crazy. He concluded that the voice was a manifestation of the guilt he felt over Hartley's firing and then death. Perfectly normal. Except the voice was a nuisance over which he had no control. Hartley made himself heard whenever the spirit moved him. As it were. David accepted the situation as a kind of penance. A temporary one that he planned soon to rectify.

There is a knock on the office door.

"Come in," David says.

Mary Balfour enters, her face wreathed in a broad smile of satisfaction. David perceives Mary as a lover of disasters. As she nears forty and her torso thickens like the aging trunk of a tree she seems to take even greater delight in making gloomy announcements.

"There's a fellow at the counter with an unemployment cheque. No I.D. of course. Expects us to cash it and he doesn't have an account here."

"Mary, you are the head teller. You know the rules. That kind of decision is within your realm of responsibility."

"It is, Mr. Renkin but there were times when you got upset with me for sending creeps like this packing."

"We have customers, Mary, not creeps."

"He's drunk out of his head. I think you should handle it. Oh, another thing, did I mention that Shirley didn't balance again last night?"

"I found your memo this morning. It was very detailed. The fourth or fifth time this month. Do you have a recommendation?"

"I think she's on drugs," Mary says with a punctuating snort.

"Her doctor prescribed valium for her when her father died."

"That was two months ago. That's no excuse for turning into an addict."

There is a pounding in David's head, an overwhelming desire

"So Renkin, you're the big shot here."

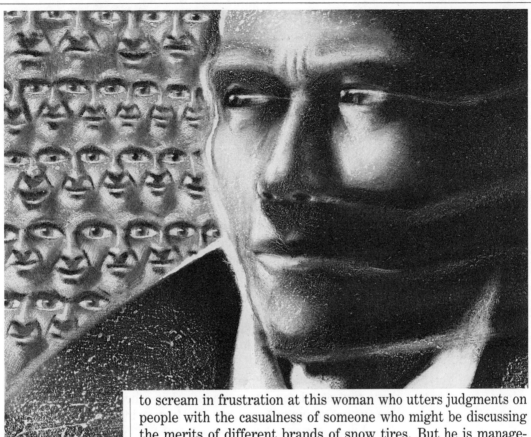

to scream in frustration at this woman who utters judgments on people with the casualness of someone who might be discussing the merits of different brands of snow tires. But he is management. He must maintain control.

"Mary, tell me, who gave the order for the air conditioner to be turned on?" he asks in a strained voice.

"That's not my department," she says.

"I know that but I thought you might have a clue as to who actually flicked the switch."

"Probably the maintenance guys did it."

"Have we ever discovered where the controls are? Just in case we might want to make our own adjustments."

"Haven't got a clue. Listen you going to do anything about this guy at the counter or should I call the police?"

David is aware of another pounding taking place beyond the parameters of his own skull. An angry customer protesting with his fist against the lack of personalized service that all the television ads promise. David can hear the man shouting and while the phrasing is colourful, it is not complimentary. He rises hastily from his chair.

"I'll deal with this, Mary."

"Good luck," she says with a smirk. He watches with fascination as she deftly swings her girth smartly about face and manoeuvres through the narrow aisle of desks back to her window, never once bumping into anything.

He strides briskly towards the counter and has to brake suddenly or he will collide with it as he has before. Last time it knocked the wind out of him and all the bank staff laughed as though it were a great joke. He successfully stops in time and greets the disgruntled customer with a smile.

"What seems to be the difficulty?" he asks the man who has been directing his loud comments to the line of people who are queued up awaiting their turn with one of the four tellers. The customers look uneasy but the woman tellers all wear expressions of amusement. David is reminded again that he is the only male working here. He is convinced if there is a robbery that he will be summoned from his office by Mary and asked to give the proper procedures that she and the others must follow in such a situation. And probably catch a thumping big bullet in his chest from the nervous crook as the female staff stand by and giggle. The man swirls around and faces David.

"I ain't no bum, mister. Followed orders all my life. That's why I'm here."

"This here's a government cheque. Good as gold," he says, waving it in front of David's face for which he is grateful since the man's breath is noxious and the fumes that are not swept away are somehow reminiscent of the vapours that linger in hospital corridors.

He is a middle-aged man, with red veined eyes, a thin pointed nose that could serve as a weapon, like a beak. His slack mouth sprays saliva when he speaks. He is wearing a heavy, old-fashioned overcoat but there is no evidence of sweat on his brow. A baseball cap pulled tightly over his head conceals whatever hair he might have. Without the energy of his anger the man would be easily dismissed as being harmless. But in his presence David feels a cold terror. This is what Hartley could have become before he died. Or his father.

"Do you have any identification, sir?" David asks calmly.

"I.D.," the man sputters indignantly. "Them buggers at the Sally Ann took my wallet, shoes, everything. The first night I was there. See!"

He holds his foot up to display the ratty looking running shoes he is wearing.

"Had ninety dollar work boots. New. Brand new. Had them tied around my neck but I guess they cut the laces. I ain't no bum, mister. Followed orders all my life. That's why I'm here."

"I'm not suggesting . . ." David begins, but the man interrupts him with a sputtering shower of words.

"C.N.R. transferred me here three months ago. Outa Oshawa, Ontario. I worked there six years but then things slacked off so they sent me here. I came like they told me and worked in the yard. Then after six weeks they gave me notice. Laid me off. Had no money to speak of. Been staying at the Sally Ann when they let me. Or sleeping on a river bank. This here's

the first real money I've had in over a month."

"You've been drinking. We have a policy . . ." David says feebly.

"You're damn right I had a drink. I was coming over here through the back lanes and I met a couple of fellas. Sittin' in a garage singin' their hearts out and they offered me a snort of this stuff they had in a coke bottle. You know what it was?"

"It smells awful," David says.

"Lysol," the man says triumphantly. "They drink it all the time. Cut it with some water and ya got a drink that ain't the nectar of the Gods but it calms ya down."

"Sounds terrible," David says. He can hear the snickering of the staff. Female voices but in their midst he thinks he hears a male chortle.

"You cash this here cheque mister and I'll take my rightful money, get myself a hotel room, a room with a T.V. and I'll pick up a bottle of rye and a bucket of chicken. And the next time you see me, you'll be talkin' to a different man."

David takes the cheque from the man, turns it over on the counter and examines the signature on the back. He hands the man his pen.

"Endorse it," he says.

"I already signed it," the man says.

"I want to make sure you can do it twice," David says.

Slowly the man scrawls his name. David looks at the writing. It matches the first signature.

"Wait a sec," he says to the man and walks over to Mary and holds out the cheque to her. She ignores him and finishes with the customer she is serving. He waits and after a long moment she turns, levels a simpy smile at him and accepts the cheque. She examines it with obvious distaste and then hands it back to him.

▼

*With strained
patience
he scribbles
on the
cheque . . .*

"Initial please," she says.

With strained patience he scribbles on the cheque and Mary scrutinizes the mark he has made as though she suspects him of trying to trick her. Finally, her eye-brows arched in disapproval she begins to count out the money into his outstretched hand.

"Thank you," he says, when she appears to be finished.

"Don't forget the twenty cents," she says. "He could use it to buy himself a razor. A little shave wouldn't hurt him."

Seething with anger, David walks back to the counter and counts out the money for the waiting man who scoops it up gleefully.

"Thank you sir," the man says. "I won't forget this." He turns and makes a lurching retreat towards the door.

"Get some identification for the next time," David calls after him. The man waves and as he disappears into the street, a young woman enters through the same doorway. David looks at his watch. Eleven o'clock on the button. He flashes his warmest smile at her. The woman returns the smile but it is more subdued. David opens the gate for her and she follows him into his office and takes a seat while he picks up her file and fiddles with it. There is no need for him to read it. All the important details are registered clearly in his memory. He sits on the corner of his desk, deliberately avoiding going behind it. He wants her to feel relaxed.

"So how's the insurance business?" he says, slapping the file closed.

"Didn't you see my last year's income tax return? I dropped it off."

He had never put it around his neck but the sight of the thing could make him weep.

"Oh yes," David says, startled and even slightly hurt. He would like to be friends with this woman. Perhaps even more. He admires her. He would like it if she admired him. He hears the sound of mocking laughter. His own. Or Hartley's. Why would she think of him beyond what he represented in her business dealings with the bank? He clears his throat and assumes what he hopes is a professional manner.

"I've seen the return and it's apparent you're doing very well."

"I've left my card with you several times but you've never called. I assumed you weren't interested."

"Insurance, you mean?" He is embarrassed by his stupid question. Of course insurance. What else? And then for no apparent reason, David thinks of his mother. Perhaps it is the letter she sent a week ago. She still lives in Toronto in the small house where he grew up. They seem to have little to say to one another. Writing is hard and most of the time David phones her. On Sundays when the rates are cheaper although they are never on the line for more than five minutes so it doesn't make much difference. Months will sometimes pass with no contact between them. David is the one who has to initiate it. Even when he was a child it was like that. After his father's funeral, David had asked her if she needed anything and she had replied, no, she was fine. She had never needed much. And then last week the letter came. Inside the envelope he found a silver chain with a small medallion. His mother had explained that this was the family's coat-of-arms. She had bought it at a booth during her annual visit to the Canadian National Exhibition. In her notes she said she hoped that he would wear it proudly. He had never put it around his neck but the sight of the thing could make him weep. It seemed to represent the awkward silence that existed between his mother and himself. A silence he was unable to fill.

The woman is laughing and this jars him from the growing sense of dread he feels. Insurance. They were talking about insurance.

"The bank has a group plan. It's not much but I have no family. Just my mother. But no wife," he says.

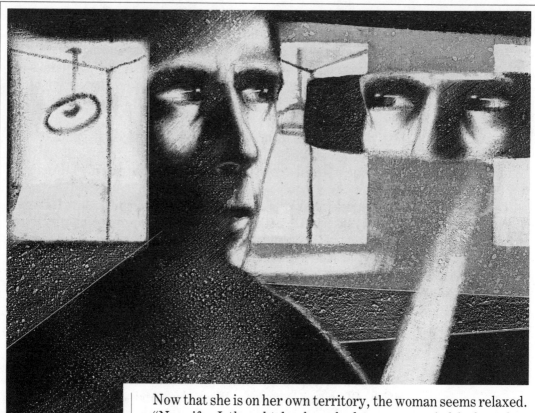

Now that she is on her own territory, the woman seems relaxed.

"No wife. I thought bankers had to get married before they were twenty-five. Otherwise they weren't considered stable."

It is his turn to laugh.

"Could be the reason my career isn't progressing the way it should, Lorinda."

He loves her name and savours it like a sweet taste in his mouth. But then he notices her attention wandering. She is looking out the window and he is afraid that his familiarity is boring her. He picks up the file again and flips it open.

"So," he says. "You're looking for thirty-five hundred. For the purchase of a car."

"Yes," she says, alert and attentive now. "My old rustbucket's had it."

"I would have thought you'd have a company car."

"Not for the lowly field representatives," she says with a smile.

"Looking over your financial picture, you seem to be operating to the limit of your resources. Over extended in fact. The mortgage payments on your five properties run at two thousand a month."

"The rents from those houses bring in three thousand," she says tightly. "Are you turning me down?"

"No," he says, afraid now that she misunderstands him. He knows how carefully she has invested. He envies her skill in acquiring these properties that he believes are part of a larger dream. But he wants her to know that he too is competent. He feels he must explain himself. "I just want to fully grasp the implications of the loan. In our credit check we learned that you're in arrears with the city tax department on three of the houses. Comes to about forty-six hundred."

"I've had to do some repairs," she says. "I let the taxes wait. Next month I've got a big commission cheque coming. I'll use that to wipe out the taxes."

"I really admire how well organized you are," he says with a burst of enthusiasm. "And your ambition. Here you are, only twenty-seven and you already have five houses. Must be a lot of work though."

"They keep me busy but they're all on the same street so it's not so bad."

He knows where the houses are. In his desire to know more about Lorinda, David drove to the street one night after work. He sat in his car and observed the people moving around inside the modest bungalows. He stayed a long time and wondered what it must feel like to own the space that other people made their lives in. When it became dark he decided to leave but just before he pulled out, Lorinda arrived and parked just a few cars in front of him. He expected her to get out and visit the houses. Collect the rent perhaps. But she just sat there in the dark. Watching, like he had. She spent over two hours, sitting in her car, staring out the window at the people living their lives in the houses she owned. And later as David drove home he decided she must be very lonely.

"Do you find it chilly in here?" he asked.

"Freezing," she says with a shudder.

"Let's go look at this car you've picked out."

"Now?" she says, surprised. "You and me?"

"Yes," he says, "I want to get outside and see if my new suit breathes."

She laughs and as they go out the door, David thinks he hears someone else laughing. Mocking him. David ignores it and is proud of himself for not informing Mary of his departure.

At the car lot, Lorinda leads him to a square shaped, imported vehicle famous for its fuel economy. It is painted blood red and has good tires. Functional is the word that comes to David's mind. His eyes wander over the lot and he spots a large American built car. He puts his hand on Lorinda's shoulder and propels her towards it. The door is open and he gets in. The key is in the ignition. He starts the motor and revs it several times until the engine settles into a gentle, throbbing rhythm. David sinks back into the deep, comfortable upholstery. He runs his hand over the thick carpeting on the floor. When he switches on the radio, the resonance of the stereo sound system thrills him. The car has

"Here you are, only twenty-seven and you already have five houses."

cruise control. And of course, air conditioning. This is luxury. This is an automobile designed with a spirit of generosity.

Lorinda runs her hand along the smooth fender with obvious admiration.

"This is some car," she says.

"Get in," he says.

"No," she says, laughing lightly. "I don't even want to consider it. Too rich for my blood. It's twice the price of the other."

"I could arrange financing for you," David says. "Spread it over a longer period of time. You work hard. Give yourself a treat. A reward."

"I wouldn't feel right," she says. "It's not me. I guess I'm just too stingy."

"Why don't we have dinner tonight and talk about it," he says.

She stiffens and steps back from the car. Hurriedly, David turns off the engine and gets out so he can face her.

"I didn't mean to offend you," he says. "I mean, I thought we could . . ."

"I keep my private life separate from business," she says curtly. She turns and begins to walk away.

"I'm sorry," David calls after her.

Later he is sitting in his office at the bank. Someone has adjusted the air conditioner and now the room is muggy. His new suit does not breathe. In front of him is Lorinda's file. He was not in when she picked up the cheque for the car. Perhaps he can call her and pretend he doesn't know she was in. But she would see through the sham and hang up on him. He thinks about phoning his mother and then decides against it. He will wait until Sunday. He wonders again as he has many times how his father came to be a man so alone. And then suddenly he remembers Hartley and is aware that he has not heard the voice for hours. He feels a longing to hear it one more time. Just for the company.

"I keep my private life separate from business."

R E A D I N G A N D R E A C T I N G

1. a) In a small group, discuss the meaning of the title "The Neutral Enemy," and explain why the author chose that title.

   b) Brainstorm other titles for the story. Compare titles with other groups and come up with the most appropriate title.

2. a) In a small group, identify the symptoms of stress that David reveals and list the sources of his stress.

b) Read "You Can Make That 'Damn Job' Better If You Try" (page 99) and discuss ways in which David can improve his work situation.

3. Imagine that you are a management consultant hired by the bank to observe David's performance. Write a report to David's supervisor in which you evaluate his handling of Mary and the man attempting to cash the unemployment cheque.

4. In a small group, list the qualities that you think are required in management, and then decide whether or not you agree with the supervisor's observation that David has "no instinct for the job."

5. In the voice of David, write a letter to your mother expressing your frustrations over your new job.

or

Script a scene in which David confides to his analyst about some of his work-related frustrations. Role-play the scene with a partner.

6. Script one of the scenes that illustrates the relationships in the story and role-play it for the class.

R E A C H I N G   O U T

1. Write a continuation of the story in which you reveal what happens to David in his job.

or

Write a memoir in the voice of David Renkin as an old man looking back on his banking career.

2. In the voice of David, write a report for your files in which you justify the loan to Lorinda. Include the repayment terms you have decided on.

3. It was Hartley's opinion that "banking was fraught with risk." Interview several middle and senior bank management personnel and ask them whether or not they agree with the statement and why. Share your findings with your group.

► RESPECT IS KEY IN WORKER SATISFACTION

Sandro Contenta and Brian McAndrew

Tony Denotaris: Head houseman at the Four Seasons Hotel dismantles a Christmas tree. Although he'd rather not have to work at all, he finds the hotel an excellent environment.

Job satisfaction. It makes people *want* to get up in the morning and go to work.

A good post used to mean security, healthy wages and benefits, and those elements are still important. But times are changing.

The *Toronto Star* conducted dozens of interviews with employers and managers and found that key ingredients also include responsibility, authority to make decisions, and opportunities to keep learning on the job. In other words, managers who trust and respect their employees.

Now many companies are trying to give workers a say in management and sometimes a piece of the profits.

The approach is common in the computer industry, typified by successful Hewlett-Packard. But service companies, like the Four Seasons Hotel are encouraging employees to contribute their views, and auto-parts manufacturer Magna International is thriving, in part, because of a co-operative spirit.

Here's what their employees say:

FOUR SEASONS HOTEL

Tony Denotaris has never liked getting up in the morning. In fact, he'd much rather be lying on a beach in his native Italy, sipping a chilled glass of white wine and just plain enjoying life.

But since coming to Toronto 26 years ago, Denotaris quickly realized the streets weren't paved with gold and only after a lot of hard work could he enjoy the *dolce vita*.

Twelve years ago he landed a job with Four Seasons Hotel in Yorkville, and since then, getting up in the morning has become a touch easier.

"Personally, I tell you, I would like to retire. I would really like that," says Denotaris, 47, a head houseman at the hotel. "Like everybody else, I have to work. I don't have a choice. But you know, this place, it's great. I know a lot of people who don't have it so good."

The opportunity to perform a variety of jobs, to air complaints at committees or directly to supervisors, and the freedom to make decisions makes Denotaris believe he can happily keep working until retirement age.

For the past two and a half years, the Four Seasons has set up what it calls "round table" committees. Every month, employees in each of the 20 departments get together with supervisors to thrash out complaints and make suggestions on how to improve service and working conditions.

Employees meet for a half-hour to discuss strategy before the manager joins in the last half of the meeting.

"We felt it would be a good idea to get employees involved," says Eileen Maxwell, Four Seasons personnel manager. "They're the ones who are closest to the guests and see what works and what doesn't."

Denotaris isn't that fond of the round table because he says the one time he came up with an idea, management didn't act on it. He prefers dealing directly with supervisors, saying he gets better results that way.

"It feels good when a manager looks at me and says, 'Tony, you know the hotel like the back of your hand. What do you think?' So at least they listen," he adds.

Nancy Bilyk, a banquet waitress at the hotel for 12 years, says the round table allows employees to fight for better working hours but most of the time is spent discussing how service can be improved.

"Sometimes it's little things like getting the manager to get more herb teas for the guests," she says.

Many employees—especially the cleaning staff—are recent immigrants. They can use the last half hour of their shift to attend English classes provided by the hotel twice a week.

The hotel will also pay tuition fees for employees who want to further their education. Employees receive free coffee and one free meal a day along with a period of free accommodation at other Four Seasons hotels.

▼

HEWLETT-PACKARD

Free coffee and snacks cost the Hewlett-Packard company $4 million for its 65,000 employees throughout the world this past year.

It wasn't a large gesture for a company with $6 billion in sales in 1984 but the return in employee satisfaction was priceless.

The "HP Way" was developed by Bill and Dave—as everyone calls company founders William Hewlett and David Packard—when they formed the business equipment and computer firm in 1939 in Palo Alto, California.

Their revolutionary approach to employee relations hasn't changed much from the days when the first few employees sat around a table with their shirt sleeves rolled up, sipping coffee, and exchanging ideas on a first-name basis.

Company policy evolved that gave employees the opportunity to establish personal goals for the upcoming year and work with a minimum of supervision.

"When you get the job done it's nice to know you got the job done without

Malcolm Gissing: President of Hewlett-Packard in Canada says he manages "by walking around."

someone standing over you," says Ian Jackson, who's set to retire at the end of January from the Canadian head office in Mississauga.

After 17 years with the company, Jackson maintains that satisfaction on the job comes from the challenge offered by Hewlett-Packard.

"There is constant change. If you can't put up with change you're dead in the water at Hewlett-Packard," says Jackson, who filled various administrative roles before taking charge last year of establishing a company library.

It's that sense of individual responsibility and challenge that has helped make Hewlett-Packard the third most-admired corporation in the United States, according to a Fortune magazine ranking.

Hewlett-Packard employs 1,100 people in Canada and is building its first Canadian manufacturing complex in Waterloo. The company has never experienced a layoff despite economic downturns.

"The philosophy of the company is not to hire and fire," explains Robert McDevitt, a company executive director. "We continued hiring in 1982 even though the economic conditions were bad."

The company has an annual turnover rate of less than 10 percent in an industry with an average of 20 percent. A profit-sharing plan provides employees with the approximate equivalent of an extra month's salary each year, and workers can purchase company stock at 75 percent of its value.

Retiring employees receive a pension fully paid by the company and all workers have free use of corporate recreation areas. The first Canadian recreation site is being built north of Kingston.

Office doors are never closed and employees can take problems or suggestions as high as the president without fear of repercussions.

"There's not a person in this building that I don't know," boasts Canadian president Malcolm Gissing who describes his administrative role as "management by walking around."

Says Gissing: "I'll walk around here and people never know when I'll stop by and ask how things are going."

▼

MAGNA INTERNATIONAL

Paul Witzleben worked for several faceless companies after bringing his trade skills with him to Canada more than 30 years ago from West Germany.

But he never used his tool-and-die maker abilities anywhere quite like Magna International Inc. where he's worked for 15 years.

"I've never worked for a company that is so well organized. They take care of people," Witzleben says of the Markham-based auto parts manufacturer with 5,000 employees at 55 plants in Canada and the United States.

What makes Magna, one of the fastest growing and most profitable companies, such an ideal corporation?

"You never have the feeling you're not wanted," says Witzleben. "They always say: 'We want your opinion.' That's why it's getting stronger and bigger all the time."

Wages comparable with unionized plants at the non-union shop also contribute to employee welfare, but Witzleben says the co-operative rather than combative relationship between workers and management puts Magna ahead of other employers.

"If you have a problem you can talk to a supervisor. They never close the door on you," Witzleben says.

In an industry especially sensitive to fluctuations in the economy, Magna has been on a steady upswing with sales in 1984 jumping 63 percent to $493 million from $302 million in 1983.

"We're far from perfect," says founder Frank Stronach, who holds majority control of the company. "But we're far different from other companies. We are perhaps the only company in the Western world with an employee charter of rights."

Stronach says you could awaken him in the middle of the night and he'll repeat the philosophy he's held since starting the Richmond Hill tool and die shop in 1954.

"Employees have a right to some of the profits," says Stronach. "I'm a strong believer in free enterprise. Business has totally failed to provide employees with the ability to build capital."

Magna shares 10 percent of its pre-tax profits—most in a deferred plan used to buy company shares and the rest in cash—with its employees.

Witzleben has accumulated more than 3,100 shares valued at about $63,000, which he plans to use for his retirement.

In 1983, Magna began to build 15 factories over three years in Newmarket. A day-care centre will open in 1985, says Stronach, and the complex will also include employee fitness facilities.

The company opened a 100-acre employee recreation centre near Stouffville in 1983 that includes a lake, fishing, sports areas, and a swimming pool.

"The whole gang is like one big family," says Witzleben.

READING AND REACTING

1. In a small group, identify the main factors that contribute to employee job satisfaction at the Four Seasons Hotel, Hewlett-Packard, and Magna International. List these factors in order of importance.

2. As a class, discuss the importance of communication in ensuring job satisfaction. Brainstorm ways in which companies can keep communication channels healthy.

REACHING OUT

1. Survey employees of different companies to determine what they feel are the key ingredients for job satisfaction. Represent your findings in a graph and post it in the class. Compare your findings with the list that was compiled in Reading and Reacting #1.

2. You have just been hired as the personnel director of a large manufacturing company. Decide on the benefits and the working environment you would provide for the workers. Outline your plans in a report that you would submit to the board of directors for approval.

   or

   You are the union leader of a large manufacturing company. Write a letter to the personnel director in which you spell out the benefits and the working conditions that you think the workers must have to ensure job satisfaction.

3. In a group of six to eight, simulate a "round-table" discussion in which employees either air their grievances or express their satisfaction over working conditions. One or two group members should assume the role of managers or employers.

4. Transfer the concept of job satisfaction to the classroom or the school. As a class, discuss ways to improve the physical environment and the work and social atmosphere of the school. Incorporate the best ideas in a formal written proposal to the principal.

SMOKING: CLEARING THE AIR

Non-smokers are pushing harder to have tobacco use banned from the workplace.

Peter Redman

Not long after Sir Walter Raleigh introduced smoking at the English court, King James I (reigned 1603-1625) wrote "A Counter-Blaste to Tobacco." Smoking, concluded the king, is "a custome lothsome to the eye, hateful to the Nose, harmefull to the braine, dangerous to the Lungs . . ." James's arguments fell on deaf ears, and it is only now, nearly 400 years later, that the tide may be turning against his "vile custome of tobacco taking."

Though cigarette smokers have dropped from 47% of the population in 1975 to 39% last year, Canadians still rank fourth in the world after Cuba, Greece, and Cyprus. Thirty-five thousand of us die each year from diseases linked to smoking. If things continue as they are now, another 500,000 Canadians will have died by the end of the century. Thousands more non-smokers are dying from exposure to second-hand smoke.

The last fact is perhaps the strongest motive behind a growing protest by the non-smoking majority against public smoking. Canada has a variety of agencies doing research on the dangers of tobacco such as the Ontario Council of Health's Task Force on Smoking. The best-known anti-smoking group, however, is the Non-Smokers Rights Association, headed by Garfield Mahood. In its fight to end public smoking, the association has agitated for non-smoking areas in restaurants and last year published a manual outlining how to go about having smoke banned from the workplace.

Studies show that alarm about the risks from inhaling others' smoke is justified. Researchers have identified more than 3,800 chemicals in tobacco smoke. Sixty of them may cause cancer, and two of them are so acutely cancer causing that the acceptable exposure limit is zero. The U.S. Environmental Protection Agency (EPA) says that 15 of 17 major studies since 1980 confirm a link between second-hand smoke and cancer. James Repace, a senior EPA scientist, says "the evidence suggests that passive smoking appears to be responsible for about one third of the annual lung cancer mortality among U.S. non-smokers." Shirley Thompson of the British Columbia Lung Association points out that in some ways sidestream smoke is more dangerous than what the smoker inhales; the smoke from the smouldering end of the cigarette has higher concentrations of some toxic chemicals and has not passed through a filter.

Pressure on North American governments from non-smokers has moved them to restrict smoking in some areas now, and more legislation is almost certainly on the way. In the United States, four states and 29 cities have passed laws—covering 7.4 million workers—which control smoking on the job. In Canada, the auditor general's office in Ottawa led the way towards a smoke-free environment last year with a ban on smoking except in separately ventilated rooms in its building. The City of Toronto recently enacted a bylaw to

The real reason dinosaurs became extinct

protect non-smokers from second-hand smoke. The law, patterned after a San Francisco regulation, forces employees to negotiate satisfactory arrangements between smokers and non-smokers in the workplace.

Without waiting for legislation, many Canadian companies are going ahead with their own plans to end or restrict smoking on the job. B.C. Telephone will extend its present clean-air policy to provide a smoke-free environment for employees next month. The company estimates there will be an annual financial saving of from $600 to $4,500 for each smoking employee based on days absent and medical costs. Halifax Insurance Co. told employees to butt out their last cigarette by last New

Year's Eve. The building will be smoke-free except for one section of the cafeteria. Other companies that have banned smoking include Maritime Telephone and Telegraph, Campbell's Soup Co., and Bell Northern Research.

Individual employees are beginning to sue employers for their right to clean air. The most important case so far is the grievance brought by Peter Wilson against the federal Health and Welfare Department. Mr. Wilson, a clerk in a government office in Toronto, argued that the government was breaking its own rules about dangerous substances in the workplace by allowing smoking. Walter Nisbet, an adjudicator with the Public Service Staff Relations

Board, after listening to expert testimony, upheld the grievance.

The federal government decided to appeal Mr. Nisbet's ruling to the Federal Court of Canada. If the court agrees that "passive tobacco smoke is a dangerous substance" which breaches the government's agreement to provide a safe workplace, the decision would be a landmark one. It would allow 670,000 Canadian public servants to demand protection from tobacco smoke on the job. In the long run, it might serve as a precedent for almost every unionized worker in Canada because it stipulates that freedom from tobacco smoke is a basic principle of safety in the workplace.

Unions and governments are pulled two ways on the smoking issue. Many union members are smokers, and leaders are sensitive to their pressure as well as to the demands of non-smokers. Ottawa's Health and Welfare Department admits the risks of smoking and does some media advertising to point them out. The Department of Agriculture, however, listens to tobacco farmers and is considering a tobacco marketing board to protect sales here and subsidize dumping the surplus crop, particularly in developing countries. It argues that the roughly $3 billion in tax revenues brought in from tobacco sales makes it important to keep the industry alive.

Health organizations say that the government's waffling over tobacco should end. The $3 billion in tobacco revenues is swamped by the $8 billion cost of tobacco consumption, they point out. That cost (figured out by government economists) includes doctors' services, other health care, income lost through premature death and disability, fires, and other related expenses. At that rate, each tobacco farm costs taxpayers around $750,000 a year. Angry opponents of a tobacco marketing board ask this question too: How can the government foist a poisonous product on Third World smokers who have not been educated about the hazards?

Progress toward eliminating Canada's No. 1 preventable health problem is slow but significant. The powerful tobacco lobbies are now up against informed, dedicated groups who speak for the non-smoking majority.

▼

R E A D I N G A N D R E A C T I N G

1. a) In a small group, summarize the reasons given in the article as to why non-smokers should be concerned about smoking in the workplace. Brainstorm other reasons not mentioned.

   b) Write an open letter to smokers expressing your opinion about second-hand smoke.

2. a) In a small group, list the kinds of policies regarding smoking in the workplace that are being implemented.

   b) Brainstorm the options an employee who is bothered by smoke has if he or she works at a place where there is no policy on smoking.

3. a) The Health and Welfare Department points out the risks of smoking; the Department of Agriculture is trying to protect the tobacco farming industry. In a class discussion, examine the smoking issue from these two opposing standpoints and explore the ways the government can resolve this conflict.

b) As a class, write a letter to your local member of parliament in which you express your concerns about the issue and offer your suggestions.

REACHING OUT

1. Poll the students in your school and people in your community to find out how they feel about smoking in public places and in the workplace. Your respondents should include both smokers and non-smokers, and you should analyse your findings based on this factor. Present your findings to the class using graphs to classify the data.

2. Interview or correspond with several businesses to determine how each handles the issue of smoking on the job (include your school and school board in your survey). In a written report, evaluate the policies and indicate what you feel is the most rational solution to the problem.

3. In the voice of (a) the personnel manager of a large business corporation or (b) the owner of a small business employing under 10 people, write a memo to your employees outlining a proposal to ban smoking on the job.

or

In the voice of a smoking employee, reply to the above memo. Protest the ban and try to justify your objections.

4. Stage a debate based on the following: Smoking in the workplace should be banned.

5. Survey a variety of magazines or other materials to find out what techniques advertisers use to persuade consumers to buy cigarettes. Analyse your material and produce either a written or oral presentation.

6. Write to the Non-Smokers' Rights Association requesting the booklet *Smoke in the Workplace—An Action Manual for Non-Smokers*. In an oral presentation to the class, summarize and assess the suggestions for courses of action given to non-smokers at work.

▶ OFFICE POLLUTION

Pauline Comeau

B reathe in. That's it, take a big, deep breath, the kind that reaches to the very bottom of your innocent lungs.

Now, if you're an office worker, you have just taken in some very, very, complicated stuff.

And it just might be killing you.

Of course, then again, it may not. No one seems to know for sure.

Office air pollution, sometimes called Sick Building Syndrome, has been in the news in the past few years. The most infamous case was in 1976 when 34 people died after attending a conference at a Philadelphia hotel. The deaths were finally linked to legionnaires disease caused by biological contaminants growing in the air-conditioning system.

But air isn't all we have to worry about,

according to a Metro Toronto group. Now you can worry about the bad lighting, some of which has been linked to some pretty scary bacteria growth and eye strain, or the radiation and electro-magnetic field coming from the computer terminal (VDT) you type on all day that might be causing cancer. Or, better still, you can spend your time fretting about the psychological and sociological implications of your open-office environment, a problem now seen as a major stumbling block to "employee happiness" which in turn causes a decline in productivity, something most employers worry about.

Phew! And you thought the only thing wrong with your job was the rotten pay and bad coffee.

PEOPLE NEGLECTED

About five years ago Dr. Howard Eisenberg, a Toronto physician, decided he wanted to apply his interest in preventive medicine to the office environment. His company, Synectia Consultants Inc., includes a group of consultants working on the premise that architects, interior designers, and employers usually forget the most important element when they put together an office design—people.

So if you thought it was tough telling your boss you didn't finish your work today

Protection for today's office worker: A Balans Chair to eliminate bad posture and backaches; a lamp to control neon glare around a desk and VDT; a lead apron to deter radiation from computer terminals that may be harmful; and a mask to protect the lungs from airborne dangers of the workplace. What dangers? Oh, little things like:

RADON: Naturally found in building materials like concrete. It attaches itself to particles in the air and gets into the lungs. May cause lung cancer.

FORMALDEHYDE: Found in all kinds of office materials like particle board, carpet underpadding, vinyl wallpaper, foam insulation, and given off by cigarettes. It's been known to cause nose bleeds, eye irritation, respiratory problems, and cancer in lab animals.

BENZINE: A cleaning solvent suspected of causing leukemia.

STYRENE: Given off by carpets and plastic products. It causes damage to the kidney and liver.

OZONE: An altered form of oxygen produced by electrical office machinery (particularly photocopying machines), that in poorly ventilated areas can prove to be highly toxic. It can attack the respiratory system, cause eye irritation and headaches, and in serious cases, cause genetic damage.

because the carbon dioxide levels made you lethargic, wait until you ask for a footstool and special chair for your aching back, a spider plant or two for your sterile desk, or a Sony walkman to help fend off boredom.

"There is a lot of scepticism," admits Eisenberg, when asked about how employers react to his holistic approach. "First of all it's a new science, and secondly, management is naturally suspicious of lower-level employees. They think they're just making excuses."

Eisenberg says some of his group's suggestions, whether it's a change in lighting, ventilation system, or the furniture, may be expensive. But it's the employer who benefits in the long run, he says. "If you want productivity, you have to try and establish an environment that makes people happy."

Eisenberg usually starts with a quick walk through an office and can usually spot obvious troubles like bad lighting, poor air circulation, and bad office design. From there he decides which consultants to call in.

LIGHTING: The key word here, according to Alex Murray, one of the Synectia's consultants and a York University environmental studies professor, is control. Many offices, especially older ones, are lit with strips of fluorescent tubes which give uniform stark lighting and cause terrible reflections on VDTs. The reflections can cause eye strain and headaches. And, Murray says, the group has noticed that people unconsciously sit in bizarre positions to avoid the reflections and end up with backaches.

Changing the overall lighting is one solution but an expensive one few employers can afford. In the perfect environment, employees would have control simply by

having their own lamps. And the company can remove a few fluorescent tubes . . . a solution that costs little.

"Age is also very important when it comes to lighting," says Murray. "By the time you're 55, even if your doctor says you have perfect eyes for a 55-year-old, you need 100 percent more foot-candles to do the same job as a 25-year-old. And these are people who don't need glasses. Employers don't take the fact that their workers are aging into consideration."

OFFICE DESIGN: Every office poses a different set of problems, says Murray. "The problem can be as simple as very old furniture or poorly designed chairs which cause backaches."

Open offices, now making up about 50 percent of office environments in Metro Toronto, have been grossly oversold, says Murray. After researching the subject extensively he says: "There is no evidence whatsoever that it increases productivity, or business communication, like it was supposed to. It tends to destroy intimate relationships between employees . . . The only advantage is that you can cram more people into the same space."

And open offices restrict privacy and interaction between employees. "Again the word is control," says Murray. "You need the ability to shut off the rest of the world when it is important to the employee . . ."

The solution can be as simple as changing the angles of desks, reorganizing partitions, or adding curtains, thicker carpets, and better ceiling tiles to handle the acoustical problems.

AIR: This is usually what prompts an employer to call Synectia, and the number of complaints, from headaches to the more serious, are on the rise. "I don't know that the problem is getting worse or people's perception has gone up," said Murray.

Many office air pollution problems can be linked to energy conservation and the "absolute mania for sealed buildings," says Murray. Add to that a movement to save money by decreasing the amount of fresh air coming in (usually 10 to 15 percent at tops) and you end up with a virtual witch's brew of chemicals floating around.

The problem is heightened by the fact that air in buildings is rarely handled by experts. Instead the complex world of filters, chemicals, boilers, air conditioners, and humidity controlling devices is controlled by stationary engineers or maintainance workers who have learned the art as they go.

COMFORT ELUSIVE

"I don't have time to worry about the people," said one man as he checked the hundreds of gadgets, buttons, readings, and filters in the dingy bowels of one downtown office. "I have people complaining because they feel a draft on their shoulders, so I close the vent. Then they tell me there isn't enough fresh air. I can't make everybody happy."

But whether or not the stuff in the air, from formaldehyde to the gases leaking from all the plastics, is really causing health problems in the small quantities found in offices is another question.

Charles Pilger, a consultant with the St. Michael's Hospital Occupational and Health Clinic, poo-poohs the notion that office air is really dangerous.

"I'm a chemist and I work in a lab with all kinds of chemical agents but I'm not terribly alarmed," said Pilger, who co-authored a report on the air quality at the *Toronto Sun*'s six-storey King St. E. office where it was discovered that the carbon dioxide levels were, at times, 50 percent higher than acceptable industrial standards.

"There have been a lot of studies but they're inconclusive. Personally I don't think there is usually anything to worry about."

But Murray isn't convinced. "There is this absurd difference in standards," said Murray. "For example, a chemical like formaldehyde. In houses they allow only one part per million . . . in industrial settings (which is how offices are classified) they allow two parts per million and it's supposed to be perfectly safe . . . The problem . . . is the less obvious build-up . . . that tends to produce low levels of toxicity that could be producing long term effects . . . We just don't know yet."

The perfect scenario would be a ventilation system triggered when specified chemicals or gases reach a certain level, says Murray. That can be triggered by something as subtle as a monthly sales meeting that pulls in more employees one day a week or renovations that bring in new equipment which give off gases. That system hasn't been developed yet, but Murray thinks it won't be long.

In the meantime, don't hold your breath.

READING AND REACTING

1. a) With a partner, read the article carefully and fill in the following chart on office pollution sickness:

Source of Problem	Effect on Workers	Solution

   b) Put the chart on an overhead projector and, in a class discussion, determine if the sources of office pollution apply to your school building. If the answer is yes, brainstorm ways to correct the situation.

   c) Appoint two class members to present the situation and possible solution to the principal.

2. With help from your science teacher find out more about the dangers associated with the following chemicals: radon, formaldehyde, benzine, styrene, and ozone. Share your findings with the class in an oral presentation.

REACHING OUT

1. a) Interview friends and relatives who work in offices about office pollution. Ask
   —if they are affected;
   —what the symptoms are;
   —what they have done to solve the problem;
   —how their employers have reacted.

   b) Imagine that you are a journalist and write a column on office pollution based on your interviews.

2. In a small group, brainstorm what employees and employers can do to reduce office pollution. Appoint a group member to record all ideas during the brainstorming. Select the best ideas and put them on a chart.

3. Work in a group of three and assume the roles of an architect, an interior designer, and an employer who is setting up a new office. Together, plan the ideal pollution-free, comfortable, efficient office. Present your ideas in a detailed plan.

4. In the voice of an employee, write a memo to your supervisor to complain of Sick Building Syndrome.

▶ Workers' Health– at Risk

David Bennett

Health dangers at work are pervasive, but too often recognized only when a disabling injury or death occurs. Time-loss due to work-related injuries in 1982 (latest figures available) totalled more than 15 million work-days; whereas the time-loss from industrial disputes was 5,795,000 days. That year more than 850 Canadian workers died from work-related injuries and disease. These are the death and injury figures reported to governments, which are probably less than the actual tragic totals.

There are verifiable epidemics of illness and death from work-related cancer. Ionizing radiation damages the reproductive organs of men and women; but this hazard is just one of the dangers from exposure to radiation. And stress is often the first symptom of disease resulting from the design of work-stations which ignores the workers who will use them.

Industrial Disease Epidemics

Every year nearly a thousand Canadian workers are killed as a result of industrial injury, a scandalously high figure. But the fact that there is an epidemic of occupational disease is indicated in examining the statistics on cancer deaths. The annual Canadian total of deaths from cancer each year is about 40,000. Of these, approximately 1,600 are due in some way to occupational risks—an estimate based on current knowledge of cancer-inducing work situations. The calculated estimate for cancer deaths is based on the fact that at least four percent are work-related. Yet these conservative estimates for death from occupational cancer are still nearly double those for occupational injury fatalities ("accidents").

In addition, respiratory illness, malfunctioning of the heart and circulatory system, diseases of internal organs as well as the nervous system, muscles and joints, can be traced to work situations. Taking cancer as one of the many causes of industrial illness, we have every reason to think that disease, disability, discomfort, and premature deaths are far more important than injury as an occupational hazard of the workplace. Yet the Accident Prevention Association's vast resources are devoted to propaganda on "careless" workers. And the doctors monitor disease with all the trappings of so called scientific medicine, rather than trying to prevent the disease at the source.

Unions have proposed protective measures to eliminate, or at least reduce, work hazards through engineering controls, not so much by monitoring the workforce or by providing personal protective equipment, but by removing the causes of industrial disease from the workplace.

The cause-and-effect relationship between poor design of work-stations and industrial disease is sometimes hard to find. There is a connection on a common sense level. But the difficulty is that the

employer, and sometimes governments, want to see a concrete, tangible connection between workplace design and ill-health. When the burden is put on workers to supply that, it is very often difficult to produce the evidence. So the best answer is to try to raise the level of awareness of union members to insist on the common sense improvements in work-station design that they need. As with any other type of hazards, unions use the evidence as and when it is actually available.

Unions can prod governments to introduce preventive health measures. However, the federal government has insisted on evidence of adverse effects on workers of specific hazards. In other words, it has demanded that unions "count the bodies."

Obviously, this is not a positive approach to a sensible occupational health policy.

RADIATION HAZARDS

The currently accepted "safe limits" of exposure to ionizing radiation are inadequate because there are no safe limits. The labour movement must get the exposure limits down as low as possible. Legislation is one method of reducing the limits of radiation exposure—a maximum to which any Canadian worker is allowed to be exposed, in the course of a year.

If the radiation equipment is not designed properly, there is a very real danger of massive single exposures. For example, the new equipment designed to irradiate food has just this sort of hazard. The equipment has to be regularly maintained and inspected, which causes a very real danger of massive single exposure, in some cases causing death. Many of the other radiation health hazards have a cumulative impact, resulting from repeated exposure over a period of time. This constant, relatively low-level dose is an even greater problem than the massive single exposure.

THE RIGHT-TO-KNOW – CHEMICAL HAZARDS

Unions attempt to persuade governments—federal and provincial—to enact legislation which will provide real protection for workers on the job.

The collective agreement is at the moment the best guarantee of the workers' right-to-know law about chemical hazards so that workers, as citizens, know exactly what substances and hazards they're dealing with in the course of work. But what the labour movement desperately wants is a national "right-to-know" law on chemical hazards.

We also see a very large and central role for the Canadian Centre for Occupational Health and Safety in supplying the information that should be disclosed under the law. In addition, there is an important role for the CCOHS in providing information and advice requested by local unions.

Some industrial diseases now are "recognized" in legislation and by inadequate protective regulations. Others, such as the stress-related effect of daily exposure to unknown chemicals or machines and work-stations that gradually cause muscle fatigue, are known only to workers.

Full recognition of all work-related hazards and acceptance of appropriate methods to reduce or eliminate these dangers are goals for all trade unionists concerned about on-the-job safety.

READING AND REACTING

1. Write four questions you would ask someone to find out if he or she understood the article. Exchange questions with a classmate and try to answer each other's questions. If your partner has trouble answering any of your questions, reword it to make it clearer.

2. In a small group, design a poster titled DANGER AT WORK that highlights all of the work-related health dangers mentioned in the article. Include statistics to make the message more effective.

3. In a small group, discuss the following statements:
   a) "The cause and effect relationship between poor design of work-stations and industrial disease is sometimes hard to find."
   b) " . . . it (the federal government) has demanded that unions 'count the bodies.' "

4. In a small group, determine the meaning of the term "collective agreement," and discuss why the author feels that it is "the best guarantee of the workers' right-to-know law about chemical hazards."

5. With a partner, note the things that unions are doing to reduce industrial health hazards.

REACHING OUT

1. With a partner, research the history of unions, and how they have affected working conditions. Consult your history teacher for sources to check. Present your findings in a formal report.

2. Request permission to sit in on a union meeting and write a brief commentary based on what you observed. Consider the issues that were dealt with, how efficiently the meeting was run, the group dynamics, and the overall atmosphere of the meeting.

or

Invite a union representative to your class to explain how that union functions. As a class, prepare a set of questions to ask the representative when he or she comes.

3. Write a letter to the Canadian Centre for Occupational Health and Safety requesting information relating to a job that interests you. When you receive a reply, share it with your group.

4. Research cases in which industrial pollution has resulted in illness or death and find out what was done to prevent their recurrence. Present your findings in an oral presentation to the class.

5. In a group, compile a glossary of terms that are specific to unions.

6. In a group, make a list of the issues that you feel unions should be concerned with. Show your list to a union representative and ask him or her to comment on the appropriateness of the issues.

► JOB-SHARING: GOOD OUTWEIGHS BAD

Margot Gibb-Clark

When Doris Lane sets off to her job in market research at the head office of London Life Insurance, she doesn't mind a tough, rushed week— she knows she'll have the next week off.

At the Beaches branch of the Toronto Public Library, Darlene McKee works two days one week and three the next. It allows her to keep up with a demanding outside schedule that includes volunteering at her children's alternative school, running counselling for LaLeche League for nursing mothers, and working in her housing co-op.

"You don't get as much burn-out as you ordinarily find in a field like ours," says a social worker who shared a job with her husband when the children were small.

Work-sharing is often regarded with a jaundiced eye, or described as "poverty-sharing," but participants say there is a variation that can lead to happy employees and satisfied employers, once they have overcome their initial qualms. It is called job-sharing.

Job-sharing—two workers deciding voluntarily to divide one job—differs from an economic tactic known as work-sharing. Work-sharing is a process in which employees agree to cut back on their hours as an alternative to laying off those with the least seniority.

Job-sharing can be done in several ways. It can involve the partners performing complementary tasks, or a total sharing of duties with each being responsible for the over-all job. Sometimes people with different talents offer themselves as a package deal.

Although women with young children are the primary candidates, job-sharing is also practised by people who want to return to school, those who seek to wind down as retirement nears, or those willing to live on less money to pursue outside interests.

Management is often reticent, fearing that extra supervision and paperwork may be necessary, or that extra work space will be required if schedules overlap. Training two people costs more than training one (but one half of a job-sharing team may train the other). Still, job-sharing doesn't work for all types of jobs. And some employees lose pensions or other benefits.

But experience indicates that the advantages outweigh the problems. There is less burn-out in stressful jobs such as social work; workers remain more alert for repetitive tasks, and some job-sharing professionals report that they often spend time off the job thinking about work. In general, productivity improves.

Doug Bratton, director of human resources at London Life Insurance, says job-sharing has meant higher productivity and less absenteeism at his company, one of the few to have formally instituted the plan. Job-sharing pairs often arrange to cover for one another during illnesses or on holidays.

Formal reports on productivity are limited, but a 1983 University of Toronto study of work-sharing (not specifically job-sharing) showed that of twelve cases with data avail-

able, productivity increased in seven and was little affected in others.

Doris Lane and Pat Muxlow have been sharing their market-survey job week-on and week-off since last September. Gathering information for the insurance industry, they communicate with each other through notes left on a tape recorder. This can take a few hours a week, but it has drawn no complaints.

Mrs. Lane says she was ecstatic when Mrs. Muxlow approached her as a partner. Now every second week is spent at home with her 18-month-old daughter. "It's hard to explain the joy I get from the time with her."

Darlene McKee's partner, Ginni Taylor, is also the mother of young children. She says the set-up allows her the best of both worlds: "I really appreciate being able to go out to work."

No Canadian statistics exist on job-sharing, says Bonnie Shiell of Labour Canada, but the American Management Association estimates that one to two percent ot the United States labour force share jobs.

By its nature, job-sharing is not an option that applies to a large number of workers. Not everybody can afford the option of a half-salary (although 15 percent of Canada's work force is employed part-time).

Sharing appears difficult in jobs that involve managing many people. "I think it would be difficult in jobs which involve a lot of coordination and exchange of information," says Noah Meltz, director of industrial relations at the University of Toronto. "What happens if both bosses are there at once? Who do you report to? What if their styles are different?"

At London Life, 28 employees have taken advantage of the job-sharing plan since September 1984. So far, all are women, and most of them are in jobs that carry average salaries of $20,000 or $22,000 a year. The company keeps a registry to help interested employees find partners.

The experience of Darlene McKee and Ginni Taylor in the library system may be more typical. Although they have been job-sharing successfully for almost nine years, the library is only now exploring expansion of the idea.

A one-year pilot project was recently approved by the library's management committee, says personnel director Margaret Kvetan, and 36 people have indicated they are interested.

"I feel the Toronto Public Library has lost an awful lot of talent by not doing it earlier," says Ms McKee. Several staffers have left rather than continue to work full-time while they have small children, she says.

Not all job-sharing works out. The failure of an attempt to share a library branch-head job, also in Toronto, evidently bore out Professor Meltz's prediction that it is difficult for managers to divide up a job. Another venture, between newspaper reporters, failed after a brief trial. Their problems included conflicting ideas about just how far one reporter would cover for the other when a child was sick. (If a child falls sick suddenly, it can be difficult for the off-duty partner to arrange emergency day-care that same day.)

It is important to choose a suitable partner to share a job, not just a colleague one gets along with. Similar styles of working and communicating are needed—the methodical notetaker is likely to be driven to distraction by a colleague who keeps information in his or her head or on scattered bits of paper.

Another potential problem is fringe benefits. Holidays and some benefits can be divided, but shared coverage for dependents under health or dental plans is unusual, and many job-sharers are excluded from pensions.

Pensions are the critical area, says Joe Surich, who has researched job-sharing in various countries for the Ontario Federation of Labour. But consulting actuary Doug Lee, a vice-president of Towers, Perrin, Forster and Crosby, says pension plans can be designed to incorporate job-sharers and other part-time employees at little or no extra cost to employers.

At London Life, which has about 100 part-time workers on its staff of 5,000, the extra cost for all of them is $7,000 a year on a total benefits bill of $17 million, says Mr. Bratton.

The Wallace Commission, a 1983 government inquiry into part-time work in Canada, suggested amendments to the labour code to require pro-rating of benefits. Employer organizations balked. Many part-time workers are not committed to the work force, but merely working temporarily for extra cash, they said. Many of them come and go and pro-rating would add to administrative work.

Successful job-sharers seem unanimous in their advice to others who would like to try: be careful in choosing a partner. And keep plugging to overcome any employer reticence, because there are benefits for both sides.

READING AND REACTING

1. In a small group, weigh the benefits of job-sharing against the disadvantages, and decide whether you agree with the title of the article: "Job-Sharing: Good Outweighs Bad."

2. With a partner, assume the roles of two co-workers who would like to share a job. Write a joint letter to your employer explaining why you have to work half-time. Do your best to convince your employer that job-sharing would be advantageous for the company.

or

In the voice of the employer, reply to the letter of the co-workers. Either agree to, or refuse, their request. Give reasons for your decision.

REACHING OUT

1. a) In a small group, determine the kinds of work in which job-sharing would be successful and the kinds of work in which it would fail.

   b) List the conditions that have to be met to make job-sharing a viable option.

2. Draw up a contract that outlines the expectations you would have of yourself and of the person with whom you would share the job of your choice.

3. a) In a small group discussion, explore potential solutions to the problem of combining a career with raising a family.

   b) Write up a contract for your future spouse in which you detail your expectations of the responsibilities each of you would have in bringing up your children.

The Toronto Star, Friday July 12, 1985

► THE STUDENTS' GUIDE TO ON-THE-JOB RIGHTS

It's great to have a summer job, but remember you are protected by labour laws from being exploited.

Leslie Fruman

Now that students have found summer jobs and taken those first precarious steps into the temporary workforce, it's time for a lesson on rights.

You probably feel you're lucky just to have a job, but you may be surprised to know that once you have it, Ontario and federal employment standards govern the way you are hired and fired, and everything in between.

Ontario laws pertain to most forms of employment, but there are special federal regulations to cover businesses within federal jurisdiction. Those rules will apply to you if you're working for employers such as Canada Post, a bank, a railway, an airline, a highway transport company, a telephone, telegraph or cable system, a pipeline, a radio or television station, a grain elevator, a flour or feed mill, or a uranium mine.

Here's a guide to the Ontario and federal laws that apply to most job situations in 1985. This information is available in a pamphlet called Employment Facts For Ontario Students, published by the Ontario Ministry of Labour, or in flyers published by Labour Canada. See phone numbers at the bottom of this story for more information.

▼ MINIMUM WAGE

There is more than one minimum wage in Ontario. Students working in general industry get $3.15 per hour if they are under 18 and work 28 hours or less in a week. Students 18 or over must be paid $4 per hour. But students working in the construction industry must earn $4.25 per hour, and students working in a place where they are selling liquor directly to customers in a licenced establishment earn $3.50 per hour.

If you're a student under 18 working during the school year and working more than 28 hours a week, you are entitled to the higher, $4-an-hour rate. But during school holidays, students work for the lower, $3.15 per hour.

For students working for employers under federal jurisdiction, the rules are slightly different. Students under 17 earn $3.25 per hour, and students 17 or older earn $3.50 per hour.

EQUAL PAY

Men and women doing the same job in Ontario must be paid the same amount by law. If you are a woman building fences this summer, you must make the same wage as your male colleagues. Differences in wages are permitted, however, if they are based on such factors as seniority, merit, or quantity or quality of work. So, if you're a better fence builder than he or she is, you might get a higher wage.

MINIMUM AGES

—In construction work, employees must be 16 years or older.
—In general industry, the minimum age is 15.
—In shops or offices, the minimum age is 14.

Students may work for businesses under federal jurisdiction if they are under 17; if they are not required by provincial law to be in school; if the work is not likely to endanger their health or safety; if they are not required to work underground in a mine; and if they are not required to work between 11 p.m. on one day and 6 a.m. on the following day.

VACATION PAY

All employees, whether temporary, part-time, or permanent, are entitled to vacation pay at the rate of four percent of all wages earned. There is no minimum period of employment required for qualification. After one year of work, employees are entitled to two weeks of vacation with pay. If your job ends at the end of the summer, you must receive your vacation pay on termination of employment.

HOURS OF WORK

If your employer wants you to work more than 48 hours a week, he or she will have to obtain a permit from the director of Employment Standards Branch of the Ministry of Labour.

After you've worked 44 hours in the one week, your employer must pay you one and a half times your regular rate for all additional hours.

Canada Day and Labour Day are the two statutory holidays during the summer months. If you have worked for three months before the holiday, worked on twelve days of the four weeks before the holiday, and work on the first regular work day after the holiday, you get the holiday off with pay.

Except in the hotel and restaurant industry where special rules apply, you will be paid one and a half times your regular pay if you work on a statutory holiday.

If you work for a business under federal jurisdiction, and work a holiday, you get your normal day's pay, plus time and a half for the time actually worked on the holiday.

But if you've worked for less than 30 days before the holiday, your employer isn't required to pay you for the holiday if you don't work that day.

And for you, overtime means any hours worked in excess of the standard hours, in most cases eight hours a day or forty hours a week.

There is a minimum overtime rate of one and a half times the regular wage. Employees of businesses under federal jurisdiction may work a maximum of 48 hours a week. These hours can be exceeded under special circumstances. Call the number below for more information.

SAFETY REGULATIONS

In Ontario, on-the-job safety is a joint responsibility of the employer and the employee. Employers must follow provincial safety legislation, and employees must work in a safe manner at all times. There are rules that must be followed by both parties, including the wearing of safety equipment if it is required by regulations or by your employer.

If you are injured on the job, you are required to report it immediately. If you see dangerous conditions, you should report them, as well. If there is no improvement in the situation, you should notify a member of your health and safety committee, a union official, or the nearest Ministry of Labour district office.

It is illegal in Ontario for an employer to discipline employees for seeking enforcement of safety legislation.

SEXUAL HARASSMENT

All employees in Canada are entitled to work free of sexual harassment, which is defined as any conduct, comment, gesture, or contact of a sexual nature that is likely to cause offence or humiliation or that might, on reasonable grounds, be perceived as placing a condition of a sexual nature on employment, or on any opportunity for training or promotion.

Every employer is required to have a written policy on sexual harassment and to make it known to employees.

TERMINATION NOTICE

If you've been working for three months or more and your employer wants to fire you, he or she must notify you in writing. The length of notice depends on the length of service. If an employee has worked less than two years, one week's notice is required. A notice is necessary for part-time, full-time, and student employees.

The notice is not required, if you're being let go for specific reasons, including wilful misbehaviour, or on completion of a specific term or task for which you were hired.

All of the above information is taken from the Ontario Employment Standards Act and the Canada Labour Code. For more information on employer/employee relations, call Labour Canada at 224-3850 for federal jurisdiction inquiries, and the Ontario Ministry of Labour at 965-5251. Check the blue pages of the phone book, under Ontario Government, Ministry of Labour, for specific phone numbers to find information for specific areas.

READING AND REACTING

1. a) In a small group, list in point-form the federal and provincial (if you live outside Ontario, contact your provincial Ministry of Labour for the labour laws of your province) labour laws covering the eight areas discussed in the article. Check with the provincial Ministry of Labour to see if there have been any changes in the laws since the article was written. Update your list if necessary.

b) Using your list, design a poster that highlights on-the-job rights for students. Obtain permission to display your poster in the guidance office.

or

Design a flyer that incorporates all the information you feel students should know about their on-the-job rights. If possible, use a computer or a word processor to produce an attractive, professional-looking flyer. Ask your principal for permission to distribute your flyer in the school.

REACHING OUT

1. In a small group, conduct a survey in the school to find out if the students are satisfied with their job situations.

a) Design a questionnaire that covers each of the eight areas discussed in the article. Try out your questions on your classmates to make sure that they are clearly worded. Leave room after each question for the answer.

b) Conduct your survey by personally interviewing your schoolmates or by distributing the questionnaire and informing the students when and where to return them.

c) Analyse the data you receive in a report. Use graphs and charts in your report wherever possible to display data effectively. Submit your report to your school newspaper or magazine for publication.

2. a) In a small group, examine the labour laws that protect student workers and decide whether or not they are fair and adequate. If there are areas that could be improved, brainstorm ways to do so.

b) In a letter to your local member of parliament, express your feelings about the labour laws and offer any suggestions you may have for improvement.

1. By monitoring a major daily newspaper for several weeks, compile a report on health issues related to the workplace. Describe each issue, identify the solution (if there is one), and evaluate the effectiveness and permanence of the solution.

   or

   Write a report in which you conduct a survey of your community to determine the major local work-related health and safety issues. Find out what is being done to deal with these issues and consider additional ways of resolving them.

2. Using "The Students' Guide to On-the-Job Rights" create an up-to-date handbook that covers everything you feel a student should know about rights on the job.

3. Undertake a detailed study of the Japanese management technique known as "quality circles." Write a report in which you explore how the application of this technique could benefit the classroom.

4. Research what literature is available on the concept of group dynamics.

   Dramatize several meetings in which different kinds of role behaviours are illustrated. Video-tape the simulations and present the performances to the class, explaining to the class what type of behaviour is being represented by each participant.

   or

   Attend a series of meetings and write a report in which you use the information you have learned about group dynamics to analyse the behaviour of the individuals you observe.

   or

   Organize and conduct a workshop on group dynamics in your class. Your workshop should involve the class in exercises which allow group dynamics to develop, and then in a follow-up, develop the class' understanding of how each individual functions in a group.

5. Write a paper in which you assess the role of unions with regard to an issue of your choice. Your paper might focus on the issue from a historical, cross-cultural, legislative, or organizational perspective, or another perspective that you feel is relevant.

▶In Praise of Entrepreneurs

Setting up your own business is an avenue to employment that you may not have considered. Starting up a business can be exciting, but it's not for everyone. Successful self-starters have to be willing to take risks and to know what that involves.

▶ IN PRAISE OF ENTREPRENEURS

Guy Lavigueur

Chris Haney and Scott Abbott are the creators of the Canadian board game "Trivial Pursuit." Although in the beginning bankers refused to give them a loan, Haney and Abbott have seen profits from their game soar beyond their wildest dreams.

I hear much talk from time to time, mostly in central Canada, about how Canadians are no longer as enterprising as they were. At the Federal Business Development Bank we are directly in touch with the thousands of Canadians who each year go into business for themselves. I can assure you that this current generation of entrepreneurs is just as enterprising, just as venturesome as the generations before it.

We have been conditioned to think of entrepreneurs as corporate wheelers and dealers, putting together the billion dollar takeovers and other transactions which have made the headlines of our financial press in recent months. But my definition of an entrepreneur includes the men and increasingly, the women who risk their savings to realize their dream of a business of their own.

The current breed of entrepreneurs are representatives of every aspect of Canada's rich ethnic mix. They tend to be better educated than the average and to come from families with a tradition of self-employment. They usually have had upwards of ten years of working experience when they make the break from working for others to working for themselves. More than half of the businesses they start will fail within the first five years. But that won't stop them. Most of those failing the first time around will try again, and again if necessary. Eventually many of them will succeed. As they do, they will be laying the foundations for the next generation of bigger businesses. They will be introducing revolutionary new products and processes. Most important of all, they will be imparting to the economy the dynamic and competitive diversity so essential to its continuing growth.

There are 1.2 million businesses in Canada, 95 percent of which are small businesses with annual sales of less than $2 million. They account for about one-third of total sales in Canada and close to half of total employment. Small businesses are to be found in every aspect of the economy. Together they can make a significant contribution to our economic progress.

An even greater contribution lies in the opportunities they present to Canadians to succeed on their own. Nothing is more important to the future of Canada than the continuing availability of such opportunities. Canada has become the country it is largely through the efforts of the early entrepreneurs who responded to its challenges. The present generation of entrepreneurs, like those that preceded it, is starting small, but who knows what these entrepreneurs will achieve in the future?

▼

R E A D I N G   A N D   R E A C T I N G

1. In a small group, discuss the following words and phrases and write a short, clear definition for each:
   entrepreneur
   enterprising
   corporate wheelers and dealers
   billion dollar takeovers
   small business
   dynamic and competitive diversity

2. The fourth paragraph discusses the role of small business in the Canadian economy. Working with a partner, produce a poster that shows, through bar graphs, pie charts, or other means, the statistics on small business.

R E A C H I N G   O U T

1. "Canada has become the country it is largely through the efforts of the early entrepreneurs who responded to its challenges."
   Ask your school librarian or history teacher for help in identifying some early Canadian entrepreneurs. Choose one entrepreneur whose story interests you and prepare an oral report about the person and his or her achievements. Present your report to your group.

▶ SHOULD YOU GO INTO BUSINESS FOR YOURSELF?

Ask yourself the following questions to see whether you have the basic requirements for starting your own business:

1. Are you afraid of risk?
2. Are you unable to put off enjoying the "good life" today because you are afraid you won't be here tomorrow?
3. Are you overly security conscious?
4. Do you have trouble getting along with people?
5. Do you lose interest in things that don't work out as quickly or as well as you thought they would?
6. Are you a thinker but not a "doer"?
7. Are you a "doer" but not a thinker?
8. Are you easily frustrated?
9. Do you have trouble coping in situations that require quick judgments?
10. Do you "cave in" under stress?
11. Does your family make heavy demands on your time?
12. Are you emotionally unstable?
13. Are you unable to learn from your mistakes?
14. Are you "too good" to do manual labour?

If you answered "yes" to several of these questions, you probably are not ready to start your own business. In any case, this sort of thinking is very important in deciding whether you have what it takes to be your own boss. If you do "measure up," then you can begin to weigh the benefits and the burdens of starting your own firm.

Brian Owen, Frederick A Starke, John A. Reinecke, William F. Schoell. *Introduction to Canadian Business.* (Allyn & Bacon, Inc. 1984)

▼ READING AND REACTING

1. In a small group, consider why having each of the above attitudes could be a disadvantage for an entrepreneur.

2. Rewrite the 14 questions into a list of the attitudes that make a good entrepreneur. Design a poster featuring the list.

▶ FAST TRACKING WITH THOSE WHO HAVE MADE IT

Blake Harris

The "Entrepreneur" is fast becoming the real hero of the eighties. His or her role as the major creator of new jobs in a continuing climate of high unemployment has given the label a new acceptability. University MBA programs are paying more attention to the entrepreneurial environment and even *Small Business Week*, organized annually by the Chamber of Commerce, Federal Business Development Bank, and local Boards of Trade across Canada, sought to pay tribute to the entrepreneur.

For the rest of the business world of regular pay cheques and job security, entrepreneurs have long been viewed with a mixture of jealousy and awe. We admire the people who create the Apple Computers of the world, envying the apparent freedom of being your own boss and respecting the kind of courage it takes to risk personal assets, however meagre, to start a new business in a competitive economy.

But just what does it really take to be a successful entrepreneur? In the United States, where entrepreneurship is akin to the American Dream, it is common for those who study the "phenomena" to draw profiles of successful entrepreneurs. One book, *The Entrepreneurial Life* by David Silver, describes these people as dissatisfied with their career paths and those who decide to make a mark on the world. Yet for every profile type, there are thousands of exceptions, each running successful enterprises.

Twenty-three years ago Don and Earl O'Born started The Printing House. The company now has 40 locations throughout Ontario, producing a total of one and a half million copies a day.

The O'Borns try not to sound too cautious when they offer advice to would-be entrepreneurs. No matter the economic climate, they believe that it is always tough to start a successful business.

"You are the one who is responsible, no one is looking over your shoulder. You've got to believe in yourself because there is no one else to turn to for advice."

"But what is often overlooked is that when you are starting a new business, and working long hours for very little money, it's fun. You are accomplishing something. We'd certainly do it all over again just for the excitement," they added.

There are particular advantages to entrepreneurship in terms of personal development: "Once you reach a certain point in your development, you know that no matter what happens, you can look after yourself. So, it's not just a matter of establishing your own business, but one of personal growth. It's a learning process."

So what else makes entrepreneurs different? In a country such as Canada where one out of every ten people is out of work, often despite their educational achievements, it is rather astonishing to find that some of the most prosperous of the entrepreneurial breed have had little formal

'Honest Ed' Mirvish

vive either, he cashed a $242.00 insurance cheque for his wife. With that, he started Honest Ed's, by renting a small store in the now famous Bloor Street location for $50 and using the remaining money for inventory.

He emphasizes that he always wanted to make something of his life: "I grew up considering this the land of opportunity. You could go out and establish something for yourself. I used to drive around Forest Hill delivering meat from 1:00 to 6:00 Sunday mornings and wonder what people did to live in houses like that."

Today the legendary father of Honest Ed's is also the owner of two thriving theatres, Toronto's Royal Alexandra and the Old Vic in England.

At the age of 70, Mirvish is still actively working to expand his empire, seeing his entrepreneurial endeavours as an exciting challenge.

"I really don't do it for the money," explained Honest Ed. "Once you've reached the point where you're making a living, you've got to be doing something that excites and interests you. I wanted to build something, to make something that would work."

"If your intention is just to make money, I suppose you could do it a lot more easily just by investing in stock or something similar," he added, "for me it was the building process, the creation of something new that always excited me."

Mirvish challenges those people who seem to think that starting a business today requires substantial money: "The first thing you need is to find something you enjoy doing. Otherwise, what's the point; you aren't going to give everything you can to it. I guess you've got to have dreams."

Mirvish maintains that it is actually easier today for an entrepreneur to start a new business than when he first launched Honest Ed's. "Today it's so difficult to get good

education. And even when they do have university degrees, their success is often derived from quite different routes than their educational career paths would have naturally dictated.

Such is the case of Ed Mirvish, who makes no secret of the fact that he came from rather humble beginnings.

"I grew up surrounded by poverty. At the age of 15 I took over the family grocery store which was always bankrupt because people would buy things on credit and then couldn't pay for them," he explained. "This was in the depression years when people either had a job, went to school or were in jail for vagrancy."

Finally, after turning the grocery store into a cleaning business which didn't sur-

Don O'Born

service in any area. If you can find a way to service people, you will stand out."

As for qualities found in a good entrepreneur, he claims that education is a tool, but common sense is far more important. "Without common sense you just aren't going to get very far."

"But it really starts by determining what you like to do," he continued. "A lot of people today don't seem to be able to figure this out."

And because he loves what he does so much, Honest Ed has no notions of retiring.

"Oh I can go to the Bahamas and lie in the sun for two or three days, but after that it just gets boring. Today, I'd live over the store if my wife would let me," he contended.

"I certainly don't need to do what I'm doing. I get a pension cheque from the government each month."

From the same downtown area where Ed Mirvish grew up in relative poverty many other prominent entrepreneurial types have risen above their economic hardships to become successful. Phil Givens, Harry Rosen, Paul Godfrey, Mel Lastman, Dan Akroyd and others graduated from the school of hard knocks to move beyond what their environment seemed to be offering.

What is often missed in attempts to profile the successful entrepreneur is that these people almost routinely have a zest for life and love playing the business game almost just for the sake of playing it. They like the money, but rarely is this their sole motivation.

For local entrepreneur Denise Neehan, the game has been well worth the risk. Over the past several years Toronto investors have had their eye on her small hamburger fast food company called "Licks." And for good reason; where else would people drive from all over the city to line up for up to half an hour just to buy a fast food hamburger?

If Ms. Neehan, the founder and owner of Licks had so chosen, there would be Licks stores across Canada within a year, for she has turned away well over a million dollars from investors and would-be franchisees.

Ms. Neehan was a high school drop-out, working as a waitress, before launching the project seven years ago on $6,000 in borrowed funds.

"I had nothing going for me," she stated, "No education, no money. And I was a woman. Just before I started the business I had gone through six jobs in three months."

She contends that the biggest hurdle any entrepreneur has to overcome is approaching the venture with self-confidence.

"I had a lot of people come in after I

Denise Neehan

opened and say, my goodness, you have such a great deal of courage," she said, "and for the longest time I couldn't figure out what they were talking about."

"I hadn't risked that much money. I had borrowed $2,000 from a friend so that I could borrow another $4,000 from a bank. The worst that could have happened was that I would be back working as a waitress again."

As she emphasized, "you have to make a certain commitment and believe in what you are doing. When I first started I had people coming in and telling me that what I was trying would never work. You couldn't mix fast food with quality."

Ms. Neehan maintains that very few people have the confidence to take such risks. "And in some cases it's not even that they may lose money, it's that they may lose face. They don't want to take a stab at getting into their own business in the event that they fail. They are concerned about what people will think of them."

Despite this focus on the classic "rags to riches" stories, it must be emphasized that today's breed of entrepreneurs originate from every level of economic comfort.

Two years ago, Ian Robertson, Ken Deaton, and Jim Darling, all in their early twenties and from middle class backgrounds, set up an electronic research and development company in Toronto.

The firm, Innovative Systems Group Ltd., is now grossing over $2 million per year designing new high tech products to serve the fields of advanced computer graphics, computer arctic pipeline controllers, and just about anything else for which they can land contracts, including military products. The three entrepreneurs all expect to be millionaires by the age of twenty-five.

"In some ways, the company grew out of a business Ian and I set up when we were 13 to handle sound systems and light shows for rock bands," explained Deaton.

"The three of us went to high school together. We got into this business seriously because we believed that we would have more independence and a different kind of lifestyle than if we worked for someone else. The money certainly wasn't the prime motivator."

Deaton contends that although the work is still as exciting today, the expectations are different. "It's as if we have given birth to a child that in the beginning was very much the product of our personalities. Now with a couple of dozen staff, the company has a momentum of its own. We are just as enthused about it but it's different. It begins to think and act for itself."

Though the three began as technical experts in the field of electronic engineering, he notes that they have had to become primarily businessmen.

"We still work often 16 hours a day or sometimes for days at a stretch without any sleep if there is a deadline to be met," he said, "we get a lot of work because no one else is willing to try to complete the projects in the time required by the military or other big contractors. We put in the energy and can feed off the activity this generates. It's part of the process for us."

"For me there is no interest in doing anything else. I don't think we will always be able to keep up this pace, but while we can, we're doing it," Deaton added.

He emphasizes, however, that one does have to make compromises. "The survival of your child, your business, starts to come first. That's just a reality. But the change comes about in part because you learn more and you grow."

While he looks forward to increasing financial prosperity, Deaton does not plan to retire, even if he can afford it: "I imagine we will just slow down a little."

The rest of us may only be beginning to recognize the contribution that entrepreneurs make to the lives of millions of Canadians. Between 1975 and 1982, for example, manufacturing companies with fewer than 50 employees created approximately 40,000 jobs while larger companies eliminated in the order of 100,000 positions.

At the same time, one of the healthy by-products of the recent recession was that newly unemployed management executives within large companies often turned entrepreneurs. In 1981, 56,000 new firms were launched in Canada, in 1982 there were 87,000 such new businesses, and by 1983, 96,000.

While the death rate for any new business is high, the majority seem to survive. And with these ventures lies the country's future economic growth. It may be melodramatic to talk of the heroism and adventurous spirit of the entrepreneur, but for almost half of working Canadians, it is to entrepreneurial dreams that they owe their jobs.

READING AND REACTING

1. In a small group, identify the characteristics and qualities that contributed to the success of the entrepreneurs in this article. List these attributes, in order of importance, on a chart titled "What It Takes to be an Entrepreneur."

2. a) In a small group, weigh the pros and cons of running your own business.

   b) In a short essay, state whether you would prefer to be an entrepreneur or an employee. Give reasons for your choice.

   c) Exchange essays with someone who took the opposite view and see if you can be swayed by his or her argument, and vice versa.

3. Ed Mirvish says that "education is a tool but common sense is far more important to the entrepreneur." In a small group, debate this issue.

4. Write a song or a ballad that looks at the "heroism and adventurous spirit" of entrepreneurs. Your piece could be about entrepreneurs in general or it could feature one of the entrepreneurs described in this article.

REACHING OUT

1. a) Interview an entrepreneur—it could be a relative, a friend, or someone in your community. Find out
   —how he or she chose that particular business;
   —the education, and/or training that was obtained in preparation for the business;
   —the challenges, frustrations, and rewards encountered in building up the business;
   —the price—if any—that he or she paid for success;
   —future plans and goals.

   b) Assume the role of a journalist and write a profile of the entrepreneur you interviewed. Obtain his or her permission to submit your article to the local newspaper for possible publication.
   or
   Compile the class effort into a booklet titled "Profiles of Local Entrepreneurs." Design a striking cover for the booklet. Offer the booklet to the school library.

▶ INVESTIGATE FRANCHISES

before investing large sums of money

Eugene Ellmen

For those who dream of owning a small business, a franchise operation may seem the answer.

Franchised chains are advertising for prospective investors in all sorts of businesses, including conventional enterprises such as stereo stores, travel agents, and restaurants. But franchises have also expanded into offbeat businesses such as pizzagrams, used car rental outlets, and children's furniture stores.

This expansion has caught the attention of government authorities who are anxious to warn prospective franchisees that they may be buying into more of a lemon than a bowl of cherries.

"Unethical franchisors prey on people's dreams of prestige, profits, and independence using unrealistic promises," says Bob Simpson, director of business practices for the Ontario Ministry of Consumer and Commercial Relations.

Questionable franchises are becoming such a problem that the Ontario ministry has issued a news release urging prospective franchisees who suspect fraud to contact its investigation and enforcement branch in Toronto. Other provinces have similar commercial investigation units.

Even when fraud isn't involved, prospective franchisees should be prepared to do a lot of homework—including spending money on lawyers and business consultants—to investigate the franchise, Simpson says.

"If you're not willing or able to investigate franchises carefully and invest some money for good advice, you shouldn't even be thinking about becoming a franchisee."

"There's no easy way to make the right

decision (about whether you should become a franchisee)," says Michael Coltman, head of hospitality at the British Columbia Institute of Technology.

But before looking at specific areas for investigation, let's define exactly what franchises are.

A franchise is a contractual arrangement between two parties under which the franchisor grants the franchisee the right to market a product or service, including the right to use a trade name or trademark.

Because other franchisees have used the same trade name or trademark, promoters may quote profits made by their most successful outlets, even though the average is much lower, Simpson warns.

He advises potential franchisees to ask for proof for all claims. In Alberta, franchisors must release financial data when offering franchises to the public.

In addition, be wary of franchisors who fail to protect your territory. They may grant franchises to other nearby outlets, which will cut into your sales.

Finally, find out what your rights and obligations are in delivering the goods or services.

Simpson says some franchisees have complained that the franchisor doesn't provide expected assistance, training, and services. Others say that the head office dictates too much, enforcing such details as staff uniforms, business hours, and advertising programs.

A quick check of some recent franchises advertised in Toronto showed a wide range in the amount of investment money required.

A video trivia franchise started for as low as $4,500, a satellite company offered franchises starting at $7,500, a travel agency offered franchises for $29,000, a stereo chain put their minimum franchises at $5,000, a home cleaning company put their "total all inclusive investment" at $75,000 and a bakery chain said they needed $150,000 in "unencumbered equity."

With such a range in the types and cost, Toronto accountant Ross McCallum advises people to choose franchises carefully.

First, be sure the income from the operation can support you and your family, he says. But second, you must find out what aptitudes and skills the business requires and decide whether you possess the aptitudes.

He says it wouldn't be surprising if only two or three franchises out of the estimated 500 offered in Canada are right for any one individual.

▼

R E A D I N G   A N D   R E A C T I N G

1. a) Without consulting a dictionary, write a short definition of the word "franchise." Get together with your group and compare definitions. Check a dictionary or a business text to see if you have correctly defined the term. Together, write a one-paragraph explanation of the term.

   b) Brainstorm five major franchise operations.

   c) Incorporate your definition and the list of franchises into an attractive poster.

2. a) In a small group, discuss the following:
  —the advantages of being a franchisee
  —why prospective franchisees are open to the risk of "buying into more of a lemon than a bowl of cherries"
  —the types of problems franchisees encounter
  —the steps franchisees can take to ensure the success of their business

  b) On your own, assume the role of a prospective franchisee and, in a journal entry, explain why you have decided to invest in a franchise operation.

  or

  In the voice of a prospective franchisee, write a letter to a franchisor stating that you have decided not to buy the franchise and giving reasons for your decision.

R E A C H I N G   O U T

1. a) Research a major franchise company. Write to the company for information on
  —how the franchise was started;
  —how successful it is and why;
  —how many franchisees it controls;
  —what is required to be a franchisee;
  —what services the company offers its franchisees.
  Incorporate your findings into a report about the company. Have a partner help you polish your writing. If a word processor is available, type out your report and send a copy to the company.

  b) Share your report with the class and find out how many people would invest in the franchise.

2. a) With a partner, create your own franchise company. Decide on the type of business you will operate, the kind of people you are looking for in franchisees, the financial investment required, the projected financial returns, and the types of services you will offer your franchisees.

  b) Incorporate the above information into a brochure that you would send to prospective franchisees to tell them more about your company. Include graphs and charts where necessary.

3. Write a short story in which a person's get-rich-quick scheme sours.

► Learning Skills to Climb the Corporate Ladder

Marianne Tefft

In hundreds of classrooms across Canada, grade eight and nine students in Junior Achievement of Canada's Project Business program are learning there's more to business than three-piece suits.

Since 1979, more than 30,000 junior-high-school students have charted the stock market, scrutinized financial statements, and pondered Canada's economic problems as part of JA's Project Business program.

During the current school year, another 22,000 students in 6 provinces are participating in the 12- to 18-week program, which aims to provide a first-hand introduction to career exploration and the principles of free enterprise.

Under Project Business, the bearers of JA's message are qualified volunteer business people who bring their expertise directly to the classroom each week.

This year, about 750 such consultants from 515 large and small businesses across Canada are sharing their knowledge of the business ladder—and the education and skills needed to reach the top.

Using work books and teaching materials developed by JA, the consultant, teacher, and students discuss topics that mesh with the school's mathematics, social studies, and guidance curricula.

Depending on the consultant's background, the sessions focus on the nature of economics, the Canadian economy, the Canadian market system, money and banking, financial statements, consumer-ism, or choosing a career.

The program's open discussions, role-playing games, and field trips bring to life the words and phrases of newspaper business-news pages—market, profit, monopoly, competition. Questions posed during the sessions also call on students to think on their feet, reinforcing language and reasoning skills.

During a recent Project Business session, for example, grade eight students put their heads together to decide—in a 20-minute period—where and how to set up fictitious car-wash and popcorn vending businesses.

As the youngsters weighed the options, consultant Glen Foote circulated through the room and answered questions such as "Sir, have you ever seen a carwash downtown?"

Foote, who is project manager, product control at IBM Canada, urged the students to concentrate their limited time on one problem: determining their market.

"If you are successful about getting your product out there before your competition, you'll get more of the market," Foote told the class. "But the company that puts out the better product is the company that'll be around tomorrow."

The program also rewards the consultants and their firms, says Ted Yohn, JA's Project Business director, Metropolitan Toronto & York Region.

"A lot of firms look at it as an opportunity

Consultant Foote (back right): "determine markets"

to increase their profile and put something back into the community—they usually participate at nearby schools," Yohn says.

"Some feel the free-enterprise system hasn't done enough to teach kids what it's all about. And others see it as an opportunity to train their people in communication skills."

In 1971, Project Business began in the U.S. as a pilot-project adjunct to JA's original learn-by-doing program for high-school students. This year, about 250,000 U.S. students are taking part in the program.

In Canada, the scheme got underway in 1979 with pilot projects in Calgary and Windsor, Ontario. By 1985, the program had been extended to take in classrooms in 11 major cities and regions.

READING AND REACTING

1. a) Determine the ways in which the Junior Achievement program benefits both students and participating businesses.

b) Assume the role of an official from Junior Achievement, and write two letters: one to businesses and the other to school principals, inviting them to participate in the program. Each letter should explain how the program operates and how it would benefit each group.

2. Working with a partner, locate all the statistics in this article. Design graphic displays of the figures that you would use if you were presenting the data at a meeting of the Junior Achievement board of directors.

3. In a small group, discuss the term *free-enterprise system*. Identify an alternative to the free-enterprise system and weigh the pros and cons of each.

REACHING OUT

1. a) Telephone Junior Achievement to invite a Junior Achievement counsellor to speak to the class about the organization.

b) Follow up the call with a letter expressing your pleasure that the speaker has agreed to come and confirming the date, time, and place. Provide clear directions for getting to the school—a simple map might be helpful.

c) Prepare questions to ask the speaker.

d) Arrange for a classmate to introduce the speaker and another to thank him or her after the presentation.

e) Tape the presentation or make notes during the session. In a written report, state whether you would like to participate in the program and give reasons for your decision.

f) Send a thank-you letter to the speaker.

▶ Give Yourself a Job – Profiles of Youth in Business

Restaurant Is His Investment in the Future

Leslie Fruman

E veryone has to eat, even struggling students.

Rob Lanni came to this conclusion a few months ago, and acted accordingly. He put aside his two university degrees, raised $25,000 in small chunks by hitting up friends and relatives, and invested the bundle on a down-payment for a business of his own. Anthony's, a small pizza restaurant on the corner of Keele St. and Finch Ave. near York University, is his.

Soon he will be changing the name to Korner Kafe, and changing the menu from strictly pizza to a more continental, deli-style cuisine. This is just the beginning of what Lanni hopes will be a successful entrepreneurial venture.

"People Have Always Needed Food."

The 24-year-old sidestepped the norm when he decided to ignore his degrees in geography and administrative studies and go into business for himself. When choosing a business, he figured it was best to go with trying to sell something people needed.

"People have always needed food, and always will," says Lanni. "The hula hoop is gone, but people still eat."

After high school, Lanni wasn't sure what he wanted to do, so he decided to spend his time thinking about it in university.

"After I finished university I was offered a job as a manager of a restaurant," says Lanni. "Even though it wasn't part of my job, I used to come in at night and do the dishes with the dishwasher, and do some bussing, and do everything you have to do in a restaurant. I didn't feel I could tell people how to do something if I didn't know how to do it myself. And I wanted to learn everything I could about the business."

When he quit that job, he took a job delivering pizzas at a restaurant down the street from the restaurant he eventually bought.

"I learned everything about the take-out and delivery business there," says Lanni.

"I did it strictly for the learning experience."

It's been a month since Lanni took over Anthony's. He's working 16-hour days, foregoing his social life, and planning for the future. It doesn't sound like much fun, but Lanni loves it.

THE RIGHT CHOICE

"I figured I should take the chances now, when I'm young and don't have a wife and kids," Lanni says. "Right now, establishing my career and my bank account is the important thing."

He still doesn't know if he made a profitable decision when he decided to go into business for himself, but he does know he made the right choice.

"There's no question about it. I'm taking a chance," says Lanni. "But I'm really happy about what I've done. It's hard work, and I'm giving a lot up, but there's something about it I really enjoy."

Lanni comes from a family of independent business people, so it was natural for him to get involved in a business of his own.

"Ten years from now I hope to still be in business for myself, but not necessarily the restaurant business," Lanni says. "A lot of people feel free when they work for someone else because at the end of the day they can leave it behind.

"I feel free by being my own boss. I don't mind the long hours. I feel I can do whatever I want.

"People my age usually don't want to take chances. I'm willing to work and make the sacrifices now."

A LITTLE BIT OF ROMANCE IS OFFERED BY 'REPLICARS'

Linda Kirby

Nostalgia is popular: Witness the enthusiasm people have for collecting antique coins, furniture, and silverware. Most of us enjoy having a special memento of another time.

Two people are doing something about recapturing a romantic era and are putting their ideas on the road.

Milton resident Brian Penman, along with Kevin Kerridge of Oakville, have realized a special dream with the creation of their company "Canadian Kit Collection."

Replicars are hardly a new idea, but with a bit of luck these two gentlemen hope to assist others who share a similar passion for such classic cars as the Jaguar SS 100, the MG T series, or Austin Healeys, the "hybrids" as Brian Penman likes to describe them.

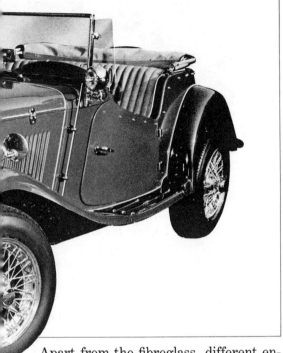

Apart from the fibreglass, different engines, and transmissions, replicars offer a very close copy of the original model.

Every detail is minutely copied and there is nothing unreal about the gleaming mahogany dash or the sumptuous leather interior.

"You get the oohs and ahhs of the original design, but you have the convenience of today's engines and parts," explained Mr. Penman, a former Austin Healey owner.

For a few thousand dollars the kit is yours.

There are additional basics one must purchase. Depending upon whether the model is a front engine or rear engine, you will require a chassis. There is also the engine and transmission, not to forget tires, leather seats, and a few other items.

Sadly, many of those who set out to recreate that dream car from the "Great Gatsby" days give up half-way through, frustrated and slightly broke after their adventure with nostalgia.

"The Kit Collection," according to its owners, hopes to prevent that all too frequent unhappy ending.

Mr. Penman and Mr. Kerridge offer a variety of services, including assisting with ordering the kit, helping to construct the model, or building the entire unit themselves from start to finish.

"People can buy these kits and then make an abortion of them, because they don't know what they are doing," noted Mr. Penman. "A lot of people start these kits, then end up offering them for sale half completed."

Friends for several years, the two decided to form a company after Brian Penman returned from a trip to Miami.

He was impressed with the market place and could see the potential for stepping up kit car production in Canada.

DIVERSE SERVICES

He is aware of only six companies in this country which build the kit cars, but none appear to offer the diverse services provided by "Canadian Kit Collection."

While Mr. Penman possesses the business and marketing techniques, Kevin Kerridge's talents lie with his mechanical and constructive abilities.

A graduate from Mohawk College, Kerridge was accepted at three different universities this fall, but declined and instead has chosen to take a year off from mechanical engineering to build cars.

He is a master craftsman according to his partner, and his nearly completed 1952 MG TD attests to his abilities.

Take for example, their next project—a Jaguar XK120G.

To own and maintain such a vehicle would require a generous budget, while the replicar can be serviced at the neighbourhood gasoline station.

The cost of having a replicar built is not

cheap (depending upon model and options it can range from $14,000 to $24,000), but once it is built, one can look forward to having a car for a good number of years.

"There are lots of women interested in them. They have more disposable income and the cars are an extension of their very personality," he explained.

"There are those who grew up with a model and now want to recapture a few memories, but there is also a growing number of 'young professionals' who are knowledgeable about cars and appreciate the older models," said Mr. Penman.

"Part of our hope is to put some fun and romance back into car ownership," he continued.

Day-Care Venture a Risk That Paid Off

Leslie Fruman

It was a big financial risk, but Rebecca Brissette was ready for it.

In 1981, she decided to leave the church basement day-care centre where she worked, and open a homey day-care/Montessori school in a house of her own.

The timing wasn't exactly right. It was near the end of the real estate boom in Toronto four years ago, when house prices were rising along with interest rates, but Brissette didn't care. She'd made up her mind to do it and went out to meet the challenge.

She approached three banks for financing to buy a big, old house on Runnymede Road in the west end of Toronto; two of them turned her down. Finally one bank decided she was worth the risk, and Brissette and her husband started renovating the house to meet the standards in the Day Nurseries Act.

"I'd worked in day-care centres with a

hundred kids and I knew parents wanted something different," says Brissette, 25. "I was especially interested in the Montessori method and wanted to offer both day-care and Montessori.

"I knew there was a need for good day-care in High Park and that a lot of parents wanted their children to have Montessori. But with both parents working, they couldn't send their children to half-day programs, which most Montessori schools are. So I decided to incorporate both."

A graduate of Sheridan College's Early Childhood Education course and Montessori training programs, Brissette was only 21 when she started the venture. Now her Stepping Stones Montessori School is expanding to include a second location in the same area, called Stepping Stones Too.

For the first three years, Brissette and her husband lived on the second floor, while the Montessori school and day-care was housed on the main floor and in the basement. Eventually, as the enrollment started to grow, the couple had to move to make room for more children.

In the meantime, Brissette had two children of her own. Her infant daughter has a daytime nanny, but her older daughter is enrolled in the school.

"It was difficult to get started," Brissette recalls. "I didn't have any business experience, but my husband is in marketing, so that helped. My father was concerned about the whole idea, and a lot of people told me to just rent a church basement, instead of getting involved in real estate.

"But it was a dream of mine. I'd had enough of working for other people, and I thought that it was the right time to get started in my own business. A lot of people thought I was just too young."

Now she has bought another house and things are running smoothly. She does the administration work now, instead of working with the children, and she misses the contact with them.

"Sometimes I just go in and read the kids a story or play with them," says Brissette. "I miss being around the kids."

FITNESS CONSULTANTS RUN FAMILY BUSINESS

Leslie Fruman

I ndre Paskauskas wanted to put her professional dance training to work but she didn't necessarily want to perform.

She thought teaching would be a good solution, but she had one more stipulation for her career: she didn't want to work for anyone else.

She took a look around, evaluated her skills, and decided to go into partnership with her sister-in-law Ilona and open a fitness and nutrition consulting business.

Energetics Inc. is the result.

As a trained dancer, Indre Paskauskas has learned a lot about fitness. Her gruelling personal workouts have taught her about working every muscle in her body and the benefits and pitfalls of all kinds of exercise.

Her sister-in-law Ilona Paskauskas is a registered dietician, and both women

believe that to do the most for your body, exercise and nutrition have to play equal roles.

"I had been working at exercise studios in Toronto, and thought there had to be an alternative," says Indre Paskauskas, 26. "We realized that not everyone wants to go out to a studio to exercise and you can't always get personalized attention when there is one instructor for 20 people."

Energetics caters to people who want to evaluate and do something about diet and fitness in their own home. The personalized

program involves both women, who go to the client's home, design specialized diet and exercise plans, and then do follow-up for as long as the client wants.

"I can come into the client's home two or three times a week to exercise and Ilona can work out a detailed diet, with menus, and even grocery lists if that's what the client wants," says Indre Paskauskas.

They charge about $25 an hour for their work, or $400 for a 12-week fitness and diet program. Rates vary depending on what the client wants, and rates drop for groups.

Starting their own business was easier than the pair thought. They went to the library and researched how to incorporate a business, then went to get the papers, and filled them out themselves. They could have used a lawyer, but that would have cost a bundle, and the young entrepreneurs didn't have it.

They enlisted friends in the graphic business to help with brochures and went to an accountant friend for some financial advice.

"We're starting small, but we do hope to build it into something bigger in the future," says Indre Paskauskas.

KETTLE CREEK CANVAS COMPANY

Joyce Carter

It all happened because Mellanie Stephens couldn't find a job.

She dropped out of high school, knocked around the world a bit, worked at a number of things including a stint cooking in a bush camp, then returned to the hometown she loves.

There aren't a lot of job opportunities in Port Stanley. It has a fishing fleet working Lake Erie, a handful of marinas for Sunday sailors. It's the kind of place where the stable population of 1,900 leaps to 10,000 in summer.

So she started her own enterprise. That was six years ago. This year the Kettle Creek Canvas Company is expecting to do $7-million worth of business. And nobody's more shocked than its 32-year-old owner.

She's the youngest of eight children, and fondly remembers her mother making all their clothes. "I think that kept her sane; she didn't have to deal with other things when she was sewing." So as soon as she was old enough, Mellanie made all her own things.

Back home and unemployed, she started sewing baby bonnets and bed comforters for a store, but the cumbersome bats of comforter filling "ate up my apartment," so she went looking for a workroom. She settled on the basement of a yacht broker's establishment. "People could see me working in there and they'd come in and say, 'Mell, would you fix this sail?' or 'would you make me a canvas bag?'" and the light bulb went on.

She rented a miniature store—250 square feet—on the main street and started sewing bags for sailors. "Then, before I was set to open on the 24th of May, I realized I couldn't make enough bags to fill the shop. So I decided, because they were quick to sew, I'd make some drawstring pants. They sold first."

Every garment in the store was of unbleached canvas—she couldn't afford colours because they only come in 77-metre lots—and she didn't have any hangers, just rough wooden (although unused) fish boxes. "For a whole year, the place looked like it was filled with sugar bags."

Her bags, of 12-ounce-a-yard cotton duck usually employed for the inside of car seats, came in colours, so the next spring she got the 8-ounce dyed to match. "I kept the natural and added kelly green, primary yellow, and primary red. In the spring of 1980 nobody was wearing primary colours; by the following spring everybody was."

"When I opened the store, I expected to sell to sailors, to the cottage crowd, but then it hit the North London market—that's a high-end market—and the business got far better than I could deal with." She was sewing all week with the door shut. Every Saturday she'd open, sell out, and head back to the machine. So she went looking for seamstresses.

She now has 68 of them on her roster, and that makes her the biggest employer in Port Stanley. Head office is a plant on Kettle Creek, a building designed as a fish house for the herring industry—"but the herring disappeared before it could be used."

It's a homey structure in grey clapboard with a store in one corner, a basement room of bargains ("our seconds and turkeys"), big rooms for cutting and serging the parts of garments that are taken home by the sewers, "because I don't want to work in a factory and I don't think other people do."

A typical seamstress has young children at home, can produce some 45 garments in a week ("though that really varies") and usually makes "$275 to $375" for her labour.

The product is now distributed to 38 stores coast to coast, most of them in the hands of franchisers, though Mellanie retains shares in the four Toronto outlets and one in Vancouver. "It's selling far better than I expected it to," she says with becoming modesty, "the product seems to have universal appeal." So she's now scanning the United States market ("we've had 400 requests for franchises there"), and she's not ruling out expansion to Europe.

It's fair comment that she was uncommonly lucky in her timing. She got into sturdy utilitarian sports clothing just when the market was ready for it. Fashion as fashion doesn't play a big role in the styling, "though it can't help but play a

part—we're inundated with it—but there is little if any detail for the sake of detail."

It's honest merchandise, suited to the sentiments of a letter once written to the Levi Strauss jeans makers which said: "You make a righteous garment." So does Melanie Stephens, though there's nothing righteous in her manner.

"I'd work here as an employee," she says simply. "I really like it. I get a charge out of hearing from consumers (she answers all letters), and we have nice employees and we're all having fun."

TEEN TAKES A FLYER ON BUSINESS VENTURE

Leslie Fruman

Shawn McGrath has turned a part-time job he had when he was eight years old into what he hopes will be a business with a future.

Several years ago, McGrath delivered flyers for his dad's business and last winter decided to start his own flyer distribution company.

There's still a lot of hand delivering involved, but now there's a lot more money to be made.

McGrath, 16, registered his business, called Unicomn, last winter, and he now has about 12 steady contracts. One contract with a large retail outlet can net him up to $400 a week.

It may not be a glamorous way to earn a living, but McGrath says it allows him to explore entrepreneurial abilities and be his own boss.

"When you're 16, it's pretty hard to get someone to hire you," he says.

He is continuing his education through home study correspondence courses, and

working the rest of the time.

"I couldn't see myself sitting in school eight hours a day," says McGrath. "This way I can do a whole spurt of school work at a time, and work at my business when I need to."

McGrath started up with about $100 in capital which he needed to get some business cards printed and to register his business.

Besides delivering the flyers, McGrath has to be constantly trying to get more contracts, by presenting prospective clients with appealing rates and services.

"I think I do the best job around, and I'm still able to undercut other operations," he says. "You'll never find a single flyer that I or one of my people deliver that is on the ground. We put each one in the door, and we do it very neatly. There isn't a door in Toronto I can't put a flyer in."

McGrath does a lot of the delivering himself, but for big jobs that require more than 2,000 deliveries, he hires students to help out. He pays them 2 cents per flyer, and he is paid 4 cents by the companies that contract his services. Since last winter, he estimates, he has delivered 25,000 flyers.

Eventually, he'd like to expand his business to include printing so he can offer a full service for his customers—both printing and delivering their flyers.

"It's tough, mainly because I'm young and my company is new," McGrath says. "I put in a bid to deliver some booklets in Cabbagetown a while back at five cents per item, but they hired someone at eight cents because the company had been around longer. I know I would have done just as good a job, but you need to create a good reputation. I haven't been at it long enough yet."

READING AND REACTING

1. Divide into six groups so that each group reads a different article from this cluster. Categorize the information in the article under the following headings:
   —type of business
   —characteristics of entrepreneur(s)
   —steps in starting the business
   —rewards of running the business
   —pressures of running the business
   —returns, both monetary and emotional
   Share summaries as a class and discuss the advantages and disadvantages of each of the business ventures.

REACHING OUT

1. Work with a partner to research the following business set-ups:
   —single proprietorship
   —partnership
   —incorporated company
   Define each type of operation and list the advantages and disadvantages of each.

2. Appoint one person to find out and present to the class the process by which a business is registered. Obtain sample registration forms for the class to fill in.

3. Invite a lawyer to visit your class to explain the procedures for

incorporating a company. Your request may be made by telephone or in writing. Preparation for the visit should include drawing up questions to ask the lawyer, and appointing a person to introduce and thank the guest speaker. Be sure to follow up the visit with a thank-you letter.

4. a) Individually, or in a small group, identify students in your school or community who have started their own businesses. Form a panel of student entrepreneurs. Invite them to give details of their endeavours. Open the panel for discussion and allow the audience to question the students about their businesses.

   b) Expand your search for entrepreneurs into the business community. Invite community entrepreneurs to join the students on the panel.

5. If you have been involved in a business venture of any kind, report on the enterprise. Graphs and charts would be useful for displaying statistics. Include the following in your report: information on how much money you originally invested, if any; how you got customers; profits you made; difficulties you had; successes you experienced; things you would do differently in the future.

6. Think about a hobby that you could turn into a business. Write a fictional account of your business. Be specific about how you went about creating your own success story. What breaks did you get? What obstacles did you overcome?

or

Write a proposal for turning your hobby into a business. Explain the venture, the investment, the locale of the business. Be honest about the problems you anticipate and be realistic about the returns you expect. Put all the information into a letter to a friend inviting him or her to be your business partner.

COMMUNICATION PROJECTS

1. a) Two teams each have an imaginary $2,000 to invest in the stock market. Team A invests in three to five stocks chosen at random. Team B invests in the same number of stocks chosen after careful evaluation of the company's records.

   b) Every day, for the period of a semester or a term, each team records (on a chart posted in the classroom) the progress made by its stocks.

   c) At the end of the period, the teams report their profit/loss situations to the class.

   d) Each group member should write a report of the experience and evaluate what he or she gained by it.

2. Present a case study that illustrates features of one of the following types of business enterprises:
   a) a partnership
   b) a co-operative
   c) a family business
   In your study, examine the advantages and disadvantages of this kind of management set-up.

3. Canada has many colourful entrepreneurs and entrepreneurial families: the Eatons, the Crosbies, the Rollands, the Simmards, the Richardsons, the Reichmanns, the Bronfmans, and others. Research one such family and write a biography. Debrett's *Illustrated Guide to The Canadian Establishment* and *The Canadian Establishment* by Peter C. Newman will be useful references. Search the magazine index in the resource centre and try to locate articles relating to your subject.

   If the entrepreneur runs a public company, write to request an annual report. Include information from the report in the biography you are writing. Advertisements of your subject's product or service, photographs, and news clippings will provide interesting current details. (These should be included as part of the appendix.) Consult a history teacher for reaction to your material and for suggestions on how to write your report as a professional, historical writer would do it.

4. a) With or without the help of a Junior Achievement counsellor, set up a real or a simulated business. Work on your own, in a small group, or as a class. Draw on the expertise of the marketing and accounting teacher, the teacher-librarian, members of the

chamber of commerce, business people in your community, parents, and any others who have knowledge that would help you.

Hold a meeting if you are working with a group or with your class, and generate a list of the decisions you will have to make in order to establish your business.

1. What is your company's business?
2. What is its name?
3. Who are its officers?
4. What company positions need to be filled?
5. Who is the market for your product or service?
6. How will you distribute your product or service?
7. What will you charge?
8. How will you keep records?
9. How will you divide the proceeds?
10. How much capital will you initially invest?
11. How will you raise this capital?
12. Do you need a logo, a letterhead, forms, and business cards? Design them if you do.

b) Check *Work and Employability Skills Program*, the Ontario Ministry of Education resource document, to find a list of steps to consider when starting a small business.

c) Write advertising copy and produce visuals for the marketing campaign for your service or product.

d) Devise and carry out a marketing survey.

e) Hire an accountant, secretaries, and sales people. Put appropriate correspondence between company personnel in memo form. Keep copies of all letters sent outside the class.

f) Draw up a set of financial statements.

5. Work individually, in a small group, or with the whole class. Suppose that you started a business of your own and it proved to be a huge success. Write an annual report, complete with financial statements, for your shareholders.

and/or

Imagine that you are the successful owner of your own business. Organize a shareholders meeting for your company. A senior office procedures text will outline the process for organizing such an event. Appoint classmates to play various roles at the meeting. Produce the written documents that would precede and follow the meeting. These would include such documents as the notice of meeting, agenda, letters to company personnel, letters arranging transportation and accommodation, memos to remind people of duties, appropriate introductions and reports to be made at the meeting, motions, and minutes.

▶ THE FRAGILE BONDS

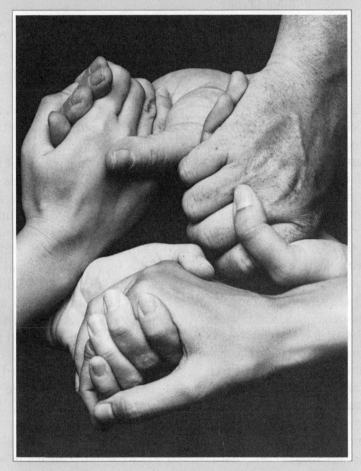

The selections in this unit ask you to reflect on some of the relationships in your life: your relationship with other people, your job, and the environment.

▶ THE FRAGILE BONDS OF FRIENDSHIP

Virginia Corner

It's the most neglected social relationship of our time, says a U.S. author who explains why we make friends and often lose them.

Friendship is a funny thing. American psychotherapist Lillian Rubin has called it "a non-event—a relationship that just *becomes*" and, too often perhaps, just fades away.

Even the word "friend" is ambiguous, says Rubin, the author of *Just Friends: The Role of Friendship in our Lives*, because it refers to a wide range of relationships with varying degrees of closeness and distance.

"We have friends, and we have 'just' friends; we have good friends, and we have best friends. Yet such is the elusiveness of the idea of 'friend' that not even the people involved can always say which is which."

What's certain though, is that we go through life making friends—and losing them.

Time, distance, envy, changing needs, unresolved conflicts, negligence, and lack of intimacy, openness, or common ground conspire to destroy a friendship. When friendships fail, we feel sad and possibly angry. We try to make sense of the experience and yet we never seem to come up with satisfactory reasons, especially if we're the one who was left.

Unlike a marriage, friendship in our society is secured by an emotional bond alone, Rubin says.

"With no social compact, no ritual moment, no pledge of loyalty and constancy to hold a friendship in place, it becomes not only the most neglected social relationship of our time but, all too often, our most fragile one as well."

Julie and Lynne were best friends in university. They went to classes, football games, and parties together. Julie was shy. She liked Lynne's self-assured manner—the way she made friends easily and seemed to be in control of every situation.

When they graduated and both got jobs in Toronto, they believed their friendship would continue, but it fell apart instead. While Lynne concentrated on getting ahead in her career, Julie married and started a family.

"A couple of times we had to cancel out of (Lynne's) parties because the baby was sick or he was being really fussy and we didn't want to leave him with the babysitter," Julie recalls. "She started getting really irritated. This happened about two or three times . . . and she just sort of said, 'That's it.' "

Toronto psychologist Sheldon Geller believes there's "a balance sheet" that has to be maintained with a friendship.

"There have to be more pluses than there are negatives," he says. "The friendship will dissolve once either party perceives that it's no longer beneficial."

When friendships go from very involved to nothing at all, it's usually because one party has been "severely injured," Geller says. "Their image of the other person and

of themselves has been altered drastically."

Geller, like Rubin, sees a disparity between people's idealized version of friendship and the reality of relations with friends, but he goes on to say that the key to maintaining a friendship is that people have the same expectations.

"As long as they both agree on what the parties contribute to the relationship, then you'll have a good friendship. Externally, a third person can say, 'Yes, but that's very abusive and manipulative and exploitive,' but as long as they each agree on what the parties' contributions are, there won't be a problem."

A true friend is somebody who is willing to accept the weaknesses and deficiencies in the other person and work within those boundaries, Geller says.

"Say you have a friend who isn't punctual, yet she has other qualities about her that are very desirable. Be prepared to put up with it. You try to impress upon her the importance of being punctual but you just accept it and sort of structure your life around it. If you're supposed to meet the person at 6, anticipate that she's not going to be there until 6:30."

Business brought Diane and Nancy together, and business split them apart.

"We got to know each other personally," recalls 28-year-old Nancy. "We had things in common. For one, we had the business. It was a growing business so we shared the joys and pains of seeing it start from nothing and really become something. Also we had great laughs. We really laughed a lot together, which to me is rare in a friendship because I'm not a big laugher. If someone can get me laughing, it's great."

Nancy was ambitious, however. She wanted Diane to make her a partner in the company, but Diane kept putting her off. Ultimately, Nancy left Diane to start her own company.

"Our falling out is sort of a tragedy. Business got in the way of our friendship. I put a lot of trust in her and when it came down to money, I didn't get the money I wanted. I didn't get the deal I wanted."

"The problem is we're competitors now and we can never ever be friends again."

We have different types of friendships for different activities and different periods in our lives, says Toronto psychologist Marty McKay. We have friends at work; friends we play tennis with; old, familiar friends we'd never give up even though we may not see them very often; and new, intimate friends with whom we can talk about our problems.

"With a real friend, you can pick up the thread of the relationship even though you may not have seen one another for 18 months," McKay says. "It's frequently happened that I'll be thinking of someone—a friend of mine who is now in Tucson—and a few days later I'll get a phone call from her.

"There seems to be just this strong bond that exists that even though you're not physically present, they're still in your thoughts and every once in a while you make actual contact."

It's McKay's impression that friendships formed when people are in their 20s are the most lasting.

"I think it becomes harder for a lot of people to make friends in their 30s than in their 20s because they don't have enough time available to give to another person to develop that foundation that's necessary."

McKay has asked a number of people for their opinions about why some friendships fade away, and she's noticed a distinct difference in the way men and women answer the questions.

"Men by and large stated that friendships faded because people outgrew each other and moved on to other things. The women said friendships fade because you get hurt by someone who does wrong by you or betrays you. The women tended to react on a more emotional level . . . whereas with men it was more a practical kind of thing."

Having the tolerance to accept the good and bad in a person and being able to give as well as take are the ingredients of a good friendship but stimulation—do you find the person interesting to be with?—is also important, says McKay. So is chemistry.

"There's some attraction there that's not that easy to define."

Twenty-three-year-old Jessica has a lot of close friends but she rarely sees them.

"I've never stayed long enough with a friend to have the friendship collapse," says the Carleton University graduate, who spent her early teens in Montreal, lived in England for a year, then in Ottawa before coming to Toronto.

Although she and a best friend may get together only once a year, Jessica claims their relationship remains "as strong as ever."

Jessica, however, recently met a girl-friend she used to chum around with years ago in Montreal, and she had to admit that things had changed between them.

"It was different because although she was the same fun girl in many respects, she was very much into another sort of lifestyle—a material lifestyle. I just couldn't really relate to that and I felt she was forsaking all her really good qualities for that shallow, materialistic goal of hers.

"She ended up moving away recently, so it never got to be a rift, but at the end there was tension."

Though we leave friends behind, we do not want to be friendless, notes author Lillian Rubin.

"To be without friends is a cause for shame, a stigma, a symptom of personal deficiency that none of us takes lightly. Indeed, in notable ways, our very sense of ourselves is connected to our ability to negotiate the world of friendship."

Rubin says we have friends—not just for fun, to replace a distant or difficult family, or as a substitute for a failed marriage—but because they help us grow as human beings.

"The turning points and transitions that are the inevitable accompaniments of living would be infinitely harder to negotiate without them."

R E A D I N G A N D R E A C T I N G

1. Lillian Rubin describes friendship as a "non-event—a relationship that just *becomes*. . . ."

a) As a class, discuss the meaning of the statement and whether or not you agree with her.

b) In a class discussion, explore the meaning of friendship.

2. "We have friends and we have 'just' friends; we have good friends and we have best friends."

a) In a small group, discuss the differences between the types of friends described in the statement.

b) Write a journal entry about your friends. Try to identify a friend for each of the four categories and explain why you think of him or her as such.

3. a) In a small group, list the qualities of a good friend as described in the article. Decide whether you agree with the author. Add any other qualities. Compare your list to other groups' to produce a class master list.

b) Write a short story in which you reveal your perception of what a good friend is through the characters and the plot.

REACHING OUT

1. a) Survey ten to fifteen peers to identify the most valuable or sought-after qualities in friends.

b) Conduct a similar survey of three adult age groups: those in their twenties, forties, and sixties.

c) Compile the results of each survey on a graph that compares the responses of all the groups.

d) Present your findings to the class. Have the class attempt to draw some conclusions about similarities or differences in the qualities that the groups valued in friends.

2. Your relationship with a friend is weakening or has ended. Write a letter to that person, identifying the reasons why the friendship faded, and then either try to rejuvenate it or say farewell. Mail the letter if you wish.

or

Write a letter to your best friend in which you explain why you value her or his friendship. Mail the letter if you wish.

3. As a group, write a report on the value people place on friends at their workplace. Base your report on a telephone or street survey of working people in which you explore the following questions:
a) To what extent do people socialize with their co-workers outside of work?
b) How many/what percent of people's friends were met through work?
c) To what extent do people need friends at their workplace? (Cite examples.)
d) To what extent do people rely on friends outside work to help them cope with work-related problems?

▶ How Money Problems Wreck Romance

Carol Colman

Disagreements about money can wreck any woman/ man relationship, from a dinner date to a marriage. More so today than ever before, now that many women bring home paycheques. That's why it's so important that all couples work out a basic money system that suits the pockets and personalities of both partners.

We all like to believe that love is enough to sustain a marriage, but unfortunately it's not true. Love is the most critical ingredient of a good relationship, but other factors are also important. Couples have to agree on the role each will perform in the relationship as well as on what their lifestyle will be like. A woman who expects to be supported will never be happy with a man who wants an equal financial partner, and vice versa.

Money fights caused by overspending or the inability to reach an agreement on a budget can be amicably resolved. It's not easy—it requires a great deal of honesty and soul-searching—but, ideally, the process can bring a couple closer together.

Every couple has to work out its own love and money balance. I know from first-hand experience that it can be a painful, difficult task. There are no short cuts. But I also know that working out the problems leads to stronger relationships—and, I believe, more romantic ones. Worrying and arguing over money the way many couples do does not promote further intimacy or help partners better understand each other.

But confronting these issues in a constructive caring manner will lead to more of both—love *and* money.

SINGLES

For most people singlehood is a temporary state; for a growing minority it is the preferred way of life. The way singles perceive marriage and the roles and lifestyles they envision for themselves in the future is reflected in how they view money, use money, withhold money, and spend money on their friends and loved ones.

Some women believe that in order for them to achieve full equality with men, they have to be willing to pay the price. That means giving up such privileges as having their doors opened for them and having their meals paid for. These women tend to be in high-paying professions in which they compete with male colleagues. For these women splitting the cheque means much more than merely paying their share of the meal—it's a declaration of independence.

As Joan Evans, a successful designer of video games, put it, "If I want to be treated as an equal, I have to behave like one."

Joan practises what she preaches. She and her boyfriend, Larry, an engineer, scrupulously split dating expenses. "When we go out to dinner, we take turns paying," Joan says, "and when we eat at home, I pay for the food at my place and he pays for the food at his."

Joan is the exception, not the rule. At least in the beginning stages of a relationship, the majority of women still allow—indeed, expect—men to foot the bill. What does this say about the relationships between men and women? Regardless of the sweeping social changes of the past decade, the rites of courtship linger on, with each sex assigned to its specific roles, rights, and responsibilities. In fact, these rituals are so ingrained that even couples who start out with egalitarian ideas about sex-determined roles often end up as traditionalists.

When Ann and Steve Elkins met 10 years ago during their first year at college, they happened to live in the same off-campus student-run residence called the Co-op. Ann remembers, "We were fanatically nonsexist and nonmaterialistic. Everybody contributed equally, and we even rotated job assignments." Men and women took turns shovelling snow in zero-degree weather, scrubbing out toilets, cooking dinner.

During their sophomore year, Ann and Steve started dating. "Nothing much changed, except Steve insisted on shovelling the snow for me, so I took over his kitchen assignments. And when we went out on a date, Steve always wanted to pay."

Ann rests her head upon her hand, revealing a diamond engagement ring, and reflects, "We started out with such bold ideas, but one by one we abandoned them. We became the kind of people we used to ridicule."

Despite the social upheavals of the past 20 years, when it comes to love and money, most men and women cling to the traditional path. Men are still the sexual aggressors, just as they are still the ones who foot the bill.

"I would never ask a man out," confesses Debbby Todd, a 26-year-old journalist who is as aggressive on the job as she is passive in a dating situation. "I would never make the first move or pick up the cheque. When you don't know someone well, you play by the rules."

From a man's point of view, "playing by the rules" means paying. Dr. Michael Perelman, clinical professor of psychiatry at Cornell Medical School in New York, says that women today are more likely to define their financial roles in the relationship than ever before. "People are aware of this as an issue and are more consciously making decisions about how to handle the cheques, how to handle money in a relationship. She's more likely to define what she wants her role to be by either offering to split the cheque, offering to pick up the next one or allowing him to pay and then deciding for herself what it means and if she wants to reciprocate."

Some women feel uncomfortable allowing a man to pay for them under any circumstances. They contend that by not sharing the financial burden of a relationship, they are being cast in a dependent role, which is not a part they care to play. If they're out with a man who feels awkward about splitting expenses, chances are the couple disagree on other sex-related issues and may not be compatible.

When a man foots the bill, what exactly is he paying for?

Andrew Wolken, a 30-year-old advertising copywriter, feels if a woman allows a man to take her out, there is, as he puts it, an "implied commitment . . . I know among my friends if they go out and spend a lot of money on a woman they could expect that it would amount to something somewhere down the line, although not

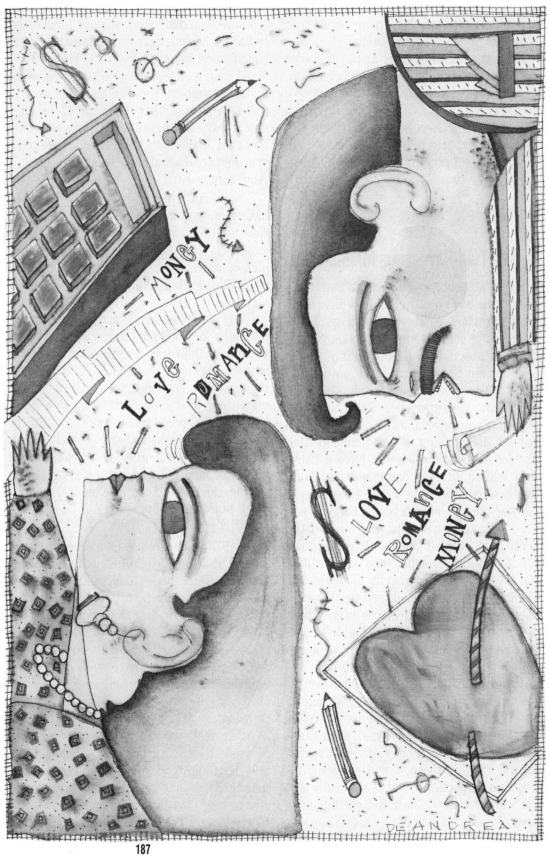

necessarily sexual. My suspicion is that women believe the same thing."

Do women feel obligated to the men who wine and dine them? Interestingly enough, most women vigorously deny that they owe anything to a man just because he has taken them out. As a 28-year-old New York secretary put it, "He may be paying the bill, but I'm giving him my most valuable commodity: my time."

THE TWO-PAYCHEQUE MARRIAGE

Some relationships can flourish under the "separate but equal" code in which partners maintain separate finances. However, many couples find that as their lives become intertwined, it's often impossible to maintain the "yours, mine, and ours" style of financial management.

Such was the experience of Joan and Alan Martin, a couple willing to share their lives but not their money. When Joan and Alan decided to get married and have a baby, they moved into an apartment they could barely afford, but just before their daughter was born, Alan received a hefty raise.[1]
. . . Since Alan was paying most of the rent, Joan decided she should pick up the tab for the housekeeper who babysat during the day when she went to work. But she found, after she had paid her share of the bills and the housekeeper's wages, there was nothing left for her. "I didn't have enough money left at the end of the month to buy a new bra when I needed one."

Joan couldn't live with their current financial situation, but she felt uncomfortable about asking Alan to revise it. "After all, I was the one who was so adamant about keeping our money apart; now that he was making more, I was suddenly interested in pooling." But what really disturbed her was the fact that she liked the idea of being supported.

Joan's dwindling bank account forced her to have a serious talk with Alan about her psychic and financial conflicts. To her surprise, he not only understood what she was going through but could relate to her desire to be supported. "I told her one of the biggest disappointments of my life was the fact that Joan didn't have a rich uncle who was going to die and leave us all his money," Alan confesses.

Since Joan felt it was very important to have money of her own, they decided that she and Alan would no longer evenly divide expenses. Rather, Joan would contribute half of each paycheque to their joint account, depositing the rest in her separate account.

Many career women admit that they have difficulty reconciling their love for their work with their love for their families. But women who don't view their jobs as careers express just the opposite feelings. They view their jobs as secondary to their husbands' and are content to take time off to raise their children. Today, however, many are shocked to learn that the "traditional" notion of family is becoming a luxury few people can afford. Many women have to work outside the home even if they don't want to.

In 1975, Len Johnson, a research scientist, married Michelle, a high-school teacher. Combined, their two modest incomes provided them with an enviable lifestyle. Five years after they were married, Michelle and Len decided it was time to start a family and agreed to buy a house for $75,000. "It seemed expensive," Len explains. "But we borrowed money and used the rest of our savings for the down-payment."

After their daughter, Chris, was born, Michelle took maternity leave from school and thoroughly enjoyed being a homemaker. Once she was back in the classroom, her thoughts would drift back to Chrissy, and like clockwork every weekend, she would slip into a depression. "I was so frustrated about having to work that I couldn't enjoy the time I had with the baby. It certainly put a damper on the time Len and I spent together. We'd get invited to visit some friends and I'd say we have to stay home with Chrissy, even though I knew she'd be sleeping by then. If Len made any romantic overtures, I'd always think of something pressing that had to be done that I didn't have time to do because I worked during the week."

One Saturday afternoon, Len angrily asked, "Why are you punishing me?"

Michelle confessed she had never realized how difficult it would be for her to leave their baby to go to work. "I feel like I'm being torn in two," she told Len. "I can't help feeling you've let me down."

Len replied, "*You've* let me down. I explained the facts to you before we bought this house. You have to take the same responsibility that I do for supporting the family. If you want to quit work, fine, go ahead and quit, but we'll have to move back into an apartment."

Michelle ran out of the room in tears. But by evening she apologized.

"I've accepted the fact that I have to work; it's made me feel a little easier about it. I'm not saying I don't feel a pang or two when I leave Chrissy, but I think because I work, Len is more involved in caring for Chrissy than he would be if I stayed home. I think we made the right decision."

▼

TRADITIONAL MARRIAGES

Despite the women's movement, there are countless wives today who have no idea how much their husbands earn.

Debby Harris, a 45-year-old homemaker, feels she would enjoy her marriage a great deal more if she didn't feel so dependent on her husband. "I feel trapped," Debby confesses with a strained smile. "Let's face it, I am."

Debby and Larry, a successful psychiatrist, live in a townhouse in a fashionable suburb with their two teen-age daughters. Everyone assumes that Larry and Debby lead an idyllic prosperous life, but Debby is constantly worried about money. Every time she uses a credit card, she frets over whether the salesclerk will tell her she's exceeded her credit line. Whenever she goes to the bank to write a cheque she hopes the teller will cash it.

According to Debby, her problem is that she's married to a man who can't say no— to himself or anyone else. "Whenever the kids want something, Larry buys it for them. Whenever we go out for dinner with friends, Larry picks up the tab.

"We have very different attitudes about money; in fact, it's the only thing we disagree on," Debby says emphatically. "Larry says I'm cheap, and I say he's a spendthrift."

The government would side with Debby. Last year the Internal Revenue Service impounded the Harris' bank account because Larry had failed to pay his full share of income tax for the past three years.

"We got into that mess because Larry could never tell me or the kids that we had to cut back," Debby recalls angrily. "It injures his image of himself if he can't give us everything we want."

Has Debby ever thought about getting a job? "I wasn't raised to have a career," Debby explains. "I was sent to college so I could be some man's well-educated wife. I can't earn enough to support myself."

At the other end of the scale from Debby is the wife who has always worked but who gives up her paycheque to be a full-time wife and mother.

Some women report experiencing a kind of identity crisis when they stop receiving a paycheque. One of them is Ilene Stevens, a 30-year-old attorney, who was pregnant when she quit her job and moved to another city so her husband, also an attorney, could accept a better position.

The only thing Ilene didn't want was an allowance. "Bob wouldn't have called it that, but I didn't want anybody putting money in my chequing account," she says emphatically. "I find the whole idea of being a dependent little girl insulting."

So Ilene and Bob decided to open one chequing account in both their names with the understanding that they would both have equal access. "It's not Bob's money, it's our money," Ilene says firmly.

Ilene knew it was time for her to go back to work when she started waking up in the morning not knowing what day of the week it was. Within two weeks Ilene had hired a babysitter and was working full time as a consultant for a large corporation.

She busily pursued her career for the next six months, and then, much to her surprise, began to find it harder and harder to leave the baby in the morning. After much soul-searching, she quit her job to be a full-time mother. "I feel I made the right choice. I think it does make a difference to the baby having me around."

Ilene now assumes more responsibility for running the household. And even though she's not bringing home a paycheque, she doesn't feel she's lost any clout in her relationship. In fact, she notes that Bob is acutely aware that she has made a sacrifice so that their baby can have the best possible childhood and Bob can have the time to pursue his career.

[1]Ellipses in the selection indicate that a portion of the original article has been deleted and rewritten by the authors of this text.

R E A D I N G   A N D   R E A C T I N G

1. a) In a small group, read the article carefully and identify the problems faced by couples who have different opinions on money management.

   b) Discuss the suggestions offered by the author for resolving money disputes; evaluate each solution for its effectiveness. Brainstorm other solutions for money disputes between couples.

   c) On a chart, list in one column the main problems couples face over money, and in the other column list the best solutions for each problem.

2. a) This article describes different types of relationships between couples. As a class, examine each type of relationship and weigh the pros and cons of each.

   b) In your journal, describe the type of special relationship you would like to have in the future. Give reasons for your decision.

3. With a partner, script a series of conversations between one of the couples described in the article. Your script should reveal their conflicts over managing money and how these conficts are resolved. Dramatize the scenes for the class.

REACHING OUT

1. Imagine that you are a financial counsellor and write a report on one of the couples mentioned in the article. Your report should describe the couple and their problems and then go on to describe how you helped them resolve these money-related conflicts. Exchange your report with someone who wrote about the same couple and compare the advice given.

2. Carol Colman states that working out money problems leads to stronger, more romantic relationships. Interview several couples and ask them if they agree. If possible, tape your interviews and play the tape for your group.

3. Colman states that women who want to be treated as equal partners economically tend to be in high-paying professions. As a class, consider whether this is a valid claim and why.

4. Imagine that you are about to embark on a long-term relationship. Make notes on how you and your partner will handle your finances. Compare your financial plans with a partner's and evaluate each plan together.

5. You have been happily married for years. Write a letter to your soon-to-be-married son or daughter in which you reveal how you and your partner manage family finances with minimal disputes.

► CHARITY

Mike Barnes

After a night of
vicious argument, in which I
struck a closet door with my
fist, splitting it in half,
and we said things
more violent and exact than that,
it was finally 7 a.m.
and time for her to go
to work. She showered,
dressed, and left.

I spent the day
in a fog of exhaustion,
standing beside windows.

Now it is 6 p.m.
and the dinner I so carefully
prepared: tuna fish and rice
and green beans vinaigrette,
will soon be cold. I look
out the bedroom window;
she is in the schoolyard,
feeding the squirrels.

She wanders, dressed in purple
and white, among the green
weeping branches, pausing
to crouch by a willow trunk.
Her movements seem stately
among the hopping squirrels.
One little black fellow,
especially, is being coaxed
to take a peanut—

I envy him her patient,
outstretched hand.

READING AND REACTING

1. Paraphrase the poem in two carefully chosen sentences which you feel capture its essence.

2. In a small group, decide on another title for the poem which best sums up what it is about.

REACHING OUT

1. a) Write a sequel to the poem in which you show how the conflict is resolved.

   b) Role-play the scene in which the two characters meet again.

2. Write an interior monologue from the perspective of the woman as she sees the other person watching her.

3. "Conflict and arguments in a relationship can be healthy." In a one-page essay, either support or refute the statement.

▶ KEY TURNS, HOUSE IS EMPTY

Ellen Roseman

Mom isn't home at 3 o'clock any more. When her kids return home from school, she's at the office.

"Latchkey children," some of whom literally go to class with a house key around their neck, have been around ever since women entered the workforce. Now, with the increase in single-parent households and the decline of the extended family, the number of children in self-care is rapidly rising.

In 1981, Statistics Canada estimated there were about 672,000 youngsters caring for themselves after school or being looked after by a school-age sister or brother. The actual number is probably far greater than surveys indicate because, out of guilt and safety concerns, many parents are reluctant to admit they aren't home until 6 p.m. or later.

For some youngsters, self-care is a positive experience, encouraging independence, responsibility, street savvy, and pride. Alone, they learn survival skills which they can put to good use in later life.

But others find the lack of parental supervision frightening and stressful. Lonely and hypersensitive to household noises, they spend hours propped in front of a television set and what they see on TV often heightens their fears.

"There are casualties as well as apparent successes," say Lynette and Thomas Long, two educators in Washington, D.C., who interviewed 75 former latchkey children, now adults.

One in five thought the isolation had a lasting negative effect, the Longs report in their *Handbook for Latchkey Children and Their Parents*.

"Many still have residual fears about staying alone," they write. "Others feel their isolation inhibited the development of their interpersonal skills; some still harbour a deep resentment against parents or siblings."

"I'd say the latchkey experience is negative for one out of every three kids," Lynette Long speculates in an interview from her home in Bethesda, Maryland.

"We'd never give out a medication that helped only two-thirds of children and harmed the other third, yet we continue to allow youngsters to stay home alone."

Elizabeth Ferguson and Mona Stephens run a support program for latchkey children in Metro Toronto; their all-day telephone service receives about 80 calls a day.

"One girl in particular sticks in my mind," says Ms Ferguson after 18 months of experience in this type of counselling. "She's 10 years old and lives up north in the city, while her parents work downtown at Queen's Park.

"She calls every Friday night because her parents don't get home until 8 p.m. They're probably out having a drink after a hard week's work, but this girl is scared and lonely.

"She never tells her parents about her fears. She doesn't want to worry them. They come home and say, 'How was your day?' and she says, 'Fine.' "

This need to protect parents is typical of

6- to 12-year-olds on their own, according to Ms Ferguson. Aware that a family's financial well-being may depend on a second income, they try to minimize the strains of self-care. Once children reach adolescence, the repressed feelings often erupt.

Kids Line, a similar telephone service in Hamilton, Ontario, receives 10 calls a day, some from children as young as five.

"We've had a lot of criticism from the school boards," says Therese Speagle, co-ordinator of the project. "They say we're encouraging parents to leave their kids. But the kids were there before we were."

By calling the hotlines, children can find help with homework, listen to stories, play trivia games, and plug into novel activities to distract them from their fears and boredom.

Kids Connection, Ms Ferguson's service, offers youngsters more than 100 diversion suggestions: pick a new name for the Cabbage Patch doll, write down 10 things they like about their best friend, devise a 20-minute exercise workout, hard-boil some eggs ("if you are allowed to") and paint them to look like your favourite singer or actor.

Parents who leave early for work face the dilemma of whether to wake up their children or let them sleep. Those roused at 6:30 a.m. often arrive at school tired if they've been watching cartoons for two hours; those whose parents reset the alarm are likely to arrive late or not at all.

One parental solution is to drop the children off early at the schoolyard, which poses a problem for the staff. "Teachers are not supposed to allow children into the classroom until 15 minutes before classes start," points out Lorna Reid, a program co-ordinator for the Toronto Board of Education. Children left outside on cold winter mornings are liable to bang on doors and windows to be let in, and fights and arguments are frequent.

While many schools provide day-care programs for children aged 6 to 9, there is a cutoff when they reach 10. "They're ready to graduate the kids, but the kids aren't ready to graduate from them," says Ms Reid.

Provincial day-care subsidies also end when a child reaches 10.

"We've urged the government to fund kids 10 to 12 years old. So far there's been no response," says John Pepin, executive director of Family Day Care Services. His agency takes up some of the slack by subsidizing certain after-school programs, but "the numbers we touch are a drop in the ocean," and without subsidies, many working parents can't afford to enrol their children. In Toronto, for example, the cost of school-age day-care ranges from $35 to $48 a week.

Latchkey children often aren't allowed to invite friends to their home or to go outside to play, so watching television tends to be the favourite activity. After-school programs help break the bonds of isolation, yet even then, some children would still opt to stay home.

"There's a whole generation of kids who are burned out on day-care," says Elizabeth Ferguson. "Kids call here all the time and say, 'I'm sick of day-care. It's for babies.' They're always in a group, programmed all the time. At a certain point, they want to be home."

How can parents make self-care a positive experience? First, suggest Lynette and Tom Long, never allow children under 10 to stay home alone or in the care of siblings.

Second, don't leave children home alone for more than 2 hours a day, and maintain telephone contact with them. "Our findings indicate that one-third of all latchkey children can't reach their parents by phone," Ms Long says. Many jobs—from grocery store clerk to doctor—just don't allow for frequent telephone contact.

Third, prepare each child, not just the

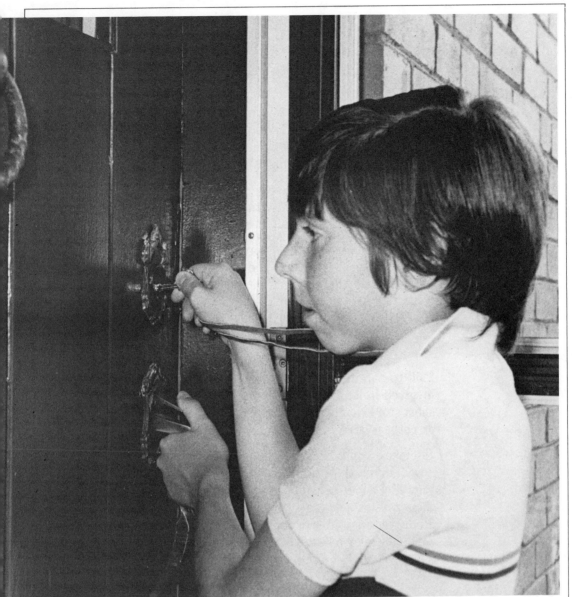

older ones. They must be taught how to handle household emergencies, use the telephone, and stay safe around the home. "Many people think that if you teach children survival skills, you'll heighten their fear," she notes. "We feel exactly the opposite way. Children are scared already. This helps them cope."

Fourth, try to find a safe part of the neighbourhood where children can go to play outside.

Fifth, don't impose too many chores. Although a few tasks help fill after-school hours, children handed too much responsibility can feel overwhelmed.

Sixth, get a pet—preferably a dog. Dogs act as burglar alarms and provide companionship.

Finally, listen to what children say. In interviews with former latchkey children, the Longs found that those who profited from the experience tended to have close relationships with their parents. "The more isolated children feel, the worse it is for them," they concluded. "Communication plays a vital role."

READING AND REACTING

1. In this article, Ellen Roseman examines some of the problems that develop when jobs keep parents away from their children. In a small group, make a point-form summary of the advantages and disadvantages of being a latchkey kid.

2. Roseman describes some services that have been created to meet the needs of latchkey kids. In a group, evaluate these services and consider how they might be improved.

3. Summarize the suggestions provided by the Longs to help children and parents adjust to the latchkey situation. Create a flyer featuring the points and offer it to elementary schools for children to share with their parents.

REACHING OUT

1. Talk to parents and/or children in your neighbourhood who are involved in latchkey situations. Write an account, a poem, or a short story that explores the feelings of the children, the parents, or both, relating to this situation.

2. Interview some latchkey children in your community. Find out how they fill their time as they wait for parents to return, how they feel about returning to an empty home, and what bothers them most about the situation. Based on the information gathered, write an interior monologue of an eight-year-old latchkey child as she or he spends an afternoon alone.

3. With a partner, script a scene between a parent and a child in which the parent explains to the child that he or she is about to become a latchkey child because of the parent's new job. In the scene, the parent sets the child's mind at ease and lays down some firm rules about what the child has to do when he or she returns from school. Role-play the scene for the class.

4. In a group, brainstorm solutions to the problems of the latchkey child. Distinguish the solutions that are easily achieved from those that are more difficult to implement.

5. Plan your own service to meet the needs of the latchkey child. List all of the steps you will have to follow in order to establish this business and include a description of staff, equipment, and location.

▶ THE RINK

Cyril Dabydeen

GEORGE SITS THERE, THINKING OF SKATING DOWN THE rink with the ease of Guy LaFleur; he, a black, black man doing this thing with ease. But the more he thinks about it, the more it begins to boggle his mind. He's thinking too that he, an islander who has come to this country to establish roots, must really learn to skate; this same skating that looks so easy because he'd stand by the boards right there and watch people, especially the young ones, floating down the ice in the hockey rink as if they had skates on their feet from the day they were born. Such an amazing thing it was. More than once he felt really ashamed of himself not being able to skate. How could a grown man living in Canada have difficulty doing such a simple thing? George is determined more than ever now. He imagines going down the ice once more, doing twists and turns.

But it seems more difficult to do than he imagines, for right then as he makes another attempt to get up from the ice, nervousness overtakes him, making him more uncomfortable in the skates by the minute the longer he has them on. At once too his heels begin to ache, burning at the ankles as well. Yet with determination he struggles to get up while he still imagines going down the ice. He steps out a few feet now; away from the boards; he sees himself going closer to the other end of the rink. This skating thing is one helluva thing to do, he says to himself, gritting his teeth.

He's really taking his time now, trying his damndest not to fall again. He remembers falling down twice yesterday, once hitting his head heavily and nearly being knocked out. This time it won't happen again; he's taking greater care, is yet more determined than ever. At the same time he's thinking, too, of Boysie coming to visit him at two o'clock in the morning; Boysie should be ashamed of himself, knocking at his door at that ungodly hour, thinking he's still back on the island. Sure, lots of other islanders often do the same, behaving without responsibility: as if they have no civilization with them. George moans a little, even as he steps out farther, becoming more confident now. Indeed, skating is an easy thing after all. He's about to smile.

How could a grown man living in Canada have difficulty doing such a simple thing?

. . . as if his feet are cast in iron . . .

But he looks ahead then too, at the few kids by the sideboards who're looking at him, studying his every move. And for a moment he imagines being one of them, being born and bred right here in Canada, in this cold, cold place. Would the cold really bother him as much as it does now if he were born right here? George doesn't really know. He takes another tentative step forward now, even as he turns and looks sideways at the kids and forces a smile, sort of. Another deliberate step, even though still tentative. George begins to feel the skates really heavy on his legs now, as if his feet are cast in iron, making him really uncomfortable. Again he looks up, mechanically sort of, this time to see the kids smiling; maybe they're really encouraging him. But his ankles are really burning now.

Yet another move forward, even as he's fully aware of the kids watching and smiling at him with increased interest. For a second, the skates feel different, almost like something fanciful in a dream, just as he'd once imagined before. Yet another step forward.

As if encouraged, the kids come closer to the boards, almost in his line of vision; these same apple-cheeked, fluffy-headed-and-handsome kids, all smiling and making him really self-conscious now. Suddenly George dares not move. He's even afraid to look up now. Something is about to happen, something he fears. It's as if his legs are moving apart of their own accord, diagonally sort of. George's heart beats faster. One of the kids bursts out laughing, nearly upsetting him fully this time. A flood of embarrassment rushes through him, like a sudden wave. George is now only five feet from the opposite end; and he's trying his damndest to make it, which he knows he must do now. He stretches out both hands, ready to hold on to anything, to something, for support. And he looks at the kids, their eyes gleaming almost, these same kids who're smiling fully; even as he tries to smile himself as a way of hiding shame. Ah, no one's going to stop him now. He'll make it. Not even Ida, his wife, will stop him; the same Ida who's been laughing at him, telling him that he—an islander—will never be able to skate since he wasn't born with ice in his veins. George asked her, "What d'you mean by that, woman?" He was angry. But Ida laughed, loudly, her typical island laughter which had echoed all around her. She added, "George, you're different, man. We are different. We've come from a hot, hot climate. We weren't born with ice in our veins as I've done told you before!" George had replied almost immediately, with anger burning in him. "But we . . . I—I want to be a—" He stopped and looked at her accusingly, questioningly. He blurted out now, "That's why I came here!" He was incoherent, he knew. Ida had a way of making him very incensed. Now he knew she wasn't even listening to him. Maybe Ida was satisfied with the way things were, still wanting to remain an

201

islander in Canada without ever changing.

The kids laugh again, now leaning forward over the boards almost, as they are really very close to him and are watching a strange show in which he—George—is on centre stage. A few seconds pass by, while George, as if by a miracle, recovers his grip. Holding onto the boards once again, he remains standing there, a little proud, thinking: he doesn't want to be like other black immigrants in Canada. He wants to integrate, fully; and he believes that before long he'll be skating like the best of the native born-and-bred Canadians. At once, he stretches out a leg again, willing himself to go out, thinking still—what's the point of living in a new country if you have no intention of conforming with its ways even though they are foreign ways? He wishes Ida would understand that sometimes. Just then he falls—*bradacks!*

At once George scurries and wriggles on the ice, spinning like a top next, eager as he is to get up, and hoping that none of the kids sees him. But the kids are already laughing, uncontrollably. George twists and scrapes, gets up and goes down once more, then up again, and once more on the ground. The kids' shrill laughter rings in the air. It's as if Ida and Boysie are also laughing with them now. The whole damn Caribbean island laughing with them too! George is not sure what to do now. In sheer frustration, he sits on the ice, casually sort of; and he looks back at them, smiling; grinning too from ear to ear to hide his increasing discomfort.

More kids appear now, laughing, some pointing to him for the benefit of the others who are still coming into the arena. George, really play-acting now, continues his grin, even though deep down he wishes he wasn't in this predicament. Now he senses the kids are watching him as if he's some sort of a performer indeed; he, acting solely for their benefit. Now they're rattling the sideboards in their excitement. George reddens. The kids come closer, some leaning over the sideboards, looking down at him. One says, "Get up, Mister." Another adds in a voice of encouragement, "Start again."

But George merely sits on the ice, as if that's all he can do now. Yet he keeps smiling his smile of embarrassment. He wishes now he never put on the blasted skates; and he grits his teeth in silent anger beneath his smiles, even as he simultaneously feels the cold seeping up under his pants. And he looks directly at these same apple-cheeked faces in agony. At once he realizes that the kids are really giving him their sympathy and encouragement, all in one: in a way too, telling him that it's no shameful thing for a man who's learning to skate to be sitting flat on the ice the way he's doing now. Once more George tries getting up; but he's having difficulty. And still with their uncontrollable laughter, the kids cluster around him, again offering encouragement. But George

. . . a strange show in which he—George—is on centre stage.

202

feels more of the cold seeping up; and at once he begins thinking that this place isn't a cricket field he's sitting on, but sheer ice! Yet he remains there, immobile: as in a sort of daze . . . even as he thinks of Boysie laughing again at him (just as Ida did); Boysie laughing the same old laugh, telling him loud and clear, "What a damn fool you are, man. You's learnin' to skate! You know full well that this ain't your kinda sport. Why you doan play cricket instead, man? Why not, eh?" Boysie's laugh echoes all around him, whirring in every cell of his brain. Another moment George imagines Ida laughing, too—she and Boysie laughing together, having fun at his expense.

"You know full well that this ain't your kinda sport."

Willing himself, George turns his attention to the kids once more—even as he sits there and looks at their winter clothes: at their gloves and red-and-blue toques. No doubt they're wondering why he doesn't get up now like any other easily would. He surveys their innocent-as-babes faces, wondering if they've ever seen a black man such as he, fully grown and learning to skate, now flat on the ice. What a ridiculous picture he must make.

Immediately he wants to shout out to them, telling them to leave him alone. Instead, he merely continues sitting there, in a way knowing that if he tries once more, he'll quickly fall again. But George also knows that he can't sit there forever. On an impulse he tries getting up; but he's unable to budge now.

What's the matter? Boysie's image again, saying now: "Man, this ain't a cricket field. This ain't like standing up straight-straight and hitting the ball on *de off side* across the green like Garfield Sobers or Clive Lloyd an' watching it shooting down to the boundary for four!"

At once George wants to tell the kids that; to tell that he, sitting-down George, used to be one of the best batsmen on the island, and of how the crowd used to cheer him loudly like thunder ringing through your ears. Oh, the sweet-sweet applause. Smiling, George reminisces happily. Right then one of the kids comes up and tries to pull him up. Then another comes, assisting. In no time three others, all around him, urging him to get up. And George, realizing he needs their help, heaves, thankful now for their assistance. In a final struggle, with skates and all, he pulls himself up. Aah! He feels the bump at the back of his head, which he remembers is the result of his falling down heavily the week he'd begun to learn to skate. He thanks the kids for their help, even though he simultaneously swears under his breath. Once more the kids laugh, a little louder this time, with satisfaction and amusement—as they look at him standing with legs splayed out, once again like a pregnant woman's.

George decides he's had enough for one day. But he will come again tomorrow, intent on becoming a skater, no matter what. Despite the taunts of Boysie. Or Ida. Or the kids. George is still swearing under his breath because of the realization of his ineptitude; swearing more than he used to as a grown-up man dreaming of coming to Canada and waiting four long years for his immigration papers to be processed. Briefly he thinks of his mother he's left behind: to whom he used to regularly send letters with a ten-dollar bill in the envelope each time and imagining the excitement on his mother's face when she opened the envelope with the bill falling out and landing on the ground like manna from heaven; but he'd stopped sending money upon realizing that his mother wasn't really receiving any (some *orangutan* postman in the district was stealing his hard-earned cash!) He remembers, too, only three months after he'd married Ida how he'd stopped writing letters to his mother, all because he'd discovered her snooping around in his pockets to read the letters before the envelope was sealed, in a way trying to censor everything he wrote. Was it because she didn't want him to have anything to do with the island again?

. . . waiting four long years for his immigration papers to be processed.

After much contemplating, George had decided to chart his own course, Ida or not. He'd decided to be a real Canadian, thinking that when he returned to the island, on vacation, he'd be flashing hundred-dollar bills before his mother's watery eyes and be telling her in his best-acquired Canadian accent that he isn't the same short-pants, barefooted fella who used to walk about the streets with a piece of raw sugar-cane sticking out of his mouth as if he was born like that, like someone having really evolved from sugar-cane as some of the native Indians believed. No siree! There'll be a real gleam in his mother's eyes, as he'll be telling her all the progress he has made. Yes, he—black as he is—will do just that. And smiling, George figures he'll be wearing collar and tie from morning to night since he'll no longer be working with his hands but with his God-given brains as man is meant to work in the first place.

Ida greets him at the door. "Well, George, you're back early today." George looks at the beautiful woman standing before him, his own wife, who's been trying to put him off his plan of action. He's about to smile, and to tell her to wait and see, that before long he'll skate as the best of the same people she's so fond of watching on TV. Instead, George looks at the skates in his hand dangling like a bunch of steel lobsters he has caught by the sea; and he remembers sitting down on the ice with his bottom freezing, with the kids laughing all around him. How can he forget that. Ignoring Ida, George walks straight past her to the storeroom to put the skates away.

Ida follows behind. George, sensing her presence, is suddenly angry, because he knows that she's about to mock and tease him now. Maybe she has become crochety since she became pregnant. As he bends down to put the skates away, he looks longingly at

them one more time (as if he's been used to wearing these same things all his life like cricket pads). But Ida's closeness, in a way, still irks. And once more the skates begin to appear now like a pair of ridiculous boots which only a strange breed of people wear; people who want to punish themselves for nothing at all. But this feeling is temporary, for just then George hears applause coming to his ears, just as before, the difference now being that he imagines he's in the NHL. And it's almost the same sound as when he's hitting the cricket ball a mighty blast in the field and watching it race down to the boundary for four. More applause splitting his ears, happily. He looks up at Ida and grins. But Ida, her lips pursed, says:

"Is it true, George? I mean, are you really skating now?" "Yes, woman!" he wants to shout to her. Instead, he only mutters, not loudly enough, and self-consciously too, the sound coming out his lips like a grunt; and he's not sure of what he's really saying now. But Ida begins to lambast him:

"But, George, you can't blasted well be able to skate! You, a black-black man doing a white thing. It isn't the sport fo' you, man!"

George angrily faces her. Yet he knows he must keep his cool because only uncivilized people lose their temper, who shout and swear like mad people even. And he's saying to her with his cold-cold civilized eyes, *Leave me alone woman. Leave me alone to do my thing in my own blasted way! Leave me, Ida, I done tell yuh!* But Ida begins to laugh in his face, telling him again that he'll never be good enough, no matter what. George is no longer able to stand the irony in her voice. She's saying this thing loudly now. "You's one helluva black man who's gonna be different in this country! You hear me, George?" And, looking at her, George sees real pain in her eyes. For a while, as if not knowing what to do, how else to react, he smiles, an odd sort of smile, because he knows full well too that there's nothing else a man can do against the onslaught of a woman's tongue, a woman born-an'-bred on the island. He looks a little sheepishly at her, studying her serious face, like some sort of pity and terror written all over it now, confusing him; for he's never seen his woman looking like this before: yes, the same beautiful woman he's married to—now looking serious, and ugly too.

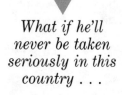

What if he'll never be taken seriously in this country . . .

Throughout supper George wonders if Ida is right. What if he'll never be taken seriously in this country, no matter how hard he tries; no matter if he goes on taking evening courses all his life as he struggles to better himself, eager as he is to match up with the best people, those same ones he and Ida often meet in the offices and stores and everywhere else, who look professional and who in one way or another sometimes make him feel inferior. And George tries to focus his mind on the rink again, as if this is the real solution, trying to imagine once more skating down with ease and joyful rhythm from one end to another. Slowly he puts food into his mouth, without speaking. Ida too isn't speaking.

In bed that night, Ida turns and twists. George is also awake, thinking. Ida asks in the unbearable silence, "What's going through your mind, George?" "Nothing," he lies. She turns again, once more to her side, still unable to sleep, this same soon-to-be heavy-bodied woman bearing his child. A three-month thing already, George is thinking, turning around right then and patting her stomach a little, then putting an arm out to caress her: to feel the living thing planted there at the same time, like some sort of miracle. Then he remembers Boysie's face: Boysie laughing and saying, "Man, George, your first-born's gonna be a genius, gonna be my God-child too. Ha-ha." George had laughed then as well, because he'd been drinking rum and coke. That was only a month ago. But now, at once almost, George makes up his mind that no *island-orangutan* is going to be the God-father of his child. He wants someone responsible, a native-born-and-bred Canadian.

Ida still twists and turns. She asks, "Are you thinking about our child, George?"

George doesn't answer right away. He only becomes more aware of her burgeoning roundness, the smoothness of her flesh under her pink nightgown, the same nightgown he'd bought for her on her last birthday. He rests a hand against her wide-awake heart (so he tells himself) which is now beating rapidly, so rapidly that he can almost hear it. And George thinks right then of a daughter being born, a child with a stout heart, this same child who'll make him (and Ida too) very proud. Ah, he imagines taking her to learn how to skate. This child's bound to learn easily because it'll be something she'll be doing every day at the rink among a number of other kids like her. Yes, there'll be no stopping her. He smiles. But the smile quickly fades because he remembers falling down earlier that day, and the kids all around him, laughing.

"Get up! Get up!" they encourage, one pulling his arm.

"Go on, sir, get up. You can make it!"

George feels more embarrassed than ever because he knows that the longer he's on the ground the more embarrassing it'll be for him; the more too he'll invite others to come an' watch him making a fool of himself.

"Get up, it's easy to do!" George hears the voice of his own child now: a black child, talking to him, urging him to get up, repeatedly. George isn't sure what's happening, as he sits there, almost bewildered. Right then he looks around and sees a large crowd of people (mostly adults), all looking at him—at him alone—who're now ready to applaud him. George pulls himself upright with the assistance of this same black child, and stands with pride. Turning, he looks at the crowd and bows. Then he looks in the middle of the rink, and there he sees this same child, his daughter, with her skates on, all alone—doing this miraculous thing as if she was born with skates on, pirouetting around to the further applause of everyone. By the boards, George applauds too, marvelling at this child he and Ida brought into the world, who's skating with such grace and ease. He's really pleased now, smiling and applauding . . . thinking . . . again, and again, and laughing too.

"George, you okay?" he hears Ida's voice.

But he's still chuckling inside, not wanting to stop this feeling inside him, welling up like a tide, making him not sure if he's still dreaming or is fully awake.

"You sure you're okay, George?" Ida turns once more, to his side. "Remember, Boysie's coming to see us again, soon. Maybe you should take him with you to learn to skate. The two o' you." Ida smiles, as he senses, still in her half-asleep state. She continues to mutter, "This skating, George, maybe you're very determined, are you not?" It's as if she's now waiting for an answer,

Turning, he looks at the crowd and bows.

turning and looking at him, now wide awake. George is thinking, and grinning too, at the same time. He's saying close to her ears, "Yes, Ida, I'm going to take Boysie to learn how to skate. It's something he's bound to know how to do. After all, this child, our newborn in a few months' time, this child right inside you now, she's gonna skate better than both of us. Ha-ha." George is unable to suppress the gladness now overtaking him, while Ida presses closer to him and looks fully at him in the dark with her eyes brimful with tears of her own sweet joy.

READING AND REACTING

1. Role-play a scene between George, Ida, and Boysie, in which George explains to the other two why it is so important that he learn to skate.

2. a) In a small group, compare and evaluate George's approach to living in Canada with that of Ida and Boysie.

   b) Discuss George's attitude toward his own culture.

3. As George's self-image shifts, so does his perception of the people around him. With a partner, trace these shifts and discuss the effect created by the author in making this link.

REACHING OUT

1. Write a short story, based on a real or imagined event, in which the pressure of a group caused you to do something that made you feel extremely uncomfortable.

2. Talk to someone you know who is a new Canadian. Find out about his or her hopes and fears on arrival, the first impressions, and the obstacles that had to be overcome. Write an interior monologue from the perspective of that person soon after arrival.

   or

   In the voice of a new Canadian, write a letter to your relatives in your homeland. Describe your new home and environment. Express your feelings about being a new immigrant.

3. Choose a symbol that you feel is most representative of Canadian culture. Write a poem or an essay in which you show why you selected that symbol.

▶ HORSE

Douglas Glover

"Samson threw me again,"

THE DRIFTS WERE THIGH-DEEP AND CRUSTY WHERE THE row of sugar maples trapped the northwesterlies and sucked the snow into the sunken laneway. The little boy stumbled slowly and painfully towards the barnyard and the red barn with its steaming manure pile and the stone farmhouse beyond. In the barnyard stood a small barrel-shaped sorrel horse, saddled, with the reins knotted over its withers. The boy stopped occasionally to rest and pull down the sleeves of his hooded overcoat that rucked up every time he fell and exposed his bright pink wrists.

The laneway ran from the barnyard to the woodlot at the back of the farm about half a mile away. On either side snowy fields rolled off towards split-cedar rail fences at the edges of the property. The fields were bordered by young spruce hedgerows at right angles to the lane. Through the barnyard gate, the lane wound between the barn and the outbuildings with green shingle roofs, rutted and chopped by hoofprints and stained with urine, up to the green clapboard woodshed at the back of the house.

The boy walked through the open gate and quickly crossed the barnyard without looking at the horse. He lifted the wire latch on the woodshed door and knocked it open with his shoulder. Hardly bothering to stamp off the snow that had balled at the top of his boots and the edges of his clothing, he went into the house.

Jeremy stood in the big farm kitchen feeling the cosy warmth filter through his several layers of winter clothing. His father was brewing coffee at the stove. A book lay open on the table. He smelled the sharp brown odour of the grounds and listened to the warm comforting roar of the electric kettle.

"Samson threw me again," he mumbled. Tears started in his eyes. "I'm scared."

"Not again?" His father stayed by the stove.

"He threw me twice. Once in the woods and once by the last windbreak."

"Are you all right? Where did you land?" Jeremy's father had caught the keen note of the boy's voice and turned to look at him closely.

"Well, get your things off and have a hot bath. That'll make you feel better," he said quietly. "Don't bother your mother about it. She's not feeling well again."

"I . . . I can't." His voice rose and fell unnaturally from the crying and he had to stop to sniffle. "He's still out there. I have to put him in the barn."

"What the . . . ? Is he tied up?" asked his father.

"He's in the barnyard. I couldn't catch him."

"Judas Priest. You mean you just let him go?"

"No, sir. I couldn't catch him."

"This is crazy. You shouldn't have had a horse. I'll have to go and get him before he gets off the farm. Haven't I told you always to get right back on?"

"Yes, sir."

"Well, you shouldn't have had a horse then."

Jeremy wasn't sure what he was scared of. He was confused. He had been afraid of the horse. He was frightened and frustrated by its immense indifference to him. He was afraid of the long fall over Samson's withers and the indifferent, dangerous hooves that fell near him. And he was afraid of the cold and the pain when he landed in the snow. Now he was afraid of his father too.

He closed his eyes so he couldn't see his father's face. He saw himself again by the spruce trees. The horse began to sidle off the trail. Its hindquarters began to rise and fall under him. Samson twisted to the right and Jeremy felt himself start to fall. It was like a slow motion movie. He hit the ground hard with his chest and couldn't breathe. Samson trotted a few yards away and waited.

It was too much, Jeremy thought. Too much. It happened all the time now. Every time he went riding. Samson somehow knew his little legs weren't strong enough to hold on. It was too much. And when he stood up finally, he felt paralyzed. He couldn't make his legs move towards the horse. He threw snowballs at it and it trotted towards the barn. But how could he make his father understand?

"I couldn't catch him. He just ran home. I'm sorry."

"That does it," said his father. "Why didn't you get him in the barnyard?"

"I'm scared."

"Well, you shouldn't have a horse then."

Jeremy could sense the disappointment as well as the anger in his father's voice. He felt ashamed and he hated himself for admitting his weakness. He suddenly realized he had seen his mother stand in exactly the same spot many times before and say the same words to his father. "I just can't do it, Jake. I can't go on. I'm not well." Jeremy was astonished. It made him feel dirty.

His father was a short, bandy-legged little man with wide shoulders and a deep chest. He was not a farmer by choice. He had set out in 1928 to study medicine at university. But the Depression

had tripped him up like a tether rope. His father had sent him a letter, the only letter that ever passed between them, and told him the money had run out. Jeremy knew the story because his mother loved to dramatize her existence. His father never said anything about it. She always said what a great surgeon he would have been if his father hadn't been such a miser.

Jeremy knew about the horses too. One morning he found a box of his father's old prize ribbons his mother had thrown in the garbage. He didn't say anything, but he kept them hidden in the back of an old pine commode in his room and he took them out from time to time. And sometimes, when his mother was in town at a tea or curling, his father would get a pitcher of water and a bottle of Canadian Club and take out the Kodak movie projector and run old movies of horse shows. Jeremy and his younger brothers used to love to sit in the darkened living room with their father, the dust motes dancing in the light of the projector and the flickering images of the little farmer and his horses. He also remembered how his mother would get upset when she found out about the movies. "You know how that frightens me, Jake," she would say. "I don't want them to get ideas about horses. It would kill me."

When Jeremy was very young, there were always horses on the farm. His father had a hired man named Billy Blake who lived in a small clapboard house across one of the fields and shared his admiration for horses. Jeremy remembered the films better than the real thing—his father dressed in a neat, brown tweed suit and a fedora, leading the colts by a halter, stopping, starting, posing, quickened by the old film. And Billy Blake, unshaven, dressed in an older suit and an old time shirt without a collar, standing aside, looking important, waiting to take the horse from his father.

Jeremy's father always said Billy had bad luck but he would give you the shirt off his back. Near the end of the time they had horses, Jeremy's father helped him buy a bit of land and gave him a beautiful black mare named Black Diamond. Billy had a daughter the same age as Jeremy, named Suzie, who had a gland problem and grew fat and white like flour. He wasn't a good farmer and couldn't keep out of debt. Eventually he went crazy so that all he could do was sit and talk and sometimes go on a weeping jag right there in your kitchen. But that all happened later.

The time for horses ended very suddenly one evening. It was really an accident, Jeremy thought now. His father had bought a colt named Ramses to train for jumping. He was a wonder, there was no doubt about it. Billy Blake never stopped talking about him until he went crazy, in that twangy toothless voice of his. But he was wild—"meaner'n bitch with litter," said old Billy.

Jeremy's father was jumping Ramses in a paddock beside the barn. The paddock had three sides of split rails and the fourth side was the barn wall. A concrete foundation ran up the wall about six feet before the red vertical boards started. At the edge of the paddock, Jeremy, his mother and his two brothers watched. The dogs were locked in the house so they wouldn't frighten the horse. The little boys were in their pajamas ready for bed. Billy Blake drove up in a battered pick-up just as Jeremy's father took Ramses cleanly over two rail jumps.

The horse took the third jump almost nonchalantly. But his feet had barely touched the earth when he pivoted like a coiled spring towards the barn. Jeremy's father didn't have a chance. All his weight went forward. Inertia carried him out of the stirrups and into the barn foundation. He hit the concrete with the side of his body. Before his feet hit the ground Ramses swung round and caught him in the stomach with his rear hooves. The man's head hit the wall like a ripe melon. Billy Blake was over the fence and running before Jeremy knew what was happening. His mother sank to the ground moaning "Oh my God" over and over again.

Jeremy was very young then. But he would always remember being sent to bed that night and watching from his window as the men carried his father through the twilight to the house. He would always remember the muffled voices from the floor below. And a few days later, a man came with a truck and gave Jeremy's

. . . he pivoted like a coiled spring towards the barn.

mother some money at the barn door. After that there were no more horses.

He knew his father was angry now. And he knew it was because he hadn't gotten back on Samson. There was something bone-hard in his father's make-up that Jeremy felt he didn't share. He watched his father put on his coat and boots. Standing there in the kitchen, the boy looked like an absurd dwarf, bundled against the cold, with big red eyes and slimy cheeks. He felt a nervous heat suffuse his body. He didn't know why he had come to the kitchen. It was a mistake. He hadn't really been afraid, but he hadn't been able to make his legs move towards the horse. Perhaps in a couple of days he could go back. He hadn't wanted to disappoint his father. And now the whole universe was spinning off like a rundown top.

He felt a nervous heat suffuse his body.

He remembered buying Samson at Blake's that summer. He couldn't think of a time when he hadn't wanted a horse despite his mother's disapproval. He had worked all his short life, it seemed, to make the fifty dollars his father had matched to pay for the horse. The night before they went to Blake's his father had surprised him in the barn with a second-hand saddle and bridle he picked up in town. He knew his father took a wry satisfaction in telling his mother, "The boy made his money. He can do what he wants with it." And he'd felt so proud riding the chunky little horse home along the abandoned railway cut through the burdock and vetch.

Maybe it was his own fault. He didn't know. But everything had gone wrong with the horse. His first week on the farm he tried to jump the pasture fence and got tangled in the barbed wire. The vet came and painted him all blue with antiseptic and dosed him with castor oil. And Jeremy had taken him for walks on a lead rope until he mended properly. When he started riding again, it was already late autumn. Samson was skittish and stubborn. The clisp clisp of windblown leaves startled him in the woods. He first threw Jeremy by accident when he bolted off the trail, shying from the shadow of an old oak that swayed in the autumn light. For Jeremy it was a bitter experience. He fed Samson himself. He petted him like a dog. He brought the horse treats, combed him and sat in the stable for hours talking to him.

He could hear his mother now saying over and over "maybe we ought to get rid of him, Jake. He's vicious like Ramses was. He was fine when we got him, but he's no good for a boy. We've got to get rid of him."

"Why didn't you catch him?" asked his father. "You could have gotten him in the barnyard easily."

"I don't know."

"You could have caught him and gotten back on in the barnyard. He couldn't throw you there."

"I was scared."

His father put his hand on the doorknob.

"No, please, I'll go."

"Stay here, I'll put him away. I'll get Billy Blake to come over in the morning and take him back. No use having a horse if you can't ride him."

"No, please," wailed Jeremy. "I'll keep him. I'm just scared *now*. I'll be all right."

His father turned toward the door in disgust and went out. Jeremy stood by himself in the kitchen. He heard the woodshed door slam shut and the wire latch fall into place. The kitchen was quiet save for the kettle and the whirring of the stove clock. He walked over and pulled the plug from the kettle. He heard his mother calling from the bedroom at the front of the house.

"Jake, Jake, is Jeremy back yet?"

Jeremy bolted for the door and ran after his father.

"There's no use you coming out here," his father said without looking as Jeremy caught up with him. "I'm calling Billy Blake to come and get his horse back."

"I'll put him away, Daddy. I'll ride him."

His father paused. For a tiny aching instant Jeremy thought he might not get the chance to ride again. He saw the hard thing rise in his father's face and then pass.

"All right. Come on."

His father strode with long steps towards the barn and Jeremy trotted along behind. The horse was standing near the barn door. He was a small sorrel gelding with a big, bony head and a straggly mane. His belly and legs were stained and matted from lying in urine-soaked straw. Beyond the horse was the red barn and the white expanse of the farm under snow. The dark leafless woods lay off in the distance surmounted by a dirty overcast sky.

The horse didn't move. It expected to be taken into the stable. Instead, Jeremy's father caught up the reins and jerked them to bring the horse round to the door where he tied him. He went into the stable without saying a word. He emerged with a long exercise rope with a chain and snap on one end and a long section of double lath that was used for hanging tobacco in kilns. He ran the length of chain through a ring on one side of the bridle, under the horse's chin, and snapped it into another metal ring on the other side. When he pulled on the rope the chain tightened against the horse's jaw. He led the horse away from the barn to the centre of the barnyard.

The lath slashed across the horse's neck with a sound like a pistol shot that echoed off the barn walls. Samson squealed in surprise and reared away from the man. He started to circle away from the lath, like a boxer moving away from his opponent's right. His eyes protruded as he tried to keep the lath in sight.

The lath slashed across the horse's neck with a sound like a pistol shot . . .

"Hold still, you bastard," muttered Jeremy's father almost to himself. "Hold still." He lashed out again with the lath and it broke against the horse's withers. Jeremy's father cursed.

"Here, hold him." He handed Jeremy the rope. The horse shied away dragging Jeremy.

"Hold him, I said," came the gruff voice from behind him.

Jeremy didn't know what to do. The horse seemed so big and wild with fear. He couldn't believe the horse wouldn't trample him. He jerked the rope. Samson jerked back and pulled Jeremy off his feet. The boy leaned back on the rope with all his weight. The horse quieted.

Jeremy's father came back with an old broom handle in his glove.

"Give me that. Get on," he said.

Jeremy didn't answer. He was more afraid of what his father

might say than of the horse. He mounted with difficulty because Samson kept circling away from the broom handle.

"Slow down, you bastard, slow down," growled his father.

Once Jeremy was mounted, his father led horse and boy out the barnyard gate into an empty field. The snow was crusty and unbroken but not very deep. The air was fresh and chill and there was no sound save for the distant rush of cars along the highway in front of the farm, the chunking sound Samson made as he chewed the bit nervously and the crunch of feet and hooves on snow. Jeremy didn't know what to expect. His mind was full of the sensation of the smooth saddle horn and his fear of what would happen if his father turned suddenly on the horse.

"Hold on."

His father stopped and faced Samson. The horse began its panicky circling again. The broom handle struck with a dull whack like the sound of carpets being beaten. Samson reared on his hind legs, almost pulling the man off the ground. Jeremy's father had the rope wound round his arm and kept shifting constantly to keep his full weight against the horse. The piece of yellow wood fell again and again like a piston arm. Samson squealed. Jeremy could hear his father's breathing and a coarse, quiet muttering. His body was being wrenched from side to side so hard he could barely breathe. He clamped himself to the saddle horn in fright.

The trio danced in what seemed the centre of the universe to Jeremy. He could almost see them, like an aerial shot in some movie, circling round and round in a tense indissoluble knot of hatred and fear. Sweat slickened Samson's coat and spattered the snow. White foam flecked his chest and mouth. His eyes stood out like golf balls. The snow all round was trampled and dirty where the horse had shit. And blood began to splash from where his spastic jerking had driven the bit into the soft flesh of his mouth.

Jeremy's father was sweating now. He stopped and threw his coat and hat out of the little circle of trampled snow. The horse stood rigidly waiting. The boy noticed how his father had trouble getting his coat off because he forgot to let go of the stick. He seemed mesmerized by the excess of emotion and the rhythmic beating. He took up the stick again and struck. Samson squealed with pain and ran in tight circles. His breath came in great slobbery bursts.

Strangely, as the beating went on, the tension and fear began to recede from Jeremy's mind. It was as if the super-charged emotion was being siphoned off or grounded in the frozen earth. They were like three amateur actors getting accustomed to their roles. The boy felt almost detached. He was used to the movement of the horse now. Samson wasn't free to back and could only rear to the extent of the rope. Jeremy sat back a little and kept his

His body was being wrenched from side to side . . .

balance by letting his hips move with the horse, holding his shoulders straight. He was surprised at the ferocity of his father's anger. And he began to worry about the blood seeping from Samson's mouth. He wanted to tell his father to stop but something held him back. The horse's panic was so abject, Jeremy knew he could never be afraid again in the same way.

Presently, the beating stopped. Exhaustion ordered a truce between man and horse and a slight breeze filtered away the last emotion like chaff from a field. Samson stood and quivered, great gasps of air rushing in and out of his nostrils, staring at the man in front of him. Jeremy's father likewise stared at the horse and breathed heavily. All at once, he seemed to recollect himself and stooped to retrieve his coat. As he turned, Samson jerked his head wearily. Without warning, like the last spasm of a dead snake, Jeremy's father swung around and smashed his fist into the horse's face. Samson was too tired to dodge the blow. He only blinked at the pain.

The farmer picked up his coat and led the horse and boy towards the barn. He let the stick drop in the snow by the little battlefield. Jeremy noticed this because his father was usually meticulous about not leaving things where they could get caught in machinery. He rode quietly holding the reins in his left hand the way Billy Blake had taught him. He glanced once over his shoulder at the patch of trampled and stained snow.

When they reached the barnyard, Jeremy slipped down and stood ready to put the horse in the stable. His father turned and gently patted Samson's nose. The horse lurched away on tired legs.

"Easy, laddy," the man crooned softly. "Easy boy. It's all over now. Easy there. Let's have a look at your mouth there. That's a good lad. It's nothing. It's nothing."

Jeremy for the second time that day was amazed. His father looked so weary. He saw his eyes; they glistened.

"Jeremy, walk him out. He's too hot to put away. Get that saddle off him and put a blanket and halter on. Mind." He paused. "Don't ever be scared of this horse again, Jeremy."

"I won't, Daddy."

Jeremy watched as the man patted the horse again. Samson almost seemed to understand and they stood together in silent communion like two tired gladiators. His father turned and walked towards the house.

Jeremy led the horse back and forth beside the barn. It was dusk. He spoke softly as his father had done. And he began to weep, partly from relief after the intense emotion of the afternoon, and partly for the unutterable inevitability of things, the iron casing of feelings and the past that binds us all, and the dark course he had only just begun.

▼

. . . they stood together in silent communion like two tired gladiators.

READING AND REACTING

1. In a few paragraphs, compare Jeremy to his father as their characters develop in the story.

2. Imagine that you are Jeremy and your teacher has assigned you the task of writing a one-page essay on your father. Describe your father and how you feel about him. Have a partner help you revise your writing.

3. In groups, discuss the characters' relationship to nature. List words and phrases used by the author to establish this relationship.

4. After Jeremy put Samson in the barn, he returned to his bedroom and wrote a very detailed account of the day and what he had learned, in his diary. Write that entry as if you were Jeremy.

5. Toward the end of the story, the author describes the barnyard as a "battlefield" and Samson and his father as "two tired gladiators." Discuss in a group, what the battle was about, what was won, and what was lost.

REACHING OUT

1. Compose another instalment for "Horse," in which you describe a day at the farm five years later, for Jeremy, his mother, and his father.

2. Write a memoir about a challenge that you overcame with the help of another person. Decide on the impact that the incident had on your outlook on life or on your relationship with that person.

3. Write an essay in which you assess how your relationship with a parent or both parents has evolved to the present. Highlight experiences that you feel best symbolize the changes that this relationship has undergone.

A PLANET FOR THE TAKING

David Suzuki

Science knows nature in bits and pieces. That is its great strength and its fundamental limitation.

Canadians live under the remarkable illusion that we are a technologically advanced people. Everything around us denies that assumption. We are, in many ways, a Third World country, selling our natural resources in exchange for the high technology of the industrialized world. Try going through your home and looking at the country of origin of your clothes, electrical appliances, books, car. The rare technological product that does have Canada stamped on it is usually from a branch plant of a multinational company centred in another country. But we differ from traditional Third World countries. We have a majority population of Caucasians and a very high level of literacy and affluence. And we have been able to maintain our seemingly advanced social state by virtue of an incredible bounty of natural resources.

Within the Canadian mystique there is also a sense of the vastness of this land. The prairies, the Arctic, the oceans, the mountains are ever present in our art and literature. This nation is built on our sense of the seeming endlessness of the expanse of wilderness and the output of nature and we have behaved as if this endlessness were real.

Today we speak of renewable resources but our "harvest" procedures are more like a mining operation. We extract raw resources in the crudest of ways, gouging the land to get at its inner core, spewing

David Suzuki

our raw wastes into the air, water, and soil in massive amounts while taking fish, birds, animals, and trees in vast quantities without regard to the future. So we operate under a strange duality of mind: we have both a sense of the importance of the wilderness and space in our culture and an attitude that it is limitless and therefore we needn't worry.

Native cultures of the past may have been no more conservation-minded than we are but they lacked the technology to make the kind of impact that we do today. Canadians and Americans share one of the great natural wonders, the Great Lakes, which contain 20 percent of the world's fresh water, yet today even this massive body of water is terribly polluted, and the populations of fish are completely mixed-up by human activity. We speak of "managing" our resources, but we do it in a way that resembles the sledgehammer-on-the-head cure for a headache. On the west coast of Canada, Natives lived for millenia on the incredible abundance of five species of salmon. Today, the massive runs are gone and many biologists fear that the fish may be in mortal jeopardy because of both our fishing and management policies. Having improved fishing techniques this century to the point of endangering runs, yet still knowing very little of the biology of the fish, we have assumed that we could build up the yield by simply dumping more back. But it wasn't known that sockeye salmon fry, for example, spend a year in a freshwater lake before going to sea. Millions of sockeye fry were dumped directly into the Fraser River where they died soon after. In Oregon, overfishing and hydroelectric dams had decimated coho populations in the Columbia River. In one year, over eight million fry were released of which only seven were ever caught. No one knows what's happening to the rest.

We act as if a fish were a fish, a duck a duck, or a tree a tree. If we "harvest" one, we renew it by simply adding one or two back. But what we have learned is that all animals and plants are not equivalent. Each organism reflects the evolutionary history of its progenitors; in the case of a salmon, each race and sub-race of fish has been exquisitely honed by nature to return to a very specific part of the Pacific watershed.

Similarly, in the enormous area of prairie pothole country in the centre of the continent, migratory birds do not just space themselves out according to the potholes that are empty. Scientists have discovered that the birds have been selected to return to a very restricted part of that area. And of course, our entire forest policy is predicated on the ridiculous idea that a virgin stand of fir or cedar which has taken millenia to form and clings to a thin layer of topsoil can be replaced after clear-cut logging simply by sticking seedlings into the ground. How can anyone with even the most rudimentary understanding of biology and evolution ignore the realities of the complex interaction between organisms and the environment and attempt to manipulate wild populations as if they were tomato plants or chickens?

I believe that in large part our problems rest on our faith in the power of science and technology. At the beginning of this century, science, when applied by industry and medicine, promised a life immeasurably better and there is no doubt that society, indeed the planet, has been transformed by the impact of new ideas and inventions of science. Within my lifetime, I've seen the beginning of television, oral contraception, organ transplants, space travel, computers, jets, nuclear weapons, satellite communication, and polio vaccine. Each has changed society forever and made the world of my youth recede into the pages of history. But we have not achieved a technological utopia. The problems facing us today are immense and many are a direct consequence of science and technology. What has gone wrong?

I believe that the core of our 20th century dilemma lies in a fundamental limitation of science that most scientists, especially those in the life sciences, fail to recognize. Most of my colleagues take it for granted that our studies will ultimately

be applicable to the "big picture," that our research will have beneficial payoffs to society eventually. That is because the thrust of modern science has been predicated on the Newtonian idea that the universe is like an enormous machine whose entire system will be reconstructed on the basis of our understanding of the parts. This is the fundamental reductionist faith in science: the whole is equal to the sum of its parts. It does make a lot of sense—what distinguishes science from other activities that purport to provide a comprehensive "world view" is its requirement that we focus on a part of nature isolated to as great an extent as possible from the rest of the system of which it is a part. This has provided enormous insights into that fragment of nature, often accompanied by power to manipulate it. But when we attempt to tinker with what lies in the field of our view, the effects ripple far beyond the barrel of the microscope. And so we are constantly surprised at the unexpected consequences of our interference. Scientists only know nature in "bits and pieces" and assume that higher levels of organization are simply the expression of the component parts. This is what impels neurobiologists to study the chemical and electrical behaviour of single neurons in the faith that it will ultimately lead to an understanding of what creativity and imagination are, a faith that I don't for a moment think will ever be fulfilled (although a lot of useful information will accrue).

Physicists, who originally set this view in motion, have this century, with the arrival of relativity and quantum theory, put to rest the notion that we will ever be able to reconstruct the entire universe from fundamental principles. Chemists know that a complete physical description of atoms of oxygen and hydrogen is of little value in predicting the behaviour of a water molecule. But biologists scream that any sense that there are properties of organization that don't exist at lower levels is "vitalism," a belief that there is some mystical life force in living organisms. And so biochemists and molecular biologists are intent on understanding the workings of organisms by learning all they can about sub-cellular organization.

Ironically, ecology, long scorned by molecular biologists as an inexact science, is now corroborating physics. In studying ecosystems, we are learning that a simple breakdown into components and their behaviour does not provide insight into how an entire collection of organisms in a natural setting will work. While many ecologists do continue to "model" ecosystems in computers in the hope that they will eventually derive a predictive tool, their science warns of the hazards of treating it too simply in management programs.

At present, our very terminology suggests that we think we can manage wild plants and animals as though they were domesticated organisms. We speak of "herds" of seals, of "culling," "harvesting," "stocks." The ultimate expression of our narrow view (and self-interested rationalizations) is seen in how we overlook the enormous environmental impact of our pollution, habitat destruction, and extraction, and blame seals and whales for the decline in fish populations or wolves for the decrease in moose—and then propose bounties as a solution!

But Canadians do value the spiritual importance of nature and want to see it survive for future generations. We also believe in the power of science to sustain a high quality of life. And while the current understanding of science's power is, I believe, misplaced, in fact the leading edges of physics and ecology may provide the insights that can get us off the current track. We need a very profound perceptual shift and soon.

READING AND REACTING

1. David Suzuki feels that we have abused our relationship with the environment. In a small group, list the ways in which we have done this.

2. a) In a small group, discuss what Suzuki means when he says, "Our problems rest on our faith in the power of science and technology."

   b) In a short essay, explain Suzuki's statement and then either support or refute it.

3. With a partner, summarize what Suzuki sees as the function of science and what its limitations are.

4. Discuss the meaning of the term "Third World" and the assumptions associated with "Third World" status. Review the reasons Suzuki gives for stating that Canada is a Third World country and decide whether you agree.

REACHING OUT

1. With a partner, research examples in which our misuse of science has had tragic results. Present your findings to the class. If possible, include posters or slides in your presentation. After the presentation, conduct a class discussion on how such tragedies can be avoided in the future.

   or

   Research some of the recent scientific discoveries that have greatly benefited humanity. Present your findings to the class.

2. Find out what the main environmental issues are in your area and what steps are being taken to address these issues. In a letter to the editor of the local newspaper, express your concern about these environmental issues. Offer suggestions on how the community can help change the environment for the better.

3. As a class, conduct an informational campaign in your school or community on environmental issues.

4. Compose a short story or a set of poems that illustrate what happens when our faith in science leads us to interact with the environment in a destructive way.

COMMUNICATION PROJECTS

1. Write a report on the ways in which male-female relationships have changed in Canada over the last 20 years. In your report,

a) research changes in the law, in attitudes and practices, what brought these changes about, and what implications those changes have for the future;

b) survey men and women to find out what they think about the changes that have taken place and how each sex copes;

c) include transcripts of interviews and survey results;

d) summarize your own impressions of the changes in male-female relationships based on your research.

2. Research a major environmental group in terms of its objectives, methods, and effectiveness. Based on your findings,

a) prepare an audio-visual presentation that might be useful for community activist groups.

b) write a formal report that you could send to a newspaper for publication.

3. Focus on one minority group, or compare two minority groups.

a) Briefly trace their history in Canada and provide an overview of their culture.

b) Interview the group or groups to determine how they feel about the treatment they have received by other groups in the past, the way they are currently treated, and what the community is doing to address the problem.

4. Explore the availability of child day-care in your community. Prepare a handbook that lists all the facilities in your area. Ask your principal if the handbook could be distributed to the parents of young children in your community.

    Deliver an oral report to the class in which you sum up your findings, evaluate whether the services provided are adequate, and make recommendations for improvements. Provide copies of your outline to accompany your talk.

5. Give an oral presentation based on either a cross-cultural comparison of family types or a comparison of contemporary family types within Canada, such as blended, single-parent, and traditional. Examine sources of cohesiveness and of conflict in family

relationships. Supplement your presentation with slides, pictures, music, or other material that might be stimulating for your class.

or

Write and stage a play that deals with some of the major issues relating to contemporary family life.

6. Prepare a handbook for young people entering the job force on how to get along with people in the work environment. Your handbook should focus on co-worker, employer-employee, and employee-client/public relationships.

a) Research available literature relating to "people skills in the workplace."

b) Survey a business and conduct confidential interviews with employer and employees. (Make sure to obtain permission beforehand.)

▶GET A GRIP ON IT

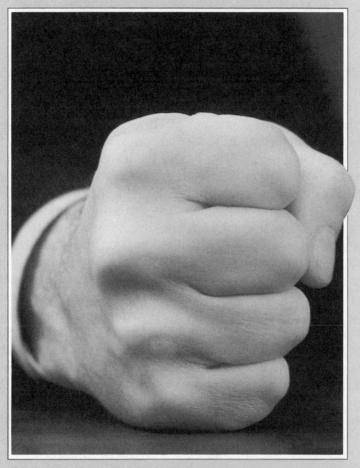

Stress is the physical and/or mental feeling people get when they are under pressure. You can't live without stress. Adventure and risk-taking involve a certain amount of tension, and that makes life exciting. But when stress interferes with your ability to function and to enjoy life, you have to know how to cope. The selections and activities in this unit are designed for you to explore sources of stress and to develop coping strategies.

STRESS BAD IF WRONGLY HANDLED

W. Gifford Jones, M.D.

When is stress the spice of life? And when does it trigger a nervous breakdown, a peptic ulcer, hypertension, arthritis, or a coronary attack?

Dr. Hans Selye, the internationally famous Canadian pioneer in the study of stress and its effect on the body, died in Montreal on Oct. 16, 1982. Among the many medical legacies he left the world was his belief that it is not stress that destroys the body, but rather how the person responds to it. Illness strikes only when the reaction to stress becomes distress.

"Suppose," Dr. Selye would say, "you meet a helpless drunk. He throws insults at you, but is too inebriated to cause bodily harm. Nothing happens if you ignore him. But if you prepare to fight, you discharge hormones that increase the heart rate and blood pressure, and the nervous system becomes tense.

"As a result of the encounter, a person with coronary heart disease might suffer a fatal attack. Who then is the murderer? The drunk who never laid a hand on the person? Or did the person commit suicide?" Dr. Selye was convinced that considerable illness is triggered by the choice of the wrong reaction.

In 1936, he began to pinpoint the physiological effect of stress. He injected extracts of cattle ovaries into rats and noted several changes. Large ulcers appeared in the stomach, the adrenal glands enlarged, and the spleen and lymph nodes decreased in size. He then discovered that other noxious substances produced the same changes. He labelled this reaction the General Adaptation Syndrome.

In GAS, stress first causes an alarm reaction or, as Dr. Selye said, "a call to arms" of the body's defensive forces. In some instances, stress is so great that death results. In most cases, the body adapts to the stress and creates resistance. Eventually, however, continued stress causes exhaustion, the defence system breaks down, and the gnawing pain of an ulcer begins, or a tension headache and other stress-related problems occur.

Avoiding stress is not the answer. As the late researcher remarked, "complete freedom from stress is death." There has never been a time in history when humans could avoid all adversity. The secret is to develop a healthy response to stress.

John H. Howard, associate professor of business administration at the University of Western Ontario in London, Ontario suggests a way to foster a healthy reaction.

He says the best technique is to build up resistance by regular sleep, exercise, and sound health habits. Work hard on the job, but blank out job-related problems at home. Use "bitch" sessions for relief and take a break from stressful situations when possible. The person who builds up physical resistance and who develops a preventive attitude about his or her health will have the energy to deal with stress rationally and effectively.

Dr. Selye's own philosophy can also

help us combat tension. He believed that the aim of life is not to work as little as possible. He wrote: "For the full enjoyment of leisure, you have to be tired first, as for the full enjoyment of food the best cook is hunger." Those who strive for shorter and shorter work hours and earlier retirement should take note.

He had other sound advice. Accept the fact that perfection is impossible, but in each category of achievement there is a "best." Be satisfied to strive for that.

At the end of his life, Dr. Selye practised what he preached. He had two artificial hips implanted and at 65 developed reticulo sarcome which is usually fatal. The disease provided him with the biggest challenge of his life. He could either slide into a death watch or adapt and squeeze as much out of life as possible. He chose the latter and beat his malignancy.

Did Dr. Selye just get lucky, or did his adaptation conquer the cancer? Doctors can't answer that question. But researchers have found that when patients have a strong will to live, they make a greater effort and use their immune system against cancer more effectively.

How Stress Hurts You

The new Canadian Institute of Stress outlines the toll stress takes on Canadians.

- As many as two million Canadians suffer hypertension or high blood pressure.
- More than one million Canadians experience insomnia on a regular basis.
- More than 40 million prescriptions for tranquilizing drugs were issued to Canadians last year.
- Premature employee death costs Canadian industry $1.9 billion a year, more than the combined 1978 profits of Canadian Business's top 10 companies.
- Alcoholism costs Canadian industry about $1.6 billion annually and mental disorders cost about $1.4 billion due to absenteeism and treatment costs.
- About 3.2 million work days and $560 million in wages and benefits are lost annually to heart related diseases in Canada.
- Stress and related psychosomatic problems account for as many as 80 percent of the problems treated by family doctors.

SHOE: **by Jeff MacNelly**

How Jobs Rate on the Stress Scale

1. Health technicians
2. Waiters, waitresses
3. Practical nurses
4. Inspectors
5. Musicians
6. Public relations
7. Clinical lab technicians
8. Dishwashers
9. Warehouse workers
10. Nurses' aides
11. Labourers
12. Dental assistants
13. Teacher aides
14. Research workers
15. Computer programmers
16. Photographers
17. Telephone operators
18. Hairdressers
19. Painters, sculptors
20. Health aides
21. Taxicab drivers
22. Chemists
23. Bank tellers
24. Social workers
25. Roofers, slaters
26. Secretaries
27. Nurses, registered
28. Operatives
29. Bakers
30. Struc. metal workers
31. Upholsterers
32. Dressmakers
33. Machinists
34. Sales managers
35. Garage workers
36. Clergy
37. Designers
38. Mechanics
39. Clerical workers
40. Office machine operators
41. Guards-watchers
42. Insurance adjusters
43. Barbers
44. Sales clerks
45. Office managers

46. Editors
47. Teachers
48. Sales representatives
49. Press operators
50. Painters, construction
    workers
51. Cooks
52. Engineers, stationary
53. Drafters
54. Mine operators
55. Tool diemakers
56. Bookkeepers
57. Food counter servers
58. Lumber workers
59. Welders
60. Meat cutters
61. Engineers
62. Brick masons
63. Insurance agents
64. Furnace workers
65. Electricians
66. Radio-TV repairers
67. Farm owners
68. Librarians
69. Mail carriers
70. Police officers
71. Shipping-receiving
72. Real estate
73. Carpenters
74. Dieticians
75. Gardeners
76. Pharmacists
77. Accountants
78. Janitors
79. Attendants
80. Truck drivers
81. Maids
82. Firefighters
83. Laundry
84. Plumbers
85. Bank financial managers
86. Lawyers
87. Child care workers
88. Dentists
89. Garbage collectors

90. Sewers
91. Bus drivers
92. College university
    personnel
93. Foresters
94. Cabinet makers
95. Clerks, counter
96. Electronic technicians
97. Supervisors
98. Farm labourers
99. Managers, administrators
100. Housekeepers
101. Vehicle washers
102. Managers—restaurant
103. Cement and concrete
     workers
104. School administrators
105. Railroad switchers
106. Physicians
107. Craftspeople
108. Firefighters, stationary
109. Sewer workers
110. Telephone lineworkers
111. Fork lift operators
112. Heavy equipment operators
113. Packers and wrappers
114. Officials and administrators
     (government)
115. Buyers
116. Electrical power liners
117. Personnel-labour relations
118. Health administrators
119. Freight handlers
120. Decorators
121. Engineering science
     technicians
122. Surveyors
123. Checkers and examiners
     (quality control)
124. Professional technicians
125. Stock handlers
126. Ticket station agents
127. Chemical technicians
128. Tailors
129. Hucksters (auctioneers and
     sales people)
130. Dyers

▶ CHECK YOUR STRESS COUNT

Here's a typical example of a scale for measuring the impact of life change. Add up the total for all the events you experienced in the last year. If you scored below 150, you're approaching the average with a one in three or better chance of serious illness. If your total is between 150 and 300, your chance of illness rises to about 50 percent. Over 300 points and the odds are 80/90 percent that you will have a serious change in your health.

EVENT	POINTS	YOUR SCORE
Death of spouse	100	
Divorce	73	
Marital separation	65	
Jail term	63	
Death of close family member	63	
Personal injury or illness	53	
Marriage	50	
Fired at work	47	
Marital reconciliation	45	
Retirement	45	
Change in health of family member	44	
Pregnancy	40	
Sex difficulties	39	
Gain a new family member	39	
Business readjustment	39	
Change in financial state	38	
Death of a close friend	37	
Change to different line of work	36	
Change in number of arguments with spouse	35	
Large mortgage	31	
Foreclosure of mortgage or loan	30	
Change in responsibilities at work	29	
Son or daughter leaving home	29	
Trouble with in-laws	29	
Outstanding personal achievement	28	
Spouse begin or stop work	26	
Begin or end school	26	
Change in living conditions	25	
Revision of personal habits	24	
Trouble with boss	23	
Change in work hours or conditions	20	
Change in residence	20	
Change in schools	20	
Change in recreation	19	
Change in church activities	19	
Change in social activities	18	
Small mortgage or loan	17	
Change in sleeping habits	16	
Change in number of family get-togethers	15	
Change in eating habits	15	
Vacation	13	
Christmas	12	
Minor violations of the law	11	
	TOTAL	

READING AND REACTING

1. In a small group, identify and list the stress-inducing factors in your lives. Compare your list with those of other groups. Together, compile a master list of common sources of stress for people of your age group.

2. a) In a group of four, read "Stress Bad If Wrongly Handled" and "How Stress Hurts You." Discuss the main issues to ensure that all group members fully understand them.

   b) Each group member should select one of the following opening statements and write a short paragraph with it, based on information from the articles.
      • STRESS IS . . .
      • STRESS IS CAUSED BY . . .
      • STRESS CAN RESULT IN . . .
      • STRESS CAN BE CONTROLLED BY . . .

   c) When every group member has finished writing, regroup and together revise and edit one another's work. Put all four polished paragraphs together as a Stress Information Sheet—use a computer or word processor if possible—and distribute copies to classmates.

3. In a small group, discuss what Dr. Hans Selye meant by these two statements in the article "Stress Bad If Wrongly Handled."
   a) "Illness strikes only when the reaction to stress becomes distress."
   b) "Complete freedom from stress is death."
   As a class, compare each group's interpretation.

REACHING OUT

1. a) Review the master list compiled in Reading and Reacting #1. Brainstorm ways to avoid or cope with each of the stress-causing situations on the list. Appoint one group member to record ideas during the brainstorming.

   b) Incorporate all the above information in a chart that lists each stress-inducing factor along with the appropriate coping strategies. Post the chart in the classroom. Each recorder should give a brief, oral report to accompany the chart.

2. In a small group, exchange accounts of situations that caused you stress, explaining how you coped. On your own, write a short

story based on the account that you found to be most interesting. Read your own story to the person who related the account and ask for his or her reaction.

3. If you are presently undergoing a stressful experience, write about it in your journal. Record your coping strategies and decide whether or not they are helping you overcome the situation.

4. Ask friends or family members to evaluate their stress level by completing the chart on page 231. Try to find out how these people are coping with stress.

5. Dr. Hans Selye founded the Canadian Institute of Stress in Toronto and the International Institute of Stress in Montreal. Write to either of these institutions and ask for the most up-to-date research on stress and how to cope with it. Share any information you receive with the class.

6. a) Study the chart "How Jobs Rate on the Stress Scale." In a small group, establish a classification system that indicates what types of jobs are most and least stressful.

   b) In a small group, compare a few of the most and least stressful jobs listed. Consider what aspects of each job make it more or less stressful.

   c) Choose two or three jobs that interest you and make a list of possible causes for stress related to each. Show your list to a partner and add any suggestions.

   d) With your partner, select one job and determine how you would handle the stress related to the job.

7. "People at the lower end of the occupational ladder are under far more stress than those at the higher end." Interview people at either end of the occupational ladder and try to establish whether the above statement is true.

► STRESS AND ADDICTION

TEEN TOBACCO ADDICTION LINKED TO STRESS

Heather Walker

A researcher here believes the results of her study of teen smoking patterns could lead to profound changes in anti-smoking campaigns.

Patricia Hadaway says the study of about 2,000 Vancouver-area junior high school students suggests they are addicted to cigarettes not because of nicotine but because cigarettes help them to deal with chronic stress.

Teens who smoke also frequently exhibit other behaviours indicative of poor ability to cope with stress she said.

A doctoral candidate in psychology at Simon Fraser University, Ms Hadaway says the data has not yet been fully analysed. However, she said: "There is some evidence that smokers are also often the students who do less well in school, who may be in trouble with the law, or may be in trouble at school, because of not showing up, for instance. Or, they may tend to use other drugs. So smoking tends to go along with other problems."

The survey covers both smokers and non-smokers and attempts to determine possible relationships between smoking and stress levels. It also looks at the students' need to be accepted by their peers and at

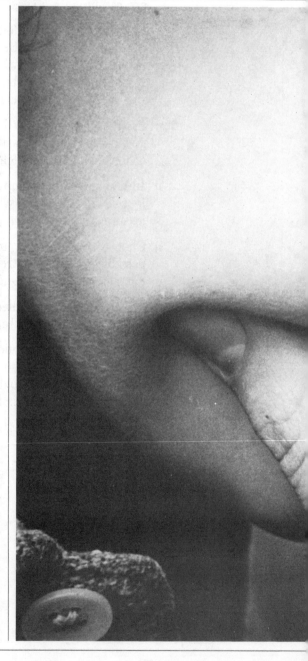

their degree of social competency.

"Smokers seem to have more of a need to be accepted. . . . There is evidence smokers are more social than non-smokers, and that acceptance from their peers is more important for them than for non-smokers."

Because she believes smoking is related to inability to cope with stress, "I also wanted to check things related to social competence, so there are questions about whether they have part-time jobs, what school activities they're involved in, things like that."

Another preliminary finding is, at least in the Vancouver area, that girls are heavier smokers than boys.

"Because it's a large sample, it could say a lot about the relationship between stress and smoking." However, she said, because it was only done in one area,

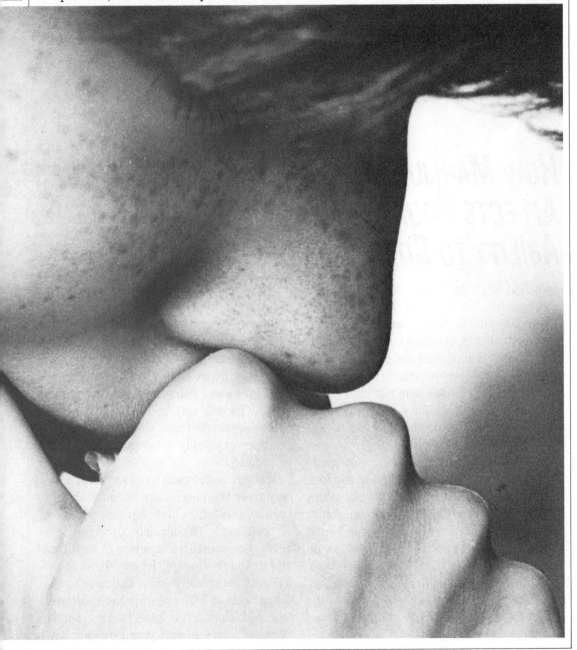

"it's not significant in terms of saying that in Canada more girls smoke."

Ms Hadaway says anti-smoking programs should include help for people in handling stress.

"We have to keep all programs that are already in existence, because there is a group who has been convinced not to smoke because of the health risks, for instance. But evidence that smoking is unhealthy will not affect those with distress and who start to smoke to cope with distress.

"We have to develop programs to help teenagers to deal with stress, and we have to give them alternatives to smoking."

How Marijuana Affects Your Ability to Cope

Addiction Research Foundation

There has been a great deal of interest in the effects of regular cannabis use on personality and behaviour. However, the research findings are not consistent and are difficult to interpret. Some researchers report that individuals who use high doses of cannabis regularly for a long time stop being contributing members of the family and community. They seem to no longer care about themselves or their surroundings; they show decreased ambition and loss of interest in the future. Some regular users do appear to experience these symptoms. However, it is unclear whether or not such problems are the result of cannabis use, or simply occur at the same time. When they do occur, such symptoms usually do not reflect a permanent change in personality, and they tend to disappear gradually when cannabis use is stopped.

The incidence of the above symptoms in regular users is not yet known. However, one recent (1981) nationwide survey of the graduating class of U.S. high school students provides evidence that the above and other behavioural symptoms may be more common than was previously thought. More than half (52%) of those 12th grade students who had stopped using cannabis after taking it frequently reported a loss of energy or ambition as one reason for their decision to quit.*

In the same survey, it was reported that many current daily users also felt their cannabis use caused a loss of energy (43%), as well as impaired school and/or work performance (34%) and decreased interest in other activities (37%). A number (37%) reported impairment of their ability to think clearly, although it is uncertain whether they meant for a few hours immediately after smoking or all the time. Finally, 39% said that cannabis interfered with their relationship with their parents.

Several studies have also found that, on average, users, and in particular regular users, make lower grades in school than non-users and are absent more often.

Sometimes, more severely disruptive symptoms are observed in regular heavy users. Extreme suspiciousness of others and emotional depression have been reported in a few cases, although many more users become increasingly irritable, nervous, and short-tempered. These symptoms also tend to clear gradually after cannabis use is terminated.

Many professionals have expressed concern over the potentially harmful effect of regular use on the developing personality of teenagers, particularly younger teenagers, because this is a period of such rapid and dramatic change. In our society, adolescence is typically one of the most stressful periods of life, even for the most well-adjusted. During this important and lengthy stage of development young people learn (or fail to learn) how to cope adequately with unpleasant but common feelings such as anxiety and depression. If they regularly use drugs, including alcohol and cannabis to avoid or to escape from normal stress, they may be depriving themselves of the opportunity to learn drug-free means of handling the everyday upsets of life. As adults, they are likely to continue to turn to drugs to deal with life's stresses.

Generally, the greater the amount of cannabis used, and the more frequently it is used, the more likely the danger of harmful psychological effects.

*In this survey, frequent users were defined as those who used cannabis 40 or more times in their life.

▼

R E A D I N G   A N D   R E A C T I N G

1. In groups, decide on a definition of (a) addiction and (b) regular use, as these terms relate to tobacco and to cannabis.

2. Write a psychological profile of a young adult who is a regular cannabis user, based on your reading of the article, "How Marijuana Affects Your Ability to Cope."

3. Design a flyer to warn teenagers of the dangers of drug use. Incorporate graphs that display the statistics in the article, "How Marijuana Affects Your Ability to Cope." Ask for permission to distribute your flyer in the school.

4. Working with a partner, design a brochure aimed at helping teenagers who "smoke to cope with stress." Offer the brochure to friends who smoke.

R E A C H I N G   O U T

1. "In our society, adolescence is typically one of the most stressful periods of life, even for the most well-adjusted."

a) In groups, brainstorm sources of teenage stress.

b) In a class discussion consider how stressful adolescence is compared with other periods in life.

2. Poll students in your school to determine their reasons for smoking and whether they feel it is stress-related. Present your findings to the class.

3. You are worried about a friend whom you think is becoming addicted to drugs. Express your concern and offer advice by

a) writing a letter to your friend
   or
b) role-playing the scene.

▶ TWO FISHERMEN

Morley Callaghan

THE ONLY REPORTER ON THE TOWN PAPER, THE *EXAMINER*, was Michael Foster, a tall, long-legged, eager young fellow, who wanted to go to the city some day and work on an important newspaper.

The morning he went into Bagley's Hotel, he wasn't at all sure of himself. He went over the desk and whispered to the proprietor, Ted Bagley, "Did he come here, Mr. Bagley?"

Bagley said slowly, "Two men came here from this morning's train. They're registered." He put his spatulate forefinger on the open book and said, "Two men. One of them's a drummer. This one here, T. Woodley. I know because he was through this way last year and just a minute ago he walked across the road to Molson's hardware store. The other one . . . here's his name, K. Smith."

"Who's K. Smith?" Michael asked.

"I don't know. A mild, harmless-looking little guy."

"Did he look like a hangman, Mr. Bagley?"

"I couldn't say that, seeing as I never saw one. He was awfully polite and asked where he could get a boat so he could go fishing on the lake this evening, so I said likely down at Smollet's place by the power-house."

"Well, thanks. I guess if he was the hangman, he'd go over to the jail first," Michael said.

He went along the street, past the Baptist church to the old jail with the high brick fence around it. Two tall maple trees, with branches drooping low over the sidewalk, shaded one of the walls from the morning sunlight. Last night, behind those walls, three carpenters, working by lamplight, had nailed the timbers for the scaffold. In the morning, young Thomas Delaney, who had grown up in the town, was being hanged: he had killed old Matthew Rhinehart whom he had caught molesting his wife when she had been berry-picking in the hills behind the town. There had been a struggle and Thomas Delaney had taken a bad beating before he had killed Rhinehart. Last night a crowd had gathered on the sidewalk by the lamp-post, and while moths and smaller insects swarmed around the high blue carbon light, the crowd

"Did he look like a hangman, Mr. Bagley?"

239

had thrown sticks and bottles and small stones at the out-of-town workmen in the jail yard. Billy Hilton, the town constable, had stood under the light with his head down, pretending not to notice anything. Thomas Delaney was only three years older than Michael Foster.

Michael went straight to the jail office, where Henry Steadman, the sheriff, a squat, heavy man, was sitting on the desk idly wetting his long mustaches with his tongue. "Hello, Michael, what do you want?" he asked.

"Hello, Mr. Steadman, the *Examiner* would like to know if the hangman arrived yet."

"Why ask me?"

"I thought he'd come here to test the gallows. Won't he?"

"My, you're a smart young fellow, Michael, thinking of that."

"Is he in there now, Mr. Steadman?"

"Don't ask me. I'm saying nothing. Say, Michael, do you think there's going to be trouble? You ought to know. Does anybody seem sore at me? I can't do nothing. You can see that."

"I don't think anybody blames you, Mr. Steadman. Look here, can't I see the hangman? Is his name K. Smith?"

"What does it matter to you, Michael? Be a sport, go on away and don't bother us anymore?"

"All right, Mr. Steadman," Michael said very competently, "just leave it to me."

Early that evening, when the sun was setting, Michael Foster walked south of the town on the dusty road leading to the power-house and Smollet's fishing pier. He knew that if Mr. K. Smith wanted to get a boat he would go down to the pier. Fine powdered road dust whitened Michael's shoes. Ahead of him he saw the power-plant, square and low, and the smooth lake water. Behind him the sun was hanging over the blue hills beyond the town and shining brilliantly on square patches of farm land. The air around the power-house smelt of steam.

Out on the jutting, tumbledown pier of rock and logs, Michael saw a little fellow without a hat, sitting down with his knees hunched up to his chin, a very small man with little grey baby curls on the back of his neck, who stared steadily far out over the water. In his hand he was holding a stick with a heavy fishing-line twined around it and a gleaming copper spoon bait, the hooks brightened with bits of feathers such as they used in the neighbourhood when trolling for lake trout. Apprehensively Michael walked out over the rocks toward the stranger and called, "Were you thinking of going fishing, mister?" Standing up, the man smiled. He had a large head, tapering down to a small chin, a birdlike neck and a very wistful smile. Puckering his mouth up, he said shyly to Michael, "Did you intend to go fishing?"

"That's what I came down here for. I was going to get a boat

240

back at the boat-house there. How would you like it if we went together?"

"I'd like it first rate," the shy little man said eagerly. "We could take turns rowing. Does that appeal to you?"

"Fine. Fine. You wait here and I'll go back to Smollet's place and ask for a row-boat and I'll row around here and get you."

"Thanks. Thanks very much," the mild little man said as he began to untie his line. He seemed very enthusiastic.

When Michael brought the boat around to the end of the old pier and invited the stranger to make himself comfortable so he could handle the line, the stranger protested comically that he ought to be allowed to row.

Pulling strongly at the oars, Michael was soon out in the deep water and the little man was letting his line out slowly. In one furtive glance, he had noticed that the man's hair, grey at the temples, was inclined to curl to his ears. The line was out full length. It was twisted around the little man's forefinger, which he let drag in the water. And then Michael looked full at him and smiled because he thought he seemed so meek and quizzical. "He's a nice little guy," Michael assured himself and he said, "I work on the town paper, the *Examiner*."

"Is it a good paper? Do you like the work?"

"Yes. But it is nothing like a first-class city paper and I don't expect to be working on it long. I want to get a reporter's job on a city paper. My name's Michael Foster."

"Mine's Smith. Just call me Smitty."

"I was wondering if you'd been over to the jail yet."

"Just call me Smitty."

Up to this time the little man had been smiling with the charming ease of a small boy who finds himself free, but now he became furtive and disappointed. Hesitating, he said, "Yes, I was over there first thing this morning."

"Oh, I just knew you'd go there," Michael said. They were a bit afraid of each other. By this time they were far out on the water which had a mill-pond smoothness. The town seemed to get smaller, with white houses in rows and streets forming geometric patterns, just as the blue hills behind the town seemed to get larger at sundown.

Finally Michael said, "Do you know this Thomas Delaney that's dying in the morning?" He knew his voice was slow and resentful.

"No. I don't know anything about him. I never read about them. Aren't there any fish at all in this old lake? I'd like to catch some fish," he said rapidly. "I told my wife I'd bring her home some fish." Glancing at Michael, he was appealing, without speaking, that they should do nothing to spoil an evening's fishing.

The little man began to talk eagerly about fishing as he pulled out a small flask from his hip pocket. "Scotch," he said, chuckling with delight. "Here, take a swig." Michael drank from the flask

241

and passed it back. Tilting his head back and saying, "Here's to you, Michael," the little man took a long pull at the flask. "The only time I take a drink," he said still chuckling, "is when I go on a fishing trip by myself. I usually go by myself," he added apologetically as if he wanted the young fellow to see how much he appreciated his company.

They had gone far out on the water but they had caught nothing. It began to get dark. "No fish tonight, I guess, Smitty," Michael said.

"It's a crying shame," Smitty said. "I looked forward to coming up here when I found out the place was on the lake. I wanted to get some fishing in. I promised my wife I'd bring her back some fish. She'd often like to go fishing with me, but of course she can't because she can't travel around from place to place like I do. Whenever I get a call to go some place, I always look at the map to see if it's by a lake or on a river, then I take my lines and hooks along."

"If you took another job, you and your wife could probably go fishing together," Michael suggested.

"I don't know about that. We sometimes go fishing together anyway." He looked away, waiting for Michael to be repelled and insist that he ought to give up the job. And he wasn't ashamed as he looked down at the water, but he knew that Michael thought he ought to be ashamed. "Somebody's got to do my job. There's got to be a hangman," he said.

"I just meant that if it was such disagreeable work, Smitty."

The little man did not answer for a long time. Michael rowed steadily with sweeping, tireless strokes. Huddled at the end of the boat, Smitty suddenly looked up with a kind of melancholy hopelessness and said mildly, "The job hasn't been so disagreeable."

"Good God, man, you don't mean you like it?"

"Oh, no," he said, to be obliging, as if he knew what Michael expected him to say. "I mean you get used to it, that's all." But he looked down again at the water, knowing he ought to be ashamed of himself.

"Have you got any children?"

"I sure have. Five. The oldest boy is fourteen. It's funny, but they're all a lot bigger and taller than I am. Isn't that funny?"

They started a conversation about fishing rivers that ran into the lake farther north. They felt friendly again. The little man, who had an extraordinary gift for story-telling, made many quaint faces, puckered up his lips, screwed up his eyes and moved around restlessly as if he wanted to get up in the boat and stride around for the sake of more expression. Again he brought out the whisky flask and Michael stopped rowing. Grinning, they toasted each other and said together, "Happy days." The boat remained motionless on the placid water. Far out, the sun's last rays gleamed

"Somebody's got to do my job."

on the water-line. And then it got dark and they could only see the town lights. It was time to turn around and pull for the shore. The little man tried to take the oars from Michael, who shook his head resolutely and insisted that he would prefer to have his friend catch a fish on the way back to the shore.

"It's too late now, and we may have scared all the fish away," Smitty laughed happily. "But we're having a grand time, aren't we?"

When they reached the old pier by the power-house, it was full night and they hadn't caught a single fish. As the boat bumped against the rocks Michael said, "You can get out here. I'll take the boat around to Smollet's."

"Won't you be coming my way?"

"Not just now. I'll probably talk to Smollet a while."

The little man got out of the boat and stood on the pier looking down at Michael. "I was thinking dawn would be the best time to catch some fish," he said. "At about five o'clock. I'll have an hour and a half to spare anyway. How would you like that?" He was speaking with so much eagerness that Michael found himself saying, "I could try. But if I'm not here at dawn, you go on without me."

"All right. I'll walk back to the hotel now."

"Good night, Smitty."

"Good night, Michael. We had a fine neighbourly time, didn't we?"

As Michael rowed the boat around to the boat-house, he hoped that Smitty wouldn't realize he didn't want to be seen walking back to town with him. And later, when he was going slowly along the dusty road in the dark and hearing all the crickets chirping in the ditches, he couldn't figure out why he felt so ashamed of himself.

At seven o'clock the next morning Thomas Delaney was hanged in the town jail yard. There was hardly a breeze on that leaden grey morning and there were no small whitecaps out over the lake. It would have been a fine morning for fishing. Michael went down to the jail, for he thought it his duty as a newspaperman to have all the facts, but he was afraid he might get sick. He hardly spoke to all the men and women who were crowded under the maple trees by the jail wall. Everybody he knew was staring at the wall and muttering angrily. Two of Thomas Delaney's brothers, big, strapping fellows with bearded faces, were there on the sidewalk. Three automobiles were at the front of the jail.

Michael, the town newspaperman, was admitted into the court-yard by old Willie Mathews, one of the guards, who said that two newspapermen from the city were at the gallows on the other side of the building. "I guess you can go around there, too, if you want to," Mathews said, as he sat down slowly on the step. White-faced, and afraid, Michael sat down on the step with Mathews and they waited and said nothing.

At last the old fellow said, "Those people outside there are pretty sore, ain't they?"

"They're pretty sullen, all right. I saw two of Delaney's brothers there."

"I wish they'd go," Mathews said. "I don't want to see anything. I didn't even look at Delaney. I don't want to hear anything. I'm sick." He put his head back against the wall and closed his eyes.

The old fellow and Michael sat close together till a small procession came around the corner from the other side of the yard. First came Mr. Steadman, the sheriff, with his head down as though he were crying, then Dr. Parker, the physician, then two hard-looking young newspapermen from the city, walking with their

hats on the back of their heads, and behind them came the little hangman, erect, stepping out with military precision and carrying himself with a strange cocky dignity. He was dressed in a long black cut-away coat with grey striped trousers, a gates-ajar collar and a narrow red tie, as if he alone felt the formal importance of the occasion. He walked with brusque precision till he saw Michael, who was standing up, staring at him with his mouth open.

The little hangman grinned and as soon as the procession reached the doorstep, he shook hands with Michael. They were all looking at Michael. As though his work were over now, the hangman said eagerly to Michael, "I thought I'd see you here. You didn't get down to the pier at dawn?"

"No, I couldn't make it."

"That was tough, Michael. I looked for you," he said. "But never mind. I've got something for you." As they all went into the jail, Dr. Parker glanced angrily at Michael, then turned his back on him. In the office, where the doctor prepared to sign a certificate, Smitty was bending down over his fishing-basket which was in the corner. Then he pulled out two good-sized salmon-bellied trout, folded in a newspaper, and said, "I was saving these for you, Michael. I got four in an hour's fishing." Then he said, "I'll talk about that later, if you'll wait. We'll be busy here, and I've got to change my clothes."

Michael went out to the street with Dr. Parker and the two city newspapermen. Under his arm he was carrying the fish, folded in the newspaper. Outside, at the jail door, Michael thought that the doctor and the two newspapermen were standing a little apart from him. Then the small crowd, with their clothes all dust-soiled from the road, surged forward, and the doctor said to them, "You might as well go home, boys. It's all over."

"Where's old Steadman?" somebody demanded.

"We'll wait for the hangman," somebody else shouted.

The doctor walked away by himself. For a while Michael stood beside the two city newspapermen, and tried to look nonchalant as they were looking, but he lost confidence in them when he smelled whisky. They only talked to each other. Then they mingled with the crowd, and Michael stood alone. At last he could stand there no longer looking at all those people he knew so well, so he, too, moved out and joined the crowd.

When the sheriff came out with the hangman and two of the guards, they got half-way down to one of the automobiles before someone threw an old boot. Steadman ducked into one of the cars, as the boot hit him on the shoulder, and the two guards followed him. The hangman, dismayed, stood alone on the sidewalk. Those in the car must have thought at first that the hangman was with them for the car suddenly shot forward, leaving him alone on the sidewalk. The crowd threw small rocks and sticks, hooting at him as the automobile backed up slowly towards him. One small stone hit him on the head. Blood trickled from the side of his head as

"It's different now, it's different,"

he looked around helplessly at all the angry people. He had the same expression on his face, Michael thought, as he had had last night when he had seemed ashamed and had looked down steadily at the water. Only now, he looked around wildly, looking for someone to help him as the crowd kept pelting him. Farther and farther Michael backed into the crowd and all the time he felt dreadfully ashamed as though he were betraying Smitty, who last night had had such a good neighbourly time with him. "It's different now, it's different," he kept thinking, as he held the fish in the newspaper tight under his arm. Smitty started to run toward the automobile, but James Mortimer, a big fisherman shot out his foot and tripped him and sent him sprawling on his face.

Mortimer, the big fisherman, looking for something to throw, said to Michael, "Sock him, sock him."

Michael shook his head and felt sick.

"What's the matter with you, Michael?"

"Nothing. I got nothing against him."

The big fisherman started pounding his fists up and down in the air. "He just doesn't mean anything to me at all," Michael said quickly. The fisherman, bending down, kicked a small rock loose from the road bed and heaved it at the hangman. Then he said, "What are you holding there, Michael, what's under your arm? Fish. Pitch them at him. Here, give them to me."

Still in a fury, he snatched the fish, and threw them one at a time at the little man just as he was getting up from the road. The fish fell in a thick dust in front of him, sending up a little cloud. Smitty seemed to stare at the fish with his mouth hanging open, then he didn't even look at the crowd. That expression on Smitty's face as he saw the fish on the road made Michael hot with shame and he tried to get out of the crowd.

Smitty had his hands over his head, to shield his face as the crowd pelted him, yelling, "Sock the little rat. Throw the runt in the lake." The sheriff pulled him into the automobile. The car shot forward in a cloud of dust.

▼

READING AND REACTING

1. In a small group, discuss how you felt as you read this story. Name the emotions that were aroused and identify the situations or incidents that caused you to feel that way.

2. a) In a small group, account for the behaviour of the following characters in the story: Michael Foster, K. Smith, James Mortimer, the town crowd.

   b) On your own, imagine that you are one of the above characters and write a journal entry on the night of the hanging. Try to capture your feelings as you relate the events: either justify your actions or pour out your guilt.

3. Imagine that you are Michael Foster and write the newspaper report on the hanging and the scene that followed. Provide a dramatic headline.

4. Dramatize one of the key scenes from the story. Be sure to highlight the inner conflicts that develop as a result of stress.

REACHING OUT

1. In the voice of Michael Foster, write a letter to Smitty. Express how you feel about him and try to explain why you failed to stand up for him on the day of the hanging.

2. You are K. Smith and you are about to retire from your job. Write a letter to your potential successor and tell him or her what to expect from the job.

3. With a classmate, script a dialogue that occurs when Michael meets Smitty two years after the hanging. Role-play this meeting for the class.

   or

   Dramatize one of the key scenes from the story. Be sure to highlight the inner conflicts that develop as a result of stress.

4. Smitty says of his job, "I mean you get used to it, that's all." With a partner, identify and interview people whose jobs involve wrestling with their conscience (e.g., scientists who must kill animals for research or doctors and nurses who must deal with disturbing situations). Find out how they cope with their jobs and whether or not they agree with Smitty's statement. Write a report on all the interviews. In your report, identify the job-related stress and then describe the person's coping strategies. Read your report to the class and ask for their comments.

5. Your job demands that you accept responsibility for an unpopular decision. Write a memo to your staff to announce your decision. Try to justify your actions.

   or

   Write the speech you would make at a general staff meeting to announce the decision. Present the speech to the class.

6. Write a short story about a person who is faced with a moral dilemma in a job-related situation. Revise and polish your writing and read it to your group.

▶ THE INTERVIEW

Margie Marks

Good thing I wore a dress today.
I think he liked me.
Was it my eyes? He said I had
beautiful eyes.
I wonder why.
We talked for a while. He asked
irrelevant questions.
I answered them.
We laughed. I chuckled at his old jokes.
He leaned back in his chair and
winked at me.
His eyes followed my dress hem
down to my shoes.
He said I had beautiful eyes.
I refused the job.

▶ SEXUAL HARASSMENT

A young woman, Gina W., was employed by a company in Metropolitan Toronto as a packer. In the course of her work, she alleged that she continually suffered sexual approaches and harassment from a male co-worker. When she complained to management, she was accused of lying, and was "told to get out."

Ms W. filed a complaint with the Ontario Human Rights Commission against the company and the co-worker, alleging sexual harassment. Following investigation, the Human Rights Commission was unsuccessful in its attempts to effect a satisfactory settlement among the parties. The commission therefore requested the Minister of Labour to appoint a Board of Inquiry. The Board of Inquiry was convened, but before any evidence could be heard, legal counsel asked for an adjournment to continue to negotiate a settlement.

After two days of deliberations, and upon agreement by all parties, the board announced that Ms W. had been awarded a cash settlement—$3000 for pain and suffering, $500 for lost wages. In addition, the company agreed to provide Ms W. with a written apology and to hold a seminar on its premises to acquaint employees with the provisions of the Ontario Human Rights Code.

▼

R E A D I N G   A N D   R E A C T I N G

1. Imagine that you are the woman in Margie Mark's poem. Write a journal entry describing your feelings as the interview progressed. Explain why you turned down the job and determine whether you did the right thing.

2. Working with a partner, script a dialogue that might have occurred between Gina W. and the male co-worker in Case No. 8. Role-play the conversation for a group.

R E A C H I N G   O U T

1. "Case No. 8, Sexual Harassment" illustrates one of the very unpleasant stresses that employees do not need to suffer. Fortunately, there are laws, such as those contained in the Canadian

Charter of Rights and Freedoms and the Ontario Human Rights Code, that prohibit sexual harassment and provide severe penalties for such behaviour. Of course, the Criminal Code also deals with the more flagrant instances of this behaviour. In a small group, research these pieces of legislation to determine what is considered to be sexual harassment. Make a summary of the legislation and present it to the class.

2. Work in a group of three. Imagine that you are the personnel manager of a large company that employs an equal number of males and females.

a) Compose a code of behaviour or a set of rules that will help prevent sexual harassment in your company. Write your code of behaviour in clear, simple sentences. Design a poster featuring the code.

b) Send a one-page memorandum to the employees, identifying the legal implications of sexual harassment and your company's position on the issue. Display your memorandum alongside the poster.

3. In a small group, exchange stories about sexual harassment that you have heard or read about. If you have a part-time job, you may wish to relate incidents that you have observed. After the discussion, write a short story about sexual harassment on the job. Remember that this kind of harassment works both ways— men, as well as women can be victims.

4. Check a clipping file or back issues of magazines for a one- or two-month period and select all articles that deal with sexual harassment on the job. Compile the information on a chart like this:

Harasser		Victim		Forms of Harassment	Outcome
Position	Sex	Position	Sex		

5. a) Sexual harassment charges are difficult to prove. In a small group, brainstorm ways that an employee can deal with the problem of being sexually harassed.

b) Invite i) a psychologist or a psychiatrist to explain why sexual harassment occurs.

ii) a human rights officer to find out what steps an employee should take when faced with sexual harassment.

Assign members of your class to
a) write letters to the speakers
b) introduce the speakers
c) thank the speakers
d) write letters of appreciation to the speakers

► COMPUTERS ZERO IN ON OUR BAD WORK HABITS

Carey English

Business is finding yet one more use for the proliferation of computers: checking up on the work of employees second by second throughout the business day.

Called computer monitoring, the process connects work stations in offices, factories and other settings to computers that keep a close watch on the individual worker's production by counting such functions as keystrokes per hour in the case of clerical personnel or the amount of time telephone operators take with callers.

Used by many employers to quicken the work pace and even determine compensation and promotion, the technique is spreading fast. At least one third of the more than 7 million workers now linked to computers through video display terminals, or VDTs, are thought to be subject to some form of monitoring. Experts think that share will grow to more than half of the 40 million workers expected to be using VDTs by 1990.

Unlike traditional supervisory techniques that measure the final production result, such monitoring goes a step further and measures how employees achieve their output. Work time can be tracked down to fractions of a second, and production goals raised.

From the employer's point of view, the advantages are often substantial. At the Maryland-based Giant Food store chain, optical scanners at checkout counters eliminate pricing guesses by employees, improve inventory control, aid in work scheduling, and track the workers' speed—all of which produce savings in excess of $15 million annually. Productivity rating sheets allow employees to personally check how they are doing. Despite enthusiasm for the system among employers, critics contend that such constant surveillance is counter-productive, leading to increased stress, fatigue, and turnover among workers. They also say that the system is easily abused, pointing to instances where employees are reprimanded and even fired for falling below time standards that accompany computer monitoring.

READING AND REACTING

1. **a)** In a small group, identify the ways that workers in various industries are being monitored by electronic devices.

   b) Describe the stresses that could arise from working on a closely monitored job.

   c) Script a scene between workers in a plant that is under electronic surveillance. Show the monitoring methods and stresses that the workers undergo on the job. Dramatize the scene for the class.

REACHING OUT

1. Interview someone who works under electronic surveillance (telephone operators, supermarket checkout clerks, and airline passenger agents are examples). Find out his or her feelings about the situation. Share your findings with the class.

2. Ray Hainsworth of the Ontario Federation of Labour says of electronic surveillance: "My bottom-line question is a simple one: Would the employer want to work under those circumstances?"

   Survey management personnel of companies that use electronic monitoring on their staff and ask them Hainsworth's question. Report your findings to the class.

3. Imagine that you are a worker in one of the monitored environments described in the article. Write a letter to your union in which you describe all the stresses that you are suffering. Ask your union leader to help convince management to remove the surveillance equipment.

   or

   As a union leader, prepare a speech denouncing the practice of electronic monitoring and its effects on your colleagues. Present this speech to the class.

4. Imagine that you are the president of an organization that is about to install electronic surveillance devices in your plant. Write a memo to the staff in which you justify your decision.

5. Prepare a policy proposal about the enlightened use of electronic surveillance in business and industry. Your suggestions should recognize the needs of employers as well as the rights and dignity of workers.

6. Read *1984* by George Orwell, and explain in a brief essay how Orwell's predictions may have come true.

▶ RISK TAKING CAN GIVE YOU A HEALTHY HIGH

While the abundance of chemicals, alcohol, and tobacco is considered a dangerous method with which to try to cope with stress, there are many healthy "highs" that can help relieve stress.

Olivia Ward

Some throw themselves out of planes. Others jump in the lake. A few sail into turbulent waters. Still others balance on wires above tall buildings, face raging bulls with drawn swords, stalk tigers through the bush, or hang dizzily from Himalayan peaks.

They are risk sport addicts. And according to a California stress expert, they are also the happiest and healthiest of men and women. If, of course, they live to tell the tale.

"The joy and euphoria you feel in a risk sport can't be equalled by anything else in modern life," says Dr. Sol Rosenthal of San Diego. "What it adds up to is a state of mental and physical well-being that is the basis of a healthy existence."

Rosenthal has recently completed a book called RE (Risk Exercise) based on an extensive study of 890 individuals participating in risk sports.

He found that 64 percent of risk-takers experience a feeling of elation that overtakes any state of depression, and that 90 percent report euphoria during the risk experience. Afterward, 20 percent remained euphoric for sustained periods.

Results far exceed ratings for nonrisk sports, in which Rosenthal found only 8.5 percent of participants are elated, and 2.5 percent euphoric.

"Physical exercise makes people feel bet-ter generally," says Rosenthal, "but there isn't the element of challenge and self-fulfilment. Risk exercise combines physical exertion with the knowledge that some sort of danger is involved. You might get hurt."

Daredevils flirt with extreme dangers. Last week German car dealer Jaromir Wagner completed a Germany-to-New York flight strapped to the outside of his plane. Stuntman Dar Robinson dived off the CN Tower clipped to a cable. And tightrope walker Jay Michael Cochrane walked suspended over Bloor St. in a high wind.

Less dramatic adventurers also count as fully-fledged RE participants. Sailors, skiers, surfers, hunters, boxers, wrestlers, ice hockey, rugby, and soccer players qualify as do skydivers, mountain climbers and water skiers, car racers, horse racers, motor bike scramblers, and explorers who risk life and limb trekking the wilds.

Competition isn't important in producing a risk-high, says Rosenthal. But there's "a certain psychic attitude that's hard to explain."

Doctors and researchers are beginning to realize that the exhilaration, joy, and well-being that risk-takers feel is a key to treating pain, illness, and depression.

In people and animals, the "danger" response triggers the pituitary hormone ACTH, which releases into the body and brain chemicals mobilizing the individual

for quick action, clear decision-making, and suppression of pain and fear.

The chemicals, called endorphins (Greek for "the morphine within"), mimic the action of opium or heroin, producing a powerful natural high. Neurobiologists say they are painkillers 100 times as potent as morphine and 40 times more effective than any other brain chemicals.

And says Rosenthal, we need our daily dose for physical and mental health.

"If you're depressed, you need more risk," he insists. "But even when you are feeling fine, you need a certain amount to keep things in balance."

Gamblers and financial risk-takers, as well as other mental adventurers, don't get their share of healthy highs, he adds.

"Consciously or unconsciously there's a feeling of insecurity. Could the performance be repeated? Will you succeed? What do other people think? Then too the body is constrained, there's no freedom of movement or physical exertion."

Rosenthal's subjects described their elated feelings from risk exercise as "deep, pure, mellow, comforting, free and joyous, unencumbered by doubts or fears."

However, those who lacked confidence about their performance were dejected and depressed—particularly if their skills were low.

"It seems to relate to a very ancient instinct," says Rosenthal. Man used to live by his proficiency in hunting and fighting. No doubt a poor performance could be fatal."

Until relatively recently, he says, our forebears took daily physical risks in foraging for food and defending their territory. Risk, in fact, was dealt with in a well-calculated way as useful stress rather than harmful "distress."

There's ample evidence, too, that physical risk enhances the feeling of being alive, and the determination to live at all costs. Records of astonishing heroism in battle or in a crisis are often accountable by the fact that the hero—euphoric—literally "felt no pain."

Indeed, many people whose outlook on life was cynical if not pessimistic, have staunchly refused to die in the face of terrible odds.

The widow of the great Russian poet Osip Mandelstam, imprisoned in a forced-labour camp in Siberia, wrote: "Whenever I talked of suicide, M. used to say: 'Why hurry? The end is the same everywhere, and here they even hasten it for you.' Death was so much more real and so much simpler than life, that we all involuntarily tried to prolong our earthly existence, even if only for a brief moment . . . ."

Sigmund Freud, too, noted the ennui that often sets in when comfort and assurance are prevalent. "Life is impoverished, it loses in interest, when the highest stake in the game of living, life itself, may not be risked. It becomes as shallow and empty as, let us say, an American flirtation."

Now that physical risk has been eliminated from daily life, scientists believe, the need for action and stimulation remains, transmitted, perhaps, genetically.

"What we have today is a deficiency," says Rosenthal. "People have less vigour and courage because we're depleted in the chemicals that help to maintain them. For instance some kinds of depression have been traced to a deficiency of norepinephrine in the brain."

Rosenthal and other researchers believe that inexplicable explosions of violence in society—rock concert riots or stadium brawls—may be caused by unexpected shots of euphoria in people accustomed to living on a dulled level.

"Action," he says, "absorbs anxiety." And the less risk-taking people are, the more stolid the country. "Canadians are even more placid than Americans," says Rosenthal. But unresolved anxiety can lead to depression and apathy, along with classically conservative political attitudes.

Recent reports in the U.S. have shown that the present demand for reduction of all environmental and social risks is part, not of a radical 1960s-style movement, but of a tendency to defensive right-wing positions.

"Physical and emotional health run closely together," says Rosenthal. Unfortunately, recent statistics show that more than half of Canadians are overweight, and 75 percent of school children are unfit—not to mention the limping young Canuck trying vainly to catch up with the 60-year-old Swede.

On the other hand, a national fitness program applied to Canada Life Assurance Co. employees for three years showed a drop of absenteeism of 42 percent among participants, and reports of improved health and spirits.

A U.S. study of aging football players showed they live longer than a comparable sedentary group—and those who remain active show no signs of coronary heart disease.

Fitness, however, is only half the solution, says Rosenthal. "You need exercise for well-being. But risk adds the bonus of euphoria. That may not be a panacea for the world's ills, but it certainly makes you better equipped to cope with them."

READING AND REACTING

1. State the reasons why risk sports are so attractive to many enthusiasts.

2. In a group, determine what Dr. Sol Rosenthal means when he says, "risk adds the bonus of euphoria."

3. In a class discussion, share your ideas about the risky activities described in Ward's article. Identify the activities that you would enjoy participating in and those activities you consider too risky. Analyse the class preference on a chart that shows the number of male/female students who felt each sport was acceptable or too risky.

REACHING OUT

1. Select one of the risk activities described in the article (or another you are aware of) and compile all the information you can about the skills, equipment, cost, etc. Produce a visual display to graphically capture the activity.

2. Interview a participant in one of the more risky activities. Establish by careful questioning what benefits the individual derives from participation. Determine how closely this information correlates with the observations made in Ward's article.

3. Without necessarily participating in the activity, compose a series of journal entries that illustrate the feelings and experiences of a participant who regularly "enjoys" a risky activity. Try to explain how the activity alleviates the stresses of your life.

4. "Risks must be taken because the greatest risk in life is to risk nothing."
   Leo Buscaglia

a) In a small group, brainstorm examples of risk that you have taken and expect to take in the future.

b) On your own, identify three risks that you will commit yourself to take in the coming year. Close your eyes and visualize yourself in the process of taking each of the risks. In a journal entry describe what you saw yourself doing and explain how it made you feel.

COMMUNICATION PROJECTS

1. Imagine that you are a counsellor; present two 30-minute workshops to high school students on "Stress in Your Life—and How to Control It." Prepare audio-visual materials and handouts for each session.
   —Begin by getting to know your audience (your class would be a good choice) so that you can tailor the workshop to their needs: find out the common stresses, fears, needs, etc.
   —Contact relevant professional organizations explaining your project. Request research material and literature that you can hand out.
   —Write to a professional counsellor for tips on how to deliver a lively, interesting workshop. If possible, request permission to observe some workshops that the counsellor is presenting.
   —Organize your research into a good workshop format. Do a trial presentation for a small group and ask for comments. Incorporate any good ideas and suggestions.
   —Deliver your workshops to your class and any other appropriate, interested audience.

2. Survey a sample of your community to determine what people know about stress, its causes, and how to cope with it.
   —Decide how you intend to conduct your survey—by questionnaire, interview, telephone interview, etc.
   —Keep questions simple and the respondents anonymous.
   —Analyse responses and show results on charts and graphs.
   —Write a detailed report entitled, "Stress in the Community—Nature, Effect, and Coping Strategies."
   —Present your report to your class.

3. a) In a group, plan an advertising campaign to discourage teenagers from (a) smoking and (b) drug use.
   —Design a newspaper/magazine advertisement with copy, graphics, and a dramatic slogan.
   —Tape a radio commercial with a catchy jingle.
   —Script and role-play a television commercial. If video equipment is available, film your advertisement.
   —Design a dramatic poster that will drive home the dangers of cigarettes and drug use through graphically produced statistics.

   b) Ask your principal for permission to launch your campaign in the school.

   c) One month after the campaign, poll students to find out the effectiveness of the campaign.

▶ FUTURE PROMISES

You will be affected by a vast number of changes in your personal and working life. In this unit you will be asked to speculate on these changes and their implications for the future. You will be challenged to examine your role in a world faced with technological revolution, scarce natural resources, and the threat of nuclear war.

▶ ROBOTS THAT MAKE ROBOTS ARE HERE AND MACHINES THAT THINK MAY BE NEXT

George Brett

No other single invention or discovery since the steam engine has had as broad an impact on all sectors of the economy as microelectronics . . . The first industrial revolution enormously enhanced the puny muscular power of man and animals; the second will similarly extend human mental capacity.
—A report to the Club of Rome

No bigger than your thumb, the microchip is revolutionizing our lives, changing the way we work, shop, bank, are educated, and think.

The microchip controls computers, automatic teller machines, supermarket checkouts, and the assembly lines in many manufacturing plants.

The chip is the tiny "brain" inside computers and other electronic devices where calculating and other functions are performed. It contains thousands—and will soon contain millions—of electronic circuits.

The blurring speed of technological developments based on the microchip means these wonders are just over the horizon if not actually in use.

• The "factory of the future" is operating now in Japan where one firm uses robots to make robots, with humans doing only maintenance chores.

• The "fifth generation" computer, boasting artificial intelligence, is only a few years away. Some say it will think. Others say it will help humans think.

• This supermachine is behind Ronald Reagan's Star Wars plan. It will have almost unlimited application in industry and will be used to translate human languages and forecast weather patterns years away.

• At a Chrysler plant in Detroit, $500,000 a year is saved by a machine that cuts cloth, vinyl, and leather to patterns set by a computer.

• The extent of miniaturization is mind-boggling. In 20 years we will be able to put the contents of a reference library into a cubic-inch device.

• The home-computer explosion will likely see us banking from home and our children learning much of their basic knowledge there.

• You'll carry your medical record on a VISA-like card that can be read by scanners in hospitals and doctors' offices.

• Computers will come to the aid of the disabled. Already a Canadian device helps blind typists by reading aloud what has been typed so errors can be caught.

"What's happening today is that we are undergoing a second industrial revolution which is as transformative, if not more so, than the first," says William Hutchison, former chairman of the Canadian

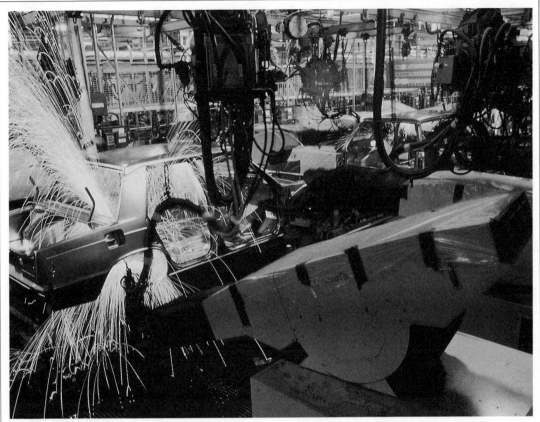

Advanced Technology Association.

"It's going to change the way we do business, the way we educate, the way we live our lives, the way we manage and operate, and even the way we think."

But it is estimated that for every six jobs the microchip creates, it will kill ten. The counter-argument: that if we don't create those six jobs they will be created in the United States or Japan.

Says David Vice, president of Northern Telecom Canada Ltd., "The issue facing Canadian industry today is performance—world-class performance. Nothing less will ensure our survival."

Vice said in a recent speech that "we are not in a recovery and we are not in a recession. What is occurring is much more important—we are changing economies" from one based on mechanical energy to an information economy.

The new information economy, he said, is dominated by "sophisticated information machines—computers and robots—rather than energy machines like the steam engine."

Nowhere is it more apparent how the new technology changes the economics of production and competition than at Chrysler Canada Ltd.'s mini-van plant in Windsor, where 128 robots paint, weld, and handle materials. On the automatic welding line, 58 robots have replaced 700 human workers.

On a smaller scale, six robots at IBM Canada Ltd.'s Don Mills plant assemble video-display terminals. Watched over by two people each on two shifts, they do a job that would require 18 people.

Robots excel in hostile environments, and Spar Aerospace Ltd. of Toronto is making use of the technology it used in developing the Canadarm for U.S. space shuttles in a $33 million joint venture with Ontario Hydro. A massive remote manipulator arm is being developed for retubing nuclear reactors.

But Denis Richards, a mechanical engineer who is involved with remote-handling systems marketing for Spar, says the ultimate use of robots is taking place at Yamanashi prefecture in Japan where robot manufacturer Fujitsu Fanuc is using robots to make robots. The factory is so automated that except for human overseers and maintenance workers, it operates for two shifts a day without human intervention.

The robot or computer, however, is an inanimate mass of parts that can do nothing for its human masters without a link between them, and that is the program, or software, stored as electrical pulses on a disc with a magnetic coating.

In the case of computers used in production, the software is often a particularly sophisticated kind called CAD/CAM.

With CAD (computer-aided design), specifications such as dimensions are entered into the computer, which then uses graphics to produce a three-dimensional image. The object can be "rotated" so the engineer can see it from different angles.

CAM (computer-aided manufacturing) refers to software used to instruct machines what to do in the manufacturing process. One of the virtues of CAM is the flexibility to replace high-volume production of identical items with the production of goods tailored to smaller markets.

"To the engineer and draftsman," says Robert Shoniker, president of Toronto-based Accugraph Corp., "computer-aided design is what word-processing is to a secretary. It takes away the drudgery of doing the drawing all over again."

"But more important to a company, it's one of the first steps into computer-aided design. It will tie manufacturing totally into the computer."

CAD can "take mathematical information on the design of say, a can, and feed it into a number of additional computer-aided systems"—for example, numerical control, systems analysis, material requirements planning, and robot manufacturing.

"It takes total control over a project."

Accugraph markets ACCU/CAD, which Shoniker describes as "a multi-purpose software package for mechanical engineers, with the capabilities of doing mechanical drawings, electrical schematics, piping diagrams, architectural drawings, and floor plans."

The impact of the microchip—representing the miniaturization to the nth degree of the technology that earlier produced the radio, radar, and television—has been astounding.

When John Leppik joined IBM Canada Ltd. in 1962 as a newly-graduated electrical engineer, his first major task was supervising the installation of an IBM 7090 computer at the University of Toronto.

"That was *the* big scientific number-cruncher in the country," he recalls. It cost about $3 million, occupied a huge room, and needed its own air-conditioning system.

"For most practical purposes," says Leppik, who left IBM Canada last year to set up a computer-applications consulting business, "today's desktop computer does the same thing."

Microelectronic devices have become workaday tools in many other ways.

There is the pocket calculator that makes everyday arithmetic painless; the greater reliability of "solid-state" entertainment equipment; the computers airlines use to make reservations and print out tickets; the terminals Bell Canada and Consumers' Gas use to quickly call up information on your account when you phone with a billing query.

Stockbrokers—who need to know prices *now*—were early and enthusiastic users of computer terminals linked to the Toronto Stock Exchange.

You probably have a plastic card that lets you make bank deposits and

withdrawals—even if you're in Montreal and your account is in Toronto. That's microelectronics at work.

It is actually a surprise these days to encounter a supermarket checkout using a manual cash register, rather than the familiar bar-code scanner that not only registers the price but gives you an itemized receipt. Scanners are also used by merchants and libraries to control inventory.

For people with home computers, the Bank of Montreal has two projects underway aimed at gathering information for the future implementation of a home-banking service. You would pay bills and get access to other banking services with the aid of a device hooked up to your personal computer.

In most offices, the IBM Selectric typewriter is still king. But the electronic office, with its word processors or linked microcomputers, is taking over in applications where there is a lot of information to store, alter, and manipulate.

This newspaper story was written on a computer keyboard, with the words appearing as they were typed on a TV-like monitor instead of on paper (though "print-outs" are available at the touch of a button). The computer lets the writer move paragraphs, insert or overwrite, and make other changes without retyping.

At the touch of a button, the story becomes available for an editor—at another terminal—to alter, then write headlines and captions. Another touch of the button and the story is "set in type" in a format the editor chooses.

Many of the electro-mechanical control mechanisms in our machines have gone electronic—in cars, dishwashers, washers and dryers, microwave ovens.

Hutchison predicts microelectronics "is going to transform just about any product we can think of, including computers, appliances, cameras, communications, mining, electrical systems, cars, trucks, trains, factory machines, office systems, forestry."

Amy Wohl, a Pennsylvania computer consultant, told a Toronto audience recently she thinks it's silly to suppose that in a few years we'll all be carrying little computers in briefcases when we travel.

"How many of you carry phones when you travel?" she asked rhetorically. Instead, Wohl said people will carry a plastic identification card which they'll use to gain access to computers installed in every hotel room so they can read electronic mail and write reports that will be flashed to their offices.

A similar technology is at the heart of a service announced last fall at six Canadian airports. Ten "teleport booths"—each consisting of a specially-equipped microcomputer—allow subscribers to send and receive electronic messages.

Computers can be the equalizer for disabled people in the job market. One example: David Kostyshyn, a Hamilton electronic consultant who is blind, has developed a device that allows a blind typist to correct errors by having a speech synthesizer read back what the person has typed.

And a program known as ACT—for Alternative Computer Training—was introduced in Toronto last year to provide training for the disabled in business-related computer programming.

Computer programs have paralleled the development of the machines themselves—from programs you needed a degree in computer science to understand to today's "user-friendly" software. William Hutchison says we're now moving toward "fifth generation" software, led by developments in Japan, the United States, and Britain.

"It will treat the computer more like a human," he says. "It'll say, 'Here are the facts; you decide'."

The concept behind artificial intelligence (AI)—the Hal of *2001: A Space Odyssey*—is that a machine with the ability to do human-like intuitive thinking in combination with enormous calculating power would give its human possessors an edge in any endeavour, industrial, or military.

With industrial applications in mind, the Japanese in 1981 launched a national effort to find artificial intelligence, with $850 million (U.S.) of public money to be spent in a decade.

And in 1983, with mainly military applications in mind, the U.S. Defense Department entered the race with a $600 million, five-year research program to develop fifth generation computers. (The first four generations are computers based on the vacuum tube, the transistor, the microchip, and the very-large-scale-integration chips, now coming into use.)

Washington's artificial intelligence program is co-ordinating the efforts of universities, industry, and the government in the development of a "completely autonomous weapons/battlefield management system."

The program would likely be the key to the space-borne strategic weapons in President Ronald Reagan's Star Wars program. But in addition the report envisages a computer of less than 225 kilograms (500 pounds) and enormous flexibility. In one application it could drive an unmanned land vehicle across country at up to 60 kilometres an hour for as much as 50 kilometres.

Computer scientist Douglas Lenat writes in Scientific American magazine that AI is likely to be developed but the challenge is tremendous. "Even a millionfold increase in computing power will not change the fact that most problems cannot be solved by brute force," he writes, "but only through the judicial application of knowledge to limit the search."

There are "professional systems" on the market using some principles of artificial intelligence, but a Calgary conference was told last year that the term artificial intelligence should be used sparingly. Dudley Allan, president of Control Data Canada Ltd., the only company in Canada to design and manufacture large-scale computers, stressed that artificially intelligent computers do not yet exist.

"Today's so-called artificially intelligent machines work only in full information domains," he explained. "A real intelligence system will work in grey areas, or partial information domains."

Leppik agrees. "I'm a believer in the immense potential (of microelectronics) but I draw a very specific line between what's possible and pure speculation.

"When you add a combination of logic and permanent memory—or active electronic storage—to the mind, you have tremendous potential. But I have never seen anything done with a computer that couldn't be done, conceptually at least, with cogs and levers.

"And I refuse to accept that anything I can build out of cogs and levers has any intelligence."

The effective work that has been done in this area is not artificial intelligence but simply pushing back the bounds of what we consider a machine capable of doing, Leppik says.

"We grew up thinking that arithmetic required intelligence, but a pocket calculator can now do all the multiplication and division you want," he says.

But Leppik has no reservations whatever about the ability of computers and their programs to "extend human mental capacity," as forecast in the quotation at the beginning.

The computer and its program "will help us think with few pains," he says. He suggests a doctor, working closely with a systems engineer, could design a program that would be a tremendous teaching aid in medical school.

By making the doctor straighten out inconsistencies in his or her thinking, the programmer and the doctor together could create a program 'smarter than he or she is'."

But this doesn't mean the machine would be thinking, Leppik stresses. What it boils down to is refining and "human interaction driven by the needs of a dumb computer. But it's purely a mechanical process."

READING AND REACTING

1. In a group, list all the applications of micro-technology described in the article. Discuss the impact of the micro-chip on business, industry, education, and on the way we live.

2. In a group, examine the ever-increasing role of robots in the workplace. Discuss the benefits and limitations of robotics.

3. a) In a class discussion, explore the concept of artificial intelligence and how it will affect our lives.

b) On your own, write a letter to the editor of your newspaper in which you express either your approval of or your fears about artificial intelligence.

4. "We are changing 'economies' from one based on mechanical energy to an information economy."
Explain to a partner what you think the speaker in the article means by this statement.

R E A C H I N G   O U T

1. Imagine that you are an engineer, and write a report in which you outline the specific ways in which you would use CAD (computer-aided design) and CAM (computer-aided manufacturing) to develop the product of your choice.

2. Correspond with several manufacturing companies to determine the extent of robotic use in each plant. If possible, arrange to interview one or two managers and workers to find out how they view the introduction of robots.

3. **a)** You are a candidate for president of the union and your platform includes job protection. Prepare a campaign speech to be delivered to union members in which you express your concern about the invasion of robots and how you plan to combat the resulting job loss. Present your speech to the class and be prepared to answer questions.

or

b) You are a personnel manager and your workers have just heard the speech in (a). Write a memo to all workers in which you explain the management's reasons for using robots and try to allay the workers' fears about job loss.

4. Write a short story that contains a warning about what can go wrong when people lose control over their inventions.

or

Write a short story set in the future when robots have replaced humans in the workplace. Convey to your readers how society functions and how people occupy their time.

5. View a videotaped series about the future of employment (e.g., T.V. Ontario's "Futurework" or Alvin Toffler's "The Third Wave"). Note the data provided, and in a class discussion, speculate on the kinds of work that will be needed in the year 2000.

▶ HEAD OF THE HOUSE

*The computerized home is smart enough
to run the household.*

Timothy Perrin

"Good morning. This is your house speaking."

"Good morning, house. What's on tap today?"

"It is now 6:30 a.m., Wednesday, October 30, 1985. You are due at work at 9 a.m. You have an 11:15 appointment with your dentist. Your daughter's birthday is Friday; have you bought her a present yet?"

"Oops! Thanks for the reminder."

"You're welcome. The bathroom is heated and your coffee will be ready when you finish your shower. Have a good day."

"Thank you house."

That conversation, while still pretty expensive, is almost within reach of current technology. In fact, the only part of it beyond an everyday price range is the talk itself. The house, without the friendly chit-chat, is available today for a lot less money than you would spend on a new car.

For example, in the southern California community of Lancaster, more than 40 percent of the buyers at a new housing project are paying an average $3,000 (U.S.) to have their homes controlled by a system called Smart Home I. One Pittsburgh-based construction company is installing a competing product, General Electric's HomeMinder system, in more than 8,000 houses across the U.S.

While these new homeowners won't be able to talk to their homes, they can program the house to wake them in the morning with gentle music, turn on lights and heat when they enter a room, prepare their morning coffee, water the lawn and, when they are out of the house, keep watch for intruders and fires. If the homeowners have health problems, the house can even call for help. Homeowners simply press switches on a small pendant worn around the neck which activate radio waves that house sensors detect.

The system being installed in the California homes, Smart Home I, is from the Boulder, Colorado company of Cyber-LYNX Computer Products Inc. It's an add-on system for Apple II and IBM computers. Using screen graphics and a floor plan of your home, you tell the computer to program the Smart Home control unit. You then disconnect the computer from the control unit and use the computer for other functions while the controller unit, usually no bigger than a standard-sized telephone, monitors the home.

You can schedule events for a particular time. For example, turning on the television for Hill Street Blues each Thursday, or arranging for things to happen when certain conditions are met, such as switching off lights and heat when your seven-year-old leaves the bedroom.

After you've gone to work, the system switches into a security mode and monitors your home for trouble. Using radio-controlled detectors on the windows and doors combined with motion detectors that sense an intruder's body heat, the system can be programmed to call the police if someone breaks in while you're away. It can even

recognize the difference between your cat or dog and a burglar. This is accomplished by aiming the motion detector higher than the animal. Most systems have a switch-off key, so if you are locked out and must break into your home, you'll be able to shut off the alarm without being taken for a burglar. Those same heat detectors, working with smoke alarms, can spot a fire and inform the fire department in time to minimize damage.

Prices for the Smart Home I start at about $1,300 (Can.) for a basic system. A full-blown system monitoring a dozen windows and doors, with two motion detectors, a thermostat device, a smoke detector, 12 devices to control lights and appliances, an alarm pendant, a 10-hour battery backup, an auto dialer to call the police and a hand-held remote controller would cost about $6,500.

The market for these kinds of home-con-

trol systems is expected to be massive. Timothy Schoechle, president of Cyber-LYNX, says studies by Apple Computer are predicting a potential billion-dollar annual market. General Electric has said that within a few years, more than half of all new homes will include some kind of computer control. But systems like the Smart Home I are still primitive. They must send signals by radio and through house wiring so they can be used in existing houses without tearing out walls. Their control of remote items in your home is fairly crude; while they can dim your lights, they are usually limited to on/off control of appliances.

However, in Rockville, Md., the National Association of Home Builders Research Foundation is working on the next generation of houses in a project called, coincidentally, the Smart House Project—the development of a computer-controlled house. It will have features similar to products like Smart Home I, but they will be built into the house wiring. Like a central vacuuming system, the program remains with the house when you sell it. (Because the Smart Home I is a unit added on to your computer, you take it with you to your next house.) "How smart it is depends on how much you want to spend," says Pieter VanderWerf of the NAHB. You do the programming, but, says VenderWerf, "You could have something that observes you going through the house, learns your lifestyle and then controls things for you."

But the Smart House is not just a computerized house. It is also a new wiring standard that is designed to takes homes into the next century. Today, many homes have half a dozen or more separate wiring systems. There is the standard 110-volt power circuitry, plus a 220-volt circuit for a stove or dryer, a 12-volt circuit for the doorbell, a heating-control system, the cable-TV system, the telephone system, and in some homes, a computer network. Each of these wiring layouts has to be installed separately, often by different contractors, and each is limited to one function.

The Smart House will have a single system that includes both power and communications capabilities in a single cable. The central computer will determine which signals go on which wires. If you want to use the outlet as a cable-TV outlet, the control system will recognize the difference and make the change.

Even the power wiring will be "smart" and designed to work with new kinds of appliances. Currently, everything in your house has to take the standard 120- or 220-volt alternating current found in house wiring. But more than 30 well-known appliance manufacturers including General Electric, Whirlpool, Carrier, Lennox, Honeywell, and Apple Computer, are designing new appliances that can tell the Smart House what kind of power they need.

Until you plug in your appliance, there will be very little power on the circuit. A computer chip on board the appliance will tell the house what power the appliance needs. One result could be cheaper, more energy-efficient appliances. Gone would be bulky, expensive components like your stereo's power supply, designed to turn 120 volts AC into the 5 volts DC the radio really needs. The system would also be safer. If your three-year-old sticks a screwdriver into a wall socket, the Smart House won't put any power into the circuit because a three-year-old holding a screwdriver doesn't have its own chip to tell the central computer what power to deliver.

Not too many years away are sophisticated voice-recognition and voice-synthesis systems that will allow you to carry on a conversation similar to that at the beginning of this article. Voice-synthesis systems are already quite impressive. Earlier this year, the University of Victoria's Centre for Speech Technology Research tested a voice-synthesis system that sounds incredibly lifelike, much more like the soothing voice of Kit, the intelligent car on TV's Knightrider, than the monotonal Cylons intoning "By your command" a few years ago on Battlestar Galactica. The big stumbling block is voice recognition. Systems currently available have high prices and limited vocabularies. The problem is programming a computer to not only recognize when one word ends and the next begins, but also to understand the nuance of inflection and to cut its way through various accents. It's a long way from the text book, "How do you do?" to "How y'all doin?"

Such systems are only five or six years from the marketplace. They are the ones that will allow you to say, "Turn up the hot tub a bit, will you? About 104 degrees Fahrenheit should be fine."

"Oh, house."

"Yes."

"Thanks. You've done a good job."

Reading and Reacting

1. In a small group, list all the features offered by Smart Home I, Homeminder, and Smart House. Develop an advertising campaign for your favourite house. Your campaign could include one or more of the following: newspaper and magazine advertisements (create eye-catching headlines, exciting copy, and appealing illustrations); television and radio spots; or a flyer for mailing. Provide as much information as you can about the house.

2. a) Prepare a summary of ten of the most intriguing features in the new houses described in the article.

   b) In a class discussion, rank the features in order of usefulness to the house owner.

   c) Conduct a survey of the class to determine how many favour the "smart" houses and how many prefer that houses remain the way they are. Present the results in a bar graph.

Reaching Out

1. In a small group, script and dramatize a comic scene in which a "smart house" malfunctions and causes (all kinds of) problems for its owners.

   or

   With a partner, compose a dialogue between a house of the future and its owner in which both parties have a disagreement about how the house is operated.

2. On your own or with a partner, plan and design your future dream house. Incorporate all the technological features you would like to satisfy your needs in terms of aesthetics, comfort, convenience, and recreation. Be as extravagant as you wish! Draw a detailed interior plan with all the features labelled. On an accompanying list, describe each special feature—its purpose and how it works. Either illustrate the exterior of the house or build a model of your dream house.

► Low Pay, Lack of a Job Carry No Stigma in Society of 2010

Lorne Slotnick

Elroy sits down at his computer terminal at the Acme Food Corp. and begins punching the buttons that control the gigantic bakery.

"You know, everything I do could have been programmed into the computer, so that my job would just mean sitting here like a bump on a log for six hours a day, waiting for an emergency to happen.

"But instead, I'm busy the whole time and, believe it or not, it's almost interesting.

"They're not stupid here. I guess they know that I could really wreck this place if I wasn't happy. So they have this big thing about 'job satisfaction.' They spend a lot of time trying to keep me happy. They still haven't caught on that I'd be a lot happier if they paid me properly, though.

"They've got this Input Committee. Every month, they want to know how we feel about our jobs and how they can make them better. I can't stand it. It's like some kind of therapy session, except sometimes you can get something accomplished.

"They had a computer keeping track of how much time we spent in the washroom. Some of us didn't like that so we made a fuss and they stopped it. At least they said they did.

"Oh, and they're so nice to our union. Meetings all the time. They want to know how we're all doing, if anything can be improved. It's just made most of us suspicious that they're trying to neutralize the union; we've had big debates about whether we should even co-operate. We do, for now. But most of us believe that a good boss is still a boss, so we still need a union."

There is no doubt that technology can destroy a skilled job and create in its place a deskilled job. In 1985, society has already seen that process at work in the manufacturing industry.

Some observers argue, however, that technology can give rise to new skills, and most experts agree that high-tech workplaces make management more dependent than ever before on the workers who run the new machines.

"This is why there will be more emphasis on loyalty," says Tom Rankin of the Ontario Quality of Working Life Centre. "There will be more dependence on workers both designing and operating systems."

And with an educated workforce, people will demand more of a say on the job. "People won't accept being treated like cogs," says Hans Van Beinum, who heads the centre. "We have to avoid what I call artificial ignorance—a dumb organization with smart machines."

This doesn't mean workers will have control over the means of production. The big decisions will continue to be made by a small minority, but smart business practice will dictate that workers have more control over their workplaces.

"The carrot-and-stick approach will increasingly break down," says D'Arcy Martin, Canadian education director for the

United Steelworkers of America. He says workers given meaningless jobs will engage in sabotage or what he calls "malicious obedience"—sticking so close to the rules that the organization is paralysed.

"Employers will have to stop it, and policing the workplace won't do it. Workers will always find a way around that. People will demand the restructuring of their jobs, and it will be done because it's more efficient."

History proves that it makes sense to keep people's minds stimulated, he says. "They made cake mixes where you just had to add water. It didn't sell. So they made cake mixes that you had to add water and an egg, and people bought it."

"You're doing a lot of talking about the workplace," Elroy says, "but you're forgetting that for many people nowadays, the workplace is right at home.

"Like my wife. She was a secretary down at the Legislature for a few years. Then they decided that, with computers, there was no reason for her to commute every day and she could do all her work on the computer at our house. There's thousands of people like that, just working from home. It saves the bosses huge amounts of money—no office space needed, for example.

"I guess there's both good and bad sides to it. Nobody's bugging you all day if you're working at home. As long as you get the work done, you can take a three-hour break, go out shopping, take care of the kids, or even drink yourself silly. And you can take on just a few hours a week if you want.

"But who wants to sit at home all day, with nobody to talk to? It's almost like a step backwards for women, who I think are most of the ones who work at home on computers.

"The pay is crummy, and there are all kinds of people waiting to do the job if you quit, because everybody knows how to use a computer. It's the classic deskilled job.

And the unions can't do anything—how are you going to organize a bunch of people who work at home? How could you get a strike going when the work can be so easily farmed out somewhere else? Where would you picket?"

Will people really need to work in 2010?

For much of society, the answer will be no. The experts tell us that even shorter work hours, longer vacations and sabbaticals for workers won't spread the work around enough for everyone to have a "job" in the current sense. "The connection between work and income, which made sense in a time of material scarcity, now leads to social inequity," says a recent report by Dr. Arthur Cordell of the Science Council of Canada. "Income distribution will in future have to take place through a variety of old, new, and as-yet-unimagined mechanisms."

The prospect of no "work" for a significant segment of society is scary.

"Whether you're conservative or radical, the reality is you can't allow people who have jobs to become an elite and the rest to become an underclass," says John Fryer, head of the National Union of Provincial Government Employees. "It would just mean a complete breakdown of our social fabric."

Proposals for a guaranteed income, such as the recent one in the Macdonald royal commission on the economy, view the idea as a way of tidying up Canada's social programs rather than as a replacement for work.

"But if you're going to design a society where there is no remunerative employment for significant numbers of people, then the guaranteed annual income has to generate a standard of living similar to those who are working."

That, as it has always been, is a political question, one that will not be determined by technology but by the battles between social forces over who will benefit from the technology.

READING AND REACTING

1. In a small group, compare Elroy's working conditions with the present situation. List the changes and consider whether they have been for the better.

2. Outline the changes that management will have to implement to ensure that job satisfaction is not lost with the advent of the new technology.

3. Elroy says that " . . . for many people nowadays, the workplace is right at home." In a group, discuss the pros and cons of working from the home instead of in an office. On your own, state your preference and explain why in one paragraph.

REACHING OUT

1. a) Discuss the implications of a guaranteed income and the difficulties future governments will face in trying to prevent a "complete breakdown of our social fabric" when a small, elite group of workers will have to support a large segment of the population.

   b) Invite a local politician to speak to the class about this issue. Prepare questions for him or her to answer.

2. Write a short story that has as its central character a person who
   a) cannot adjust to the concept of not working for a living

   or

   b) thoroughly enjoys receiving a guaranteed income and makes intelligent use of his or her time.

   Read your story to a small group and ask whether you have created a convincing protagonist.

▶ FUTURE PROMISES MORE LEISURE TIME BUT LESS MONEY

Mark Kingswell

It's the weekend. Another rough-and-tumble 25-hour work week is out of the way, and it's time to unwind and enjoy what really makes life worth living.

So what's it going to be this time?

Well, there's always Rent-a-Sub in Tobermory, Ont. It might be pleasant to spend a couple of days scouring the bottom of Lake Huron for shipwrecks in one of those submarines built for two. A little cramped, perhaps, but a lot more comfortable—and warmer—than scuba diving.

Or maybe a 48-hour canoe trip in one of the wilder corners of Canadian Shield National Park. It's becoming harder and harder to get away from all the other wilderness buffs, and the federal Government is starting to restrict the number of people in each park.

How about three days at Fantasy World, pretending to be a medieval knight, wielding a sword, saving the fair damsel from the mechanical dragon? But that costs a lot of money, and there isn't much to spare these days.

Perhaps a game of tennis, or bicycling with some friends. That wouldn't cost much and it should be possible to get some time on one of the 30 courts in your area.

The only problem is finding someone who isn't in the library, busy studying for the finals. Everyone seems to be going back to school or at least taking self-improvement courses.

"Leisure is the basis of culture," philosopher Josef Pieper said in 1947. In 2010, it will be the basis of most people's lives as well.

Not only will there be more people in the work force than in 1985, there will be less work available for them to do. Automation and computer aids will have eliminated many jobs, creating a burgeoning population of techno-peasants and reducing the average work week by 15 hours.

As most of us spend about 112 hours of each week awake (assuming an average of 8 hours of sleep each night), a 25-hour work week will leave 87 hours for personal maintenance and leisure.

Jobs no longer will form the centre of life, and recreation will be pursued for its own sake.

More people will take part in sports—especially less stressful or less demanding ones such as sailing, golf, swimming, and cycling—and get back to the land through camping and hiking.

More people will attend the theatre, opera, and concerts and more will go back to school to acquire new skills or knowledge.

But with a consumer-oriented, better-educated society, this might not be enough. The leisure industry might have to become more daring and creative in attracting the beloved buck, perhaps taking a tip from 1985 forecasts.

Charles Lemmon, a professor in the business school at the University of Western Ontario in London, Ontario, thinks that

"small, personal submarines will be as popular as snowmobiles are now. The next move from scuba diving is people out for a weekend in a submarine.

"And trips to space are going to be common. Also helicopters and gliding—they're both physically and mentally challenging."

Mr. Lemmon also thinks an aura of challenge will surround the leisure time of 2010; people will want to expand their horizons by exposure to the exotic and physically demanding.

Role-playing games such as those practised now by the Society for Creative Anachronism and "murder weekenders" will rise in popularity, he says.

"There will be a willingness to accept new leisure activities, and technological developments will make it easier to experiment."

But others are more cautious.

Thomas Atkinson, senior project manager for Hay Business Consultants in Toronto, sees an internal contradiction in the "leisure ethic" of Mr. Lemmon's scenarios.

"The reason the work week is going to be reduced is so the lower available income can be spread across the board," he says. "You can't have both increased leisure time and increased income. The economy doesn't work that way. People, by and large, aren't going to have more disposable income than they do now.

"I think the tendency is to work out ways to distribute the amount of available work more equitably, rather than allow a possibly violent two-class system. You won't have people who work and people who don't."

The result? More leisure hours but a lower dollar-to-hour ratio, meaning that people will spend a lot of time watching television.

Still, Mr. Atkinson predicts that such activities as car travel, hiking, camping, and individual sports will be the most popular.

"The population will be older, but they will be more fit," he said, referring to the phenomenon of the "baby boomer bulge" making its way up the age scale (the median age in 2010 will be 41 years, compared with 31 now). "They will favour inexpensive but healthy types of activities."

Apart from sports, most interest will focus on getting back to the land, but with a degree of relative comfort.

"There's going to be a much greater demand for access to national and provincial parks," Mr. Atkinson said. "There may have to be a certain amount of rationing or control of access by the government."

Stephen Smith, chairperson of the University of Waterloo's department of recreation and leisure studies, agrees that parks are going to be one of the keys in a revitalized Canadian tourist industry—perhaps expanding the system substantially by creating new parks in remote areas of the Canadian North.

"We'll see greater numbers of people in the parks, but the park experience will be strictly managed in new and imaginative ways. And we'll be exploring new environments, but using technology to ensure comfort."

So a submarine tour weekend isn't unlikely?

"Sure, there will be underwater parks, submarine tours, exploration of the Arctic in comfort. Regular trips to outer space will not be common, but they'll be something like a trip to Europe in our parents' or grandparents' day.

"The heavily motorized, powerful machine is also coming back," Mr. Smith suggests. "People will buy motor homes, sailboats, machines that they can add to and spend more money on."

He also thinks the increase in leisure time will be used for culturally significant purposes—cultivating the arts, applauding creative achievements, emphasizing individual development.

"Where we're going to see dramatic growth is in arts and culture. There will be fairly good times for publishing, newspapers, bookstores."

Mr. Smith, who has acted as a consultant to the federal Department of Tourism, thinks the ailing service industry will have to change some fundamental preconceptions if it is to meet the exigencies of the 21st century.

A renewed emphasis on Canada's big cities, together with good play for park land and natural leisure, will be the formula for success.

And, as some experts predict, such success will be necessary if Canada's economy—less and less able to be competitive in manufacturing—is to survive the projected atrophy of its primary and secondary industries.

Both Mr. Smith and Mr. Atkinson believe continuing adult education will occupy much of the available leisure time, with the traditional few weeks of vacation a year being replaced by extended leaves of absence and sabbatical years.

"This will work in part to reduce the number of people who are working," Mr. Smith predicts. "It will also contribute to a more well-rounded lifestyle. Mental health will probably be better, as well as physical health."

So there we'll be in 2010—healthier, better educated, more active, and better adjusted. It all sounds so wonderful, even without the personal submarines.

Is the world in for a golden age of intelligent, cultured activity carried out by fit, degree-laden baby boomers?

Not likely. The base facts of economic reality weigh against it. Even ancient Greece needed its slaves to function, and it simply won't be possible for Canada's deficit-prone economy to support an independent cultured leisure class—even if social pressures would allow it.

So competitiveness in the workplace will probably increase as the number of available work hours drops. Self-improvement may come to mean simple selfishness, those extra university courses just to step up the corporate ladder. Consumerism and materialism are here to stay.

"Yes, there will be a continued emphasis on consumerism—on shopping, buying, spending," Mr. Smith says. "Customers will be increasingly knowledgeable and conscious of trends. And spiritual pursuits will be manifested in reading or special interest clubs, not in meditation or reflection."

Mr. Pieper's hope—that increased leisure time would allow the freedom to tackle life's more profound metaphysical problems—will remain unrealized.

"There will be greater leisure time, yes," Mr. Atkinson says. "But mostly people will be doing the same kinds of things they are now."

READING AND REACTING

1. In a small group, discuss the implications of the term "techno-peasant." Define the term in one clear sentence.

2. With a partner, explore the possibilities of the leisure activities described in the article. Choose two of your favourite activities and create an inviting slogan to advertise each.

3. In a small group, examine the predictions of Charles Lemmon, Thomas Atkinson, and Stephen Smith about lifestyles in 2010. List those predictions that you think will be most likely to come true.

REACHING OUT

1. In a group of three or four, script a conversation between technocrats as they plan their weekly activities. Include both leisure and work activities. Role-play the scene for the class and ask for their views on the future lifestyle you have created.

2. "Jobs will no longer form the centre of life, and recreation will be pursued for its own sake."
   Survey a group of elderly people and a group of young people to find out whether they like or dislike this future scenario. Try to get your respondents to explain their reaction. Compile your data and present a report (of the survey) to the class. Is there a significant difference in perception between the two groups?

3. Select a business that can capitalize on people's new needs in the year 2010. Describe the product or service you would offer and how you plan to market it. If you have not already done so, you might like to read "Robots That Make Robots . . ." (p. 260), "Head of the House" (p. 267), and "Low Pay, Lack of a Job . . . " (p. 272) for some ideas.

THE FEELING OF POWER

Isaac Asimov

JEHAN SHUMAN WAS USED TO DEALING WITH THE MEN in authority on long-embattled Earth. He was only a civilian but he originated programming patterns that resulted in self-directing war computers of the highest sort. Generals consequently listened to him. Heads of congressional committees, too.

There was one of each in the special lounge of New Pentagon. General Weider was space-burnt and had a small mouth puckered almost into a cipher. Congressman Brant was smooth-cheeked and clear-eyed. He smoked Denebian tobacco with the air of one whose patriotism was so notorious, he could be allowed such liberties.

Shuman, tall, distinguished, and Programmer-first-class, faced them fearlessly.

He said, "This, gentlemen, is Myron Aub."

"The one with the unusual gift that you discovered quite by accident," said Congressman Brant placidly. "Ah." He inspected the little man with the egg-bald head with amiable curiosity.

The little man, in return, twisted the fingers of his hands anxiously. He had never been near such great men before. He was only an aging low-grade Technician who had long ago failed all tests designed to smoke out the gifted ones among mankind, and had settled into the rut of unskilled labour. There was just this hobby of his that the great Programmer had found out about and was now making such a frightening fuss over.

General Weider said, "I find this atmosphere of mystery childish."

"You won't in a moment," said Shuman. "This is not something we can leak to the firstcomer—Aub!" There was something imperative about his manner of biting off that one-syllable name, but then he was a great Programmer speaking to a mere Technician. "Aub! How much is nine times seven?"

Aub hesitated a moment. His pale eyes glimmered with a feeble anxiety. "Sixty-three," he said.

Congressman Brant lifted his eyebrows. "Is that right?"

"Check it for yourself, Congressman."

The congressman took out his pocket computer, nudged the milled edges twice, tooled at its face as it lay there in the palm of his hand, and put it back. He said, "Is this the gift you brought us here to demonstrate? An illusion?"

"More than that, sir. Aub has memorized a few operations and with them he computes on paper."

"A paper computer?" said the general. He looked pained.

"No sir," said Shuman patiently. "Not a paper computer. Simply a sheet of paper. General, would you be so kind as to suggest a number?"

"Seventeen," said the general.

"And you, Congressman?"

"Twenty-three."

"Good! Aub, multiply those numbers and please show the gentlemen your manner of doing it."

"Yes, Programmer," said Aub, ducking his head. He fished a small pad out of one shirt pocket and an artist's hairline stylus out of the other. His forehead corrugated as he made painstaking marks on the paper.

General Weider interrupted him sharply. "Let's see that."

Aub passed him the paper, and Weider said, "Well, it looks like the figure seventeen."

Congressman Brant nodded and said, "So it does, but I suppose anyone can copy figures off a computer. I think I could make a passable seventeen myself, even without practice."

"If you will let Aub continue, gentlemen," said Shuman without heat.

Aub continued, his hand trembling a little. Finally he said in a low voice, "The answer is three hundred and ninety-one."

Congressman Brant took out his computer a second time and flicked it. "By Godfrey, so it is. How did he guess?"

"No guess, Congressman," said Shuman. "He computed that result. He did it on this sheet of paper."

"Humbug," said the general impatiently. "A computer is one thing and marks on paper are another."

"Explain, Aub," said Shuman.

"Yes, Programmer—Well, gentlemen, I write down seventeen and just underneath it, I write twenty-three. Next I say to myself: seven times three—"

The congressman interrupted smoothly, "Now, Aub, the problem is seventeen times twenty-three."

"Yes, I know," said the little Technician earnestly, "but I *start* by saying seven times three because that's the way it works. Now seven times three is twenty-one."

"And how do you know that?" asked the congressman.

"I just remember it. It's always twenty-one on the computer. I've checked it any number of times."

"That doesn't mean it always will be though, does it?" said the congressman.

"Maybe not," stammered Aub. "I'm not a mathematician. But

"Humbug, . . . A computer is one thing and marks on paper are another."

281

I always get the right answers, you see."

"Go on."

"Seven times three is twenty-one, so I write down twenty-one. Then one times three is three, so I write down a three under the two of twenty-one."

"Why under the two?" asked Congressman Brant at once.

"Because—" Aub looked helplessly at his superior for support. "It's difficult to explain."

Shuman said, "If you will accept his work for the moment, we can leave the details for the mathematicians."

Brant subsided.

Aub said, "Three plus two makes five, you see, so the twenty-one becomes a fifty-one. Now you let that go for a while and start fresh. You multiply seven and two, that's fourteen, and one and two, that's two. Put them down like this and it adds up to thirty-four. Now if you put the thirty-four under the fifty-one this way and add them, you get three hundred and ninety-one and that's the answer."

There was an instant's silence and then General Weider said, "I don't believe it. He goes through this rigmarole and makes up numbers and multiplies and adds them this way and that, but I don't believe it. It's too complicated to be anything but hornswoggling."

"Oh no, sir," said Aub in a sweat. "It only *seems* complicated because you're not used to it. Actually, the rules are quite simple and will work for any numbers."

"Any numbers, eh?" said the general. "Come then." He took out his own computer (a severely styled GI model) and struck it at random. "Make a five seven three eight on the paper. That's five thousand seven hundred and thirty-eight."

"Yes, sir," said Aub, taking a new sheet of paper.

"Now," (more punching of his computer), "seven two three nine. Seven thousand two hundred and thirty-nine."

"Yes, sir."

"And now multiply those two."

"It will take some time," quavered Aub.

"Take the time," said the general.

"Go ahead, Aub," said Shuman crisply.

Aub set to work, bending low. He took another sheet of paper and another. The general took out his watch finally and stared at it. "Are you through with your magic-making, Technician?"

"I'm almost done, sir. Here it is, sir. Forty-one million, five hundred and thirty-seven thousand, three hundred and eighty-two." He showed the scrawled figures of the result.

General Weider smiled bitterly. He pushed the multiplication contact on his computer and let the numbers whirl to a halt. And then he stared and said in a surprised squeak, "Great Galaxy, the fella's right."

The President of the Terrestrial Federation had grown haggard in office and, in private, he allowed a look of settled melancholy to appear on his sensitive features. The Denebian war, after its early start of vast movement and great popularity, had trickled down into a sordid matter of manoeuvre and countermanoeuvre, with discontent rising steadily on Earth. Possibly it was rising on Deneb, too.

And now Congressman Brant, head of the important Committee on Military Appropriations, was cheerfully and smoothly spending his half-hour appointment spouting nonsense.

"Computing without a computer," said the president impatiently, "is a contradiction in terms."

"Computing," said the congressman, "is only a system for handling data. A machine might do it, or the human brain might. Let me give you an example." And, using the new skills he had learned, he worked out sums and products until the president, despite himself, grew interested.

"Does this always work?"

"Every time, Mr. President. It is foolproof."

"Is it hard to learn?"

"It took me a week to get the real hang of it. I think you would do better."

"Well," said the president, considering, "it's an interesting parlour game, but what is the use of it?"

"What is the use of a newborn baby, Mr. President? At the moment there is no use, but don't you see that this points the way towards liberation from the machine. Consider, Mr. President," the congressman rose and his deep voice automatically took on some of the cadences he used in public debate, "that the Denebian war is a war of computer against computer. Their computers forge an impenetrable field of counter-missiles against our missiles, and ours forge one against theirs. If we advance the efficiency of our computers, so do they theirs, and for five years a precarious and profitless balance has existed.

"Now we have in our hands a method for going beyond the computer, leapfrogging it, passing through it. We will combine the mechanics of computation with human thought; we will have the equivalent of intelligent computers: billions of them. I can't predict what the consequences will be in detail but they will be incalculable. And if Deneb beats us to the punch, they may be unimaginably catastrophic."

The president said, troubled, "What would you have me do?"

"Put the power of the administration behind the establishment of a secret project on human computation. Call it Project Number, if you like. I can vouch for my committee, but I will need the administration behind me."

"But how far can human computation go?"

"There is no limit. According to Programmer Shuman, who first introduced me to this discovery—"

"I've heard of Shuman, of course."

"Yes. Well, Dr. Shuman tells me that in theory there is nothing the computer can do that the human mind cannot do. The computer merely takes a finite amount of data and performs a finite number of operations upon them. The human mind can duplicate the process."

The president considered that. He said, "If Shuman says this, I am inclined to believe him—in theory. But, in practice, how can anyone know how a computer works?"

Brant laughed genially. "Well, Mr. President, I asked the same question. It seems that at one time computers were designed directly by human beings. Those were simple computers, of course, this being before the time of the rational use of computers to design more advanced computers had been established."

"Yes, yes. Go on."

"Technician Aub apparently had, as his hobby, the reconstruction of some of these ancient devices and in so doing he studied the details of their workings and found he could imitate them. The multiplication I just performed for you is an imitation of the workings of a computer."

"Amazing!"

"What is the use of a newborn baby, Mr. President?"

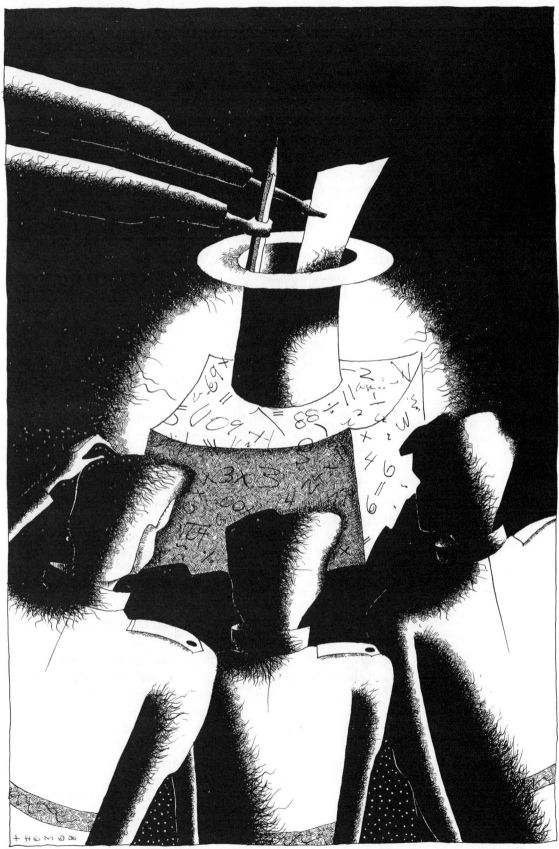

The congressman coughed gently. "If I may make another point, Mr. President—The further we can develop this thing, the more we can divert our Federal effort from computer production and computer maintenance. As the human brain takes over, more of our energy can be directed into peacetime pursuits and the impingement of war on the ordinary man will be less. This will be more advantageous for the party in power, of course."

"Ah" said the president, "I see your point. Well, sit down, Congressman, sit down. I want some time to think about this.—But meanwhile, show me that multiplication trick again. Let's see if I can catch the point of it."

Programmer Shuman did not try to hurry matters. Loesser was conservative, very conservative and liked to deal with computers as his father and grandfather had. Still, he controlled the West European computer combine, and if he could be persuaded to join Project Number in full enthusiasm, a great deal would be accomplished.

But Loesser was holding back. He said, "I'm not sure I like the idea of relaxing our hold on computers. The human mind is a capricious thing. The computer will give the same answer to the same problem each time. What guarantee have we that the human mind will do the same?"

> "The human mind is a capricious thing."

"The human mind, Computer Loesser, only manipulates facts. It doesn't matter whether the human mind or a machine does it. They are just tools."

"Yes, yes. I've gone over your ingenious demonstration that the mind can duplicate the computer, but it seems to me a little in the air. I'll grant the theory but what reason have we for thinking that theory can be converted to practice?"

"I think we have reason, sir. After all, computers have not always existed. The cave men with their triremes, stone axes, and railroads had no computers."

"And possibly they did not compute."

"You know better than that. Even the building of a railroad or a ziggurat called for some computing, and that must have been without computers as we know them."

"Do you suggest they computed in the fashion you demonstrate?"

"Probably not. After all, this method—we call it 'graphitics,' by the way, from the old European word 'grapho' meaning 'to write'—is developed from the computers themselves so it cannot have antedated them. Still, the cave men must have had *some* method, eh?"

"Lost arts! If you're going to talk about lost arts—"

"No, no. I'm not a lost art enthusiast, though I don't say there may not be some. After all, man was eating grain before hydroponics, and if the primitives ate grain, they must have grown it in soil. What else could they have done?"

"I don't know, but I'll believe in soil-growing when I see some-one grow grain in soil. And I'll believe in making fire by rubbing two pieces of flint together when I see that, too."

Shuman grew placative. "Well, let's stick to graphitics. It's just part of the process of etherealization. Transportation by means of bulky contrivances is giving way to direct mass transference. Communications devices become less massive and more efficient constantly. For that matter, compare your pocket computer with the massive jobs of a thousand years ago. Why not, then, the last step of doing away with computers altogether? Come, sir, Project Number is a going concern; progress is already headlong. But we want your help. If patriotism doesn't move you, consider the intellectual adventure involved."

Loesser said sceptically, "What progress? What can you do beyond multiplication? Can you integrate a transcendental function?"

"In time, sir. In time. In the last month I have learned to handle division. I can determine, and correctly, integral quotients and decimal quotients."

"Decimal quotients? To how many places?"

Programmer Shuman tried to keep his tone casual. "Any number!"

Loesser's lower jaw dropped. "Without a computer?"

"Set me a problem."

"Divide twenty-seven by thirteen. Take it to six places."

Five minutes later, Shuman said, "Two point oh seven six nine two three."

Loesser checked it. "Well, now, that's amazing. Multiplication didn't impress me too much because it involved integers after all, and I thought trick manipulation might do it. But decimals—"

"And that is not all. There is a new development that is, so far, top secret and which strictly speaking, I ought not to mention. Still—we may have made a breakthrough on the square root front."

"Square roots?"

"It involves some tricky points and we haven't licked the bugs yet, but Technician Aub, the man who invented the science and who has an amazing intuition in connection with it, maintains he has the problem almost solved. And he is only a Technician. A man like yourself, a trained and talented mathematician, ought to have no difficulty."

"Square roots," muttered Loesser, attracted.

"Cube roots, too. Are you with us?"

Loesser's hand thrust out suddenly. "Count me in."

General Weider stumped his way back and forth at the head of the room and addressed his listeners after the fashion of a

". . . I'll believe in soil-growing when I see someone grow grain in soil."

savage teacher facing a group of recalcitrant students. It made no difference to the general that they were the civilian scientists heading Project Number. The general was the overall head, and he so considered himself at every waking moment.

He said, "Now square roots are all fine. I can't do them myself and I don't understand the methods, but they're fine. Still, the Project will not be sidetracked into what some of you call the fundamentals. You can play with graphitics any way you want to after the war is over, but right now we have specific and very practical problems to solve."

In a far corner, Technician Aub listened with painful attention. He was no longer a Technician, of course, having been relieved of his duties and assigned to the project, with a fine-sounding title and good pay. But, of course, the social distinction remained and the highly placed scientific leaders could never bring themselves to admit him to their ranks on a footing of equality. Nor, to do Aub justice, did he, himself, wish it. He was as uncomfortable with them as they with him.

The general was saying, "Our goal is a simple one, gentlemen: the replacement of the computer. A ship that can navigate space without a computer on board can be constructed in one-fifth the time and at one-tenth the expense of a computer-laden ship. We could build fleets five times, ten times, as great as Deneb could if we could but eliminate the computer.

"And I see something even beyond this. It may be fantastic now, a mere dream; but in the future I see the manned missile!"

There was an instant murmur from the audience.

"A man is much more dispensable than a computer."

The general drove on. "At the present time, our chief bottleneck is the fact that missiles are limited in intelligence. The computer controlling them can only be so large, and for that reason they can meet the changing nature of anti-missile defences in an unsatisfactory way. Few missiles, if any, accomplish their goal and missile warfare is coming to a dead end; for the enemy, fortunately, as well as for ourselves.

"On the other hand, a missile with a man or two within, controlling flight by graphitics, would be lighter, more mobile, more intelligent. It would give us a lead that might well mean the margin of victory. Besides which, gentlemen, the exigencies of war compel us to remember one thing. A man is much more dispensable than a computer. Manned missiles could be launched in numbers and under circumstances that no good general would care to undertake as far as computer-directed missiles are concerned—"

He said much more but Technician Aub did not wait.

Technician Aub, in the privacy of his quarters, laboured long over the note he was leaving behind. It read finally as follows:

"When I began the study of what is now called graphitics, it

was no more than a hobby. I saw no more in it than an interesting amusement, an exercise of mind.

"When Project Number began, I thought that others were wiser than I; that graphitics might be put to practical use as a benefit to mankind, to aid in the production of really practical mass-transference devices perhaps. But now I see it to be used only for death and destruction.

"I cannot face the responsibility involved in having invented graphitics."

He then deliberately turned the focus of a protein-depolarizer on himself and fell instantly and painlessly dead.

They stood over the grave of the little Technician while tribute was paid to the greatness of his discovery.

Programmer Shuman bowed his head along with the rest of them, but remained unmoved. The Technician had done his share and was no longer needed, after all. He might have started graphitics, but now that it had started, it would carry on by itself overwhelmingly, triumphantly, until manned missiles were possible, with who knew what else.

Nine times seven, thought Shuman with deep satisfaction, is sixty-three, and I don't need a computer to tell me so. The computer is in my own head.

And it was amazing the feeling of power that gave him.

READING AND REACTING

1. In a small group, compare the social and political structure of the Terrestrial Federation with that of our society. List the similarities and differences.

2. On a chart, show the class distinctions in the Terrestrial Federation.

3. Imagine that you are Congressman Brant and write a letter to the President in which you argue in favour of human computation and explain how you propose to use it to benefit the Terrestrial Federation.

4. You are a book illustrator and you have been commissioned to draw pictures of these characters: Myron Aub, General Weider, and Congressman Brant. Try to show their personalities through your illustrations.

5. Imagine that you are Aub and record, in a series of journal entries, the events on the day of your presentation to General Weider; the changes in your life after your "discovery"; and why you decided to end it all in suicide. Your journal entries should reveal your feelings while recording events.

REACHING OUT

1. In a small group, speculate on the possible loss of our present faculties and skills and the development of new skills as technology takes over. List the "losses" and "gains" and provide a brief rationale for each item.

2. Interview elderly relatives and friends to find out the kind of education they received in mathematics. Compare the skills that they were taught with those that you are being taught. Identify similarities and differences and in a class discussion try to explain why things have changed.

▶ IN THE NEXT WAR

Robert Priest

In the next war don't drop the bomb
drop the excess wheat
drop the sacks of grain
and the powdered milk we have too
     much of
Send our best men over
in daring flights
their bombers full
of fish eggs, huge cheeses
and birthday cake icings
Don't machine gun our enemies
rather let us scrape off our plates
and pelt them with our leftover squash
we must inundate them with sauces
     and gravies
every day a new and better recipe
We have the technology to do this
We have the invisible aircraft
now we must make an undetectable
     red rocket
a holy sky train that drops a mountain
of Kraft dinners and Coke
Bury the Kremlin in spaghetti
minute rice and mashed potatoes
This will be a new kind of war
it will take sacrifice and patience
every one will have to put something
     aside
for the enemy
we will start
with the ham and eggs
saving for the very end
our big weapon
the hamburger

READING AND REACTING

1. In a class discussion, examine the concept of irony and how Priest uses it in this poem.

2. In a small group, identify the enemy in this poem. Justify your interpretation in a short paragraph. Exchange your writing with other groups and compare interpretations.

3. You are a television reporter who "survived" the bombardment described in the poem. File a first-hand report of the scene. Read your account to the class in your best newscaster's voice.

4. Illustrate a scene of the aftermath of the war described in the poem.

REACHING OUT

1. In a small group, define the words "war" and "enemy," and compare your definitions with those of other groups.

a) In a small group, predict the nature of the next war and brainstorm innovative ways of dealing with the enemy.

b) Write your own "war poem" in which you express your view about war. Exchange poems and compare perceptions about war.

c) Choose the best poems and compile a class anthology of these "war poems."

2. In a small group, collect information on famine and world poverty.

a) Compile a report describing the current situation. Illustrate with graphs, pictures, and maps. In a blueprint for change, suggest solutions to the problems.

b) Write to various hunger relief programs for information. Compare services offered, advantages, distribution, and financial administration of each charity.

c) Choose a charity to support, based on your information. As a class/school project raise funds to support the organization.

▶ THE HORSES

Edwin Muir

Barely a twelvemonth after
The seven days war that put the world to sleep,
Late in the evening the strange horses came.
By then we had made our covenant with silence,
But in the first few days it was so still
We listened to our breathing and were afraid.
On the second day
The radios failed; we turned the knobs; no answer.
On the third day a warship passed us, heading north,
Dead bodies piled on the deck. On the sixth day
A plane plunged over us into the sea. Thereafter
Nothing. The radios dumb;
And still they stand in corners of our kitchens,
And stand, perhaps, turned on, in a million rooms
All over the world. But now if they should speak,
If on a sudden they should speak again,
If on the stroke of noon a voice should speak,
We would not listen, we would not let it bring
That old bad world that swallowed it's children quick
At one great gulp. We would not have it again.
Sometimes we think of the nations lying asleep,
Curled blindly in impenetrable sorrow,
And then the thought confounds us with its strangeness.

The tractors lie about our fields; at evening
They look like dank sea-monsters couched and waiting.
We leave them where they are and let them rust:
"They'll moulder away and be like other loam."
We make our oxen drag our rusty ploughs,
Long laid aside. We have gone back
Far past our fathers' land.
                                    And then, that evening
Late in the summer the strange horses came.
We heard a distant tapping on the road,
A deepening drumming: it stopped, went on again

And at the corner changed to hollow thunder.
We saw the heads
Like a wild wave charging and were afraid.
We had sold our horses in our fathers' time
To buy new tractors. Now they were strange to us
As fabulous steeds set on an ancient shield
Or illustrations in a book of knights.
We did not dare go near them, yet they waited,
Stubborn and shy, as if they had been sent
By an old command to find our whereabouts
And that long-lost archaic companionship.
In the first moment we had never a thought
That they were creatures to be owned and used.
Among them were some half-a-dozen colts
Dropped in some wilderness of the broken world,
Yet new as if they had come from their own Eden.
Since then they have pulled our ploughs and borne our loads,
But that free servitude still can pierce our hearts.
Our life is changed; their coming our beginning.

READING AND REACTING

1. a) In a small group, list the words and phrases that the poet uses to convey the feeling of desolation in the first part of the poem and the sense of regeneration in the second half.

   b) On your own, express the same feelings in two prose paragraphs.

   or

   Capture the feelings of desolation and regeneration in two illustrations or a collage that accurately depicts the scenes as they are described in the poem.

2. In a group, discuss the significance of the strange horses that came "Barely a twelvemonth" after the war.

3. With a partner, discuss what the poet means by the following lines:

   a) "We have gone back
   Far past our fathers' land."

   b) "But that free servitude still can pierce our hearts.
   Our life is changed; their coming our beginning."

   Express your interpretation of each set of lines in one paragraph. Compare your interpretations with those of your classmates.

REACHING OUT

1. With a partner, role-play a conversation between the narrator of the poem and his or her grandchild, in which the grandparent describes the events that followed the seven day war and the regeneration process, and also answers questions from the child.

2. In a small group, brainstorm other titles for the poem.

3. In a small group, make a taped reading of the poem with appropriate musical accompaniment.

   or

   Develop a sound poem to dramatize the story in "The Horses." Use any sounds that you think best capture the moods and events of the poem. Perform your composition for the class or divide the class into sections (with each section producing one set of sounds) and lead your classmates through your choral interpretation of the poem.

   or

   Make a tape collage of the poem. Use music, voices, and sounds to represent the events of the poem.

EXTINCTION IS FOREVER

Louise Lawrence

VANYA STARED ACROSS THE VAST RUINS OF A CIVILIZATION,
devastated miles of tumbled concrete, twisted girders and the
blackened remains of walls. It was nothing to do with the venge-
ance of God, Kermondley said. It was the result of a nuclear
holocaust. All her life Vanya had known about the holocaust and
many times she had played among the ruins of towns and cities
on the edge of the lifeless land. But this time it was different or
maybe she was different . . . older and more understanding. She
had listened to Kermondley teaching history as once she had
listened to the sea-wives telling fairy tales but now, suddenly, it
all became real and she sensed the almighty meaning.

The Ancients were not simply a legendary race, just marble
statues in the sea-museums, cold carved forms of men and women,
art works and artefacts and strange-sounding names. Rodin and
Renoir and Richard Burton had really existed, as real and alive
as she was now. Here, where the wind mourned and sighed across
a loneliness of bones and dust, had been a city full of people.

"They called themselves *homo sapiens*," Kermondley said. "Who
can tell me the meaning of *homo sapiens*?"

"Wise man?" someone said.

Kermondley nodded.

"They were joking, of course."

The students laughed.

Everyone knew that the Ancients had engineered their own
extinction. Such appalling termination was nothing to laugh at,
Vanya thought. Even Kermondley showed no respect for history,
no reverence for his ancestors, no grief for the various millions
of life-forms that had been lost. What Vanya felt was a terrible
pity for the stupidity of *homo sapiens*. But all around the laughter
rose like mockery, shrill as the cries of extinct birds drifting inland
from the shore, carried by the wind towards the silence.

Steven moved among the wreckage of the Third World War. The
dial on his time-machine had stopped midway through the thirty-
first century and time on his wrist watch showed a quarter
past noon. Two hours ago it had been 1995 and himself a student
of physics at the University of London, watching the peace

> *Rodin and
> Renoir and
> Richard Burton
> had really
> existed.*

campaigners marching to Trafalgar Square.

"Are they right to demand the abolition of nuclear weapons?" Professor Goddard had murmured. "Or is it, as the government claims, only the threat of nuclear war that guarantees world peace?"

Steven shrugged, loaded the video-camera.

It took proof, not opinions, to convince governments.

"I'll bring back a film of the end of the world," he had promised.

"I prefer to hope you will film the future of the human race," the old professor had replied.

But that had been in 1995.

Then it was still possible to hope.

It was even possible to believe the human race had a future.

But Steven had seen them commit the unforgivable act. He had seen the white clouds mushroom over England and the black ash falling on the land. He had witnessed the whimpering aftermath of the war they said would never happen, the hell of human dying and genetic decline. What new life was born sickened and failed . . . plant, animal and human. It seemed that nothing survived. After a thousand years there was only ruins and silence, the moan of the wind and the wash of the waves against the shore. What Steven had on film was proof of destruction, desolation without hope. But suddenly, far away and strangely incongruous . . . he heard laughter.

"Don't laugh at them!" Vanya cried.

It was an odd thing to say, an odd reaction . . . as if she believed the Ancients listened, a city full of ghostly souls made vulnerable by genocide and shame. There were tears in her eyes as she turned away. And then Kermondley understood . . . Vanya had realized that history had really happened and all his years of teaching were suddenly worthwhile.

He watched her swim towards the shore, the line of wharfs and rusting wrecks of ships and fallen warehouses. He saw her reach the flight of crumbled steps, her webbed hands heaving herself up in one lithe arching motion of water and light, reflections of sky on wet scales.

"Where's she going?" someone asked him.

"Do we follow?" asked another.

Kermondley shook his head.

He remembered himself at Vanya's age. He remembered the moment when history had come alive for him too. In another city, just like this one, he had felt the anguish of the Ancients dying, heard the scream of unborn generations echoing through time. He too had been felled by feelings of horror and grief. But now Kermondley could laugh at the arrogance of those who had called themselves wise . . . for his kind had been formed among the ashes of their world and he was glad they had not survived.

"I'll bring back a film of the end of the world."

Steven walked towards the sound of distant voices, his footsteps silent in the dust. He came to water and acres of drowned streets, a great river estuary where Thames-side London had been. In a stench of sea-weed and barnacles he saw her haul herself on to the land. He realized then that she was human . . . or had been.

He closed his eyes, leaned against the vitrified remains of a doorpost, waited for the horror and repulsion to subside and his thoughts to become rational. He should have expected it. He should have known if anything survived the holocaust it was bound to be a mutation. He remembered the banners the peace campaigners had carried . . . EXTINCTION IS FOREVER, they said.

And maybe it was not enough to build a time-machine, not enough to present the governments of the world with evidence of genocide. Maybe it would not persuade them to disarm. And simply by establishing their nuclear arsenals they had already accepted the possibility that untold millions of people would die. The public too had already accepted it. Mass destruction was a box office hit. Earthquakes, infernos, nuclear war itself was being shown in every local cinema. People actually paid to watch it!

Sometimes Steven believed that the human race was willing its own annihilation, that it was a suicide instinct triggered naturally whenever the species put too great a strain upon the environment. Rabbits failed to breed . . . lemmings flung themselves from a cliff and drowned in the sea . . . and human beings went to war. It was a biological fail-safe, a way of preserving the species by reducing the number of individuals. But this time they would go too far.

Extinction was forever.

But maybe if they knew what they would become . . .

Steven raised the video-camera. This was the hope Professor Goddard had asked for. This was the future of the human race, a true daughter of the holocaust . . . a scaly mutant, mackerel-coloured, sea-dwelling. And out in the estuary a whole shoal of them!

Vanya let the dry dust trickle through her fingers. The past belonged to her and all that once lived was as real and precious as she was now. She saw a sungleam break through the clouds, gold light touching the crumbled heart of the city, making it sacred. The stillness was so intense she was almost afraid. Out in the estuary the swimmers turned towards the distant beach. Vanya was tempted to rejoin them but something moved within the darkness of a broken doorway. Something emerged from the shadows and became a man.

Homo sapiens was not extinct!

The camera whirred and clicked.

And Vanya's voice was a scream across the open water.

"Kermondley! Come back!"

Steven gaped at her.

He realized then that she was human . . . or had been.

Her voice was beautiful, clear as a bell or a bird call, a sonar echo or a siren's song . . . each word pure and distinct in perfect English. She was not some kind of human subspecies. She was a being in her own right who perceived and communicated and was aware. Her bright aquamarine eyes regarded him nervously, her curiosity tinged with fear.

"I won't hurt you," Steven assured her.

One webbed finger pointed to the camera.

"You carry a weapon!" she said.

"It's a video-machine," he corrected.

"You used to kill," she said. "All the Ancients did. They killed everything that lived upon the land . . . including themselves."

"Hell!" said Steven. "Is that all that has survived of us . . . our blasted murderous reputation?"

Kermondley would never know what caused him to look back. Perhaps unconsciously he heard her cry or sensed her fear. For a while he could see nothing but the dazzle of light on water and waves swilling around the broken dome of St. Paul's cathedral. But then on the sky-line of land he saw that Vanya was not alone. Someone was with her, framed in a sunlit doorway . . . the dark silhouette of a man.

Kermondley blinked.

He was reminded of the small bronze statuette he had dredged from the silt of sunken towns around Southampton water. But this was no museum piece. This man was alive . . . a figure that moved as Vanya moved, approached as she retreated, paused and raised his hands in the age-old gesture of peace or surrender.

Above the drowned spans of antique bridges Kermondley trod water and could not believe his eyes. The Ancients had become extinct a thousand years ago . . . like dodos and mastodons they were gone from the world. World-over the land had decayed to deserts of dust, supported no life larger than lizards and sandflies and forests of sparse vegetation that clung to the rivers' reaches. Not even birds had survived. Yet Kermondley saw a man.

He called the students back.

"Tell me I'm dreaming," Kermondley said.

They looked at him, puzzled.

"Over on the shore where Vanya is . . . what do you see?" Kermondley asked them. "What do you make of that shape in the doorway that looks to me like a man?"

Not even birds had survived. Yet Kermondley saw a man.

"Everything died of radiation," Vanya said. "But the oceans diffused it and the seas contained our only source of food. So we had to adapt and become aquatic. We had to hunt the shoals of fish hundreds of miles from the nearest shore, and cultivate seaweed . . ."

Steven stared at her.

It was not mutation she talked of.

It was evolution.

Natural selection, which should have taken millions of years, had created a different species within a few generations. Men had to swim for survival . . . their skin turning to scales, feet to flippers. Now, looking at Vanya, not much remained of her human ancestry . . . just her voice, her aquamarine eyes and the pale breasts that made her female.

"Do you breed under water?" he asked her.

Vanya felt embarrassed.

The way Steven looked at her, the way he questioned her . . . it was as if he regarded her as some kind of biological specimen, as if sea-people were no different from dolphins or seals. Maybe he imagined her among a colony, hauled up like sea-cows on a barren beach to wait for the breeding season. He did not seem to realize . . .

"There are cities under the sea," she said primly.

"Half of London by the look of it," Steven said.

"Not ruins!" said Vanya. "Living cities! Pressurized domes full of warmth and light! Sea gardens bloom beyond our windows in colours like the land has never known. We have music and drama, museums and galleries and schools of learning. Under the sea we eat and sleep and, yes, we breed."

An underwater civilization!

Incredulity showed on Steven's face, turned to nervousness as he saw Kermondley re-crossing the estuary, his dark shape speeding through the water followed by a dozen more. Suddenly Steven realized that *he* was the alien, the intruder, out of place and out of time. And if the sea-people could build cities under the ocean they were even more accomplished than the human race, more advanced, more intelligent . . . maybe more dangerous.

Muscles rippled, flashed and shone with blue-green sheen as Kermondley gained the lower steps and started to climb. Steven backed away. Stones from a wall slipped and fell as he knocked against it and the video-camera hung heavy and useless around his neck. He wished he had brought a gun, or a harpoon . . . something to defend himself with . . . anything. His fingers gripped a jagged lump of concrete as the rest of the sea people crowded on to the land.

"Stay right where you are!" Steven howled.

"Stay right where you are!" Steven howled.

Vanya laughed.

"We're all quite harmless," she said. "It's only the history class and Kermondley who teaches us. He always said history was alive but I bet he never expected to meet a real live *homo sapiens* who should have been extinct!"

Kermondley stopped, not because he was afraid of being struck by a lump of concrete but because he sensed the Ancient was afraid. He probably recognized the sea-people as aquatic descendants of his own race and expected them to display the same mistrust, the same tendency to attack first and ask questions afterwards. He motioned the students to stay behind him, waited as Vanya laughed her reassurances, then bowed his head in greeting. Not by the flicker of an eyelid did Kermondley betray his own, more terrible fear.

"Be welcome, *homo sapiens*," Kermondley said.

"His name's Steven," said Vanya.

"And we were hardly wise," Steven admitted.

Kermondley smiled.

"It's a little late to realize that, my friend."

"Not where I come from," Steven said.

"Space?" Kermondley said hopefully.

"Time," said Steven. "1995."

Kermondley nodded.

His fear was established now.

"I thought perhaps you had returned from the stars," Kermondley said. "A space traveller cryogenically frozen for ten centuries. I didn't know the Ancients actually invented a machine that could travel time."

"Officially we haven't," Steven told him.

"But unofficially you have?" Kermondley prompted.

It was Steven's turn to smile.

Apart from himself no one knew they had invented a time

machine, either officially or unofficially. Even Professor Goddard waiting in the laboratory could not know until Steven returned. Government departments, heads of the armed services and scientists all over the world waited with baited breaths. Should time travel become a proven reality its effects on the past and future of the human race seemed virtually unlimited.

"This is our first experiment," Steven said. "We needed to know what would happen in the future in order to prevent it. Many of us predicted it, of course, but now I have proof." He patted the video-camera. "Proof of the war and what happens afterwards . . . you and Vanya and all of this."

Kermondley understood.

Steven's eyes said what his words did not, stared bitterly and fixedly out across the estuary to the fallen dome of the cathedral. He could not accept human extinction. He would return to his own time, present this evidence of the future, and the nuclear holocaust would never happen. The London Steven loved would rise again from the sea and all Kermondley's kind would never exist.

The thought touched Vanya too, triggered the same fear. She had always accepted the legacy of barren land and living ocean and never wished it could be different . . . but Steven did. Steven hated everything he saw because all he saw was the terrible ruins of his own world, his own civilization. He did not see Vanya's world . . . the green perpetual beauty and peace of the undersea cities. He did not understand how good it was to be alive in the present time. He just wanted it gone . . . everything restored to what it was. Steven was trying to change the future and it did not occur to him that his future was Vanya's past.

"History is a living process," Kermondley had said.

Vanya could feel it.

History contained inside herself.

For her the universe had formed and spread. For her the Earth revolved around the sun and life evolved. She was the reason why countless millions of species had become extinct. She was the reason why the Ancients had dropped their bombs and died over decades of terror and pain. The whole of history had happened that she might exist.

"And no one can change it," Vanya thought. "No one can change history!"

But maybe Steven could.

Across the dusty space of land she met Kermondley's gaze, teacher and pupil in a moment of recognition. The thought was the same in both of them. But she was the only one on the landward side, the only one who could act. Vanya hesitated, appalled by the awfulness of what she must do. But Kermondley's eyes urged her, willed her to go. She turned away, searched for

Steven's footprints in the dust and followed them into the city.

Steven squatted on his heels on the cliff edge of the street, watching the water swill against the old foundations, a slow relentless erosion. The ebb tide left its line of green weed on the dome of St. Paul's and sea voices whispered around him, alien, inhuman, Kermondley's students crowding the steps, restless and waiting. Steven had been in their time for less than half an hour and already he had seen all he wanted to see and was ready to go. The loneliness depressed him, the immense absence of everything he knew. The silence grated on his nerves. He had no reason to stay in this godforsaken future any longer but Kermondley delayed him.

"This being a history lesson," Kermondley said, "we would like to take this unique opportunity . . . would you mind?"

"Sure," said Steven. "What can I tell you?"

"What was it really like in 1995?" one of the students asked.

They had no idea.

They could not even imagine trees in St. James's Park or Christmas lights glittering along Oxford Street. They had never tasted chestnuts or potato chips or strawberries and cream. They had never smelled roses, touched cat's fur, heard a blackbird sing, ridden the fun-fair rides or the rush-hour train. All the things Steven took for granted were meaningless to them.

Surrounded by ocean and empty lands Kermondley's students could grasp very little of everyday human existence. It was like trying to describe colours to people born blind, or spinning them fairy tales. They had thought all Ancients were violent, that everyone went around attacking everyone else . . . that tanks and guns and atom bombs were personal possessions. It was not easy to convince them that most Ancients had not wanted war.

"If no one wanted it how come it happened?" they asked him.

"Maybe it won't," he said.

"It already has," said Kermondley.

"Not in my time," said Steven. "In 1995 we can still prevent it and my evidence will make the vital difference. Now I must go. It's been nice meeting you."

He turned towards the ruins of the city.

Vanya stood in the broken doorway.

Sea-green tears shimmered in her eyes.

"I'll wait for you, Steven," Vanya said.

And he thought she was crazy.

No one waited for a thousand years!

The future was dependent on the past.

If anyone should change the past . . .

"We had to make sure," Kermondley said.

"There was nothing he could have done," said Vanya. "We know

"What was it
really like
in 1995?"

that! We're here! If he had succeeded we wouldn't exist!"

"We had to make sure," Kermondley repeated.

"One nuclear war guaranteed!" Vanya said bitterly.

"The Ancients still have a choice," Kermondley reminded her.

"Steven doesn't" she said dully.

Kermondley sighed.

"At least he's alive."

But Vanya knew that being alive would be no consolation to Steven. Heavy on her conscience was the sick knowledge of what she had done to him. She followed Kermondley down the steps. Her skin felt itchy and dry. She needed the silk sweet water to wash the dust from her scales. She needed to swim away, far out to sea, and forget.

Her fellow students waited and called.

"Hurry up, Vanya!"

"It's way past lunch time!"

"And Kermondley said we can go!"

"We'll race you to the restaurant!"

"Are you coming?"

"You go," Kermondley said quietly. "I'll wait for Steven."

Vanya shook her head.

She too would wait.

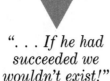

". . . If he had succeeded we wouldn't exist!"

And his cry rose from the heart of the ruined city making a pain in her heart like she had never known before. It was a cry of anguish and despair that went on and on, a terrible human sound. Vanya sobbed inconsolably knowing what he had found. She had smashed the workings of his time machine. He was trapped here now for the rest of his life . . . *homo sapiens* on the verge of extinction, the only one of his kind.

Professor Goddard switched off the laboratory light and closed the door. He had waited all afternoon and evening but Steven had not come back. The experiment had failed. His theory of time travel remained unproven and a young man was missing, presumed dead.

Professor Goddard sighed and shook his head. It was not only guilt that troubled him. He also knew the consequences of academic failure. He would not get a second chance to build a time machine. His research grant would not be renewed and he would have to accept retirement from the university, an old discredited scientist exiled to a bungalow in Bognor Regis . . . growing zinnias perhaps.

He sighed again, buttoned his jacket and went out into the night. He was just one more old man whose life had not amounted to very much. He did not read the writing on the banner which someone had tied to the front railings.

EXTINCTION IS FOREVER, it said.

READING AND REACTING

1. a) In one paragraph, explain the government claim, expressed by Professor Goddard, that only the threat of nuclear war guarantees world peace. Conclude with a statement explaining whether or not you agree with the claim and why you feel the way you do.

b) In a small group, read aloud your paragraphs and compare interpretations.

2. Imagine that you are Steven and, in a letter to Professor Goddard, describe Vanya, both in terms of her physical appearance and her personality.

or

Draw a picture of Vanya that Steven could send to his friends. Your picture should be based as closely as possible on the details in the story.

3. In a small group, discuss the meaning of the following terms: mutation, genocide, and natural selection. Cite examples of each.

REACHING OUT

1. Stage a debate on the following statement: "Nuclear weapons should be abolished."

2. a) In a small group, discuss who and/or what is likely to survive a nuclear war and what skills would be required of the new breed.

b) Write your own short story based on these speculations. Edit your story with a partner and share the polished version with the group.

3. Imagine that you could take Vanya back in time to continue the lesson that "History is a living process." Plan an itinerary of what you would want her to see.

4. Script a dialogue between Steven and Vanya in which Vanya tries to explain to the distraught Steven why she and Kermondley destroyed his time machine. Role-play the scene for the class.

5. Imagine that you have travelled to a time in the future. Records of your era have been destroyed. You are captured by strange creatures who demand an explanation of who you are and where you come from. Prepare a statement that you will read aloud at a public hearing. In your statement, try to convey the essence of what was important about your era.

The Toronto Star, Sept. 1, 1985

►"WE TEENAGERS FEEL THE OLDER GENERATION LEFT US A POOR WORLD"

I am writing this letter to comment on the world today. It doesn't look good. I am a 17-year-old female living each day and questioning whether I'll live to see the next. Our world has been flooded with a mountain of problems. Being a teenager entering the 12th grade, I am also looking forward to the future.

I know of many students who have spent years in college and university only to find that there are not any jobs out there for them.

Many of these students are faced with the difficult task of paying back loans they took out to pay for their education. Now they are educated bums in debt—a terrible way to be starting off your life.

We are also being told of how everything has changed and the "good old days" are gone. Today's young people haven't experienced the same type of good old days as our parents did. We are constantly being faced with the increasing pressures of society to succeed and be better than others. As a result, many turn to drugs, alcohol, and other forms of "relief" to escape the peer pressure.

It is also difficult to believe that there are people starving in a world of such abundance. We don't need all the luxuries we have in fortunate countries and we take it all for granted. Our society wastes so much without a second thought. Striving to obtain more luxury seems senseless, when it can all be taken away in a matter of moments.

The constant threat of nuclear war is also a great fear of my generation. It is very unreal that harmful weapons are being produced at an enormous cost while there are hungry people in Canada and other countries.

Another disadvantage to the future is the possibility of the destruction of plants, lakes, trees, humans, and animals as a result of harmful toxic chemicals being needlessly produced.

We are supposed to look to the future with hopes of accomplishing our dreams. With all that is going on in the world, is it really surprising that teen suicide numbers have risen 400 percent?

Personally, I'm going to take each day one at a time—no long-range plans, and not very many dreams. The one thing I can't understand is, how our parents can brag to us of the "good old days" when they are passing on to us the remains of the world they've created to date; a world full of hate, anger, frustration, and famine.

Kitty R.
Beamsville, Ont.

READING AND REACTING

1. In a full class discussion, determine how you feel about the sentiments expressed by Kitty R. in her letter.

2. Write a letter to Kitty R. in which you assess the validity of her observations and agree or disagree with her thesis. Attempt to send your letter to Kitty through *The Toronto Star*.

REACHING OUT

1. In a group of three, imagine that you are government ministers and have been given the task of developing a series of concrete proposals to correct the problems described in Kitty's letter. Decide which ministry (real or fictitious) each of you would represent. Brainstorm plans and then evaluate each one carefully. Present your best plans in an official announcement at a press conference with your classmates as journalists. Be prepared to answer their questions and defend your plans.

2. Write a letter to the editor of your local newspaper in which you highlight the positive aspects of your world.

3. Conduct a debate on the topic: "We teenagers feel the older generation left us a poor world."

4. The following list from the novel *Fahrenheit: 451* identifies conditions necessary for the perfect society. In a group, determine five conditions that you think are most important for an ideal world—you could incorporate ideas from this list. Compare lists with other groups and identify common conditions. Compile a class list of what makes a Utopia.
   —High quality of education for all
   —End to all war
   —Absolute freedom of choice
   —Great medical advancements, with treatment at home
   —Soothing music
   —Perfect crime detection
   —Censorship of all unpleasant facts, occurrences
   —Instant availability of all types of information
   —Increased speed of travel
   —More forms of entertainment and amusement
   —More time- and work-saving devices
   —Increased friendship and interaction between people
   —Equality of all people

▶ Young People Strive for Peace

They say they have the power to stop threat of war.

Leslie Fruman

I t is an issue that touches everyone, but the threat of nuclear war especially demoralizes those who traditionally have the most hope—young people.

For some young people, however, there is a feeling of hope and commitment to peace, and a perception that they really can do something to help make a change.

In interviews with young people involved in various peace organizations and networks in Metro Toronto, one theme emerged. The feeling among youth is that if they don't demonstrate and educate about the need for peace, they'll be partly to blame if war occurs.

Karen Ruttimann got involved in the peace movement, first through Youth Corps, a group for young Christians, and then through the Toronto Disarmament Network's (TDN) youth committee, in order to overcome what she calls "psychological numbing."

"Every day we are bombarded with information about another crisis in the Middle East, or the number of dollars being spent on defence, or some other war-torn story," says Ruttimann, 23. "You become numb to it after a while. You start thinking it doesn't matter. I don't want that to control me. I don't want to think that war is inevitable."

Ruttimann says she has overcome the numbness by reaching out to others and helping them understand the importance of the peace movement. Through her work with Youth Corps and TDN youth, she has gone to speak to high school groups interested in getting involved.

In a recent study of 1,000 public school children and high school students in Metro, 10 percent said they worried every day about the threat of nuclear war. It was these young people who believed they had the most power to change the threat of war to the promise of peace by becoming involved.

About 60 percent said they worried about the threat, but shrugged it off because they felt there was nothing they could do about it. About 28 percent said they felt there was no point planning for the future if there might not be one.

"What the study suggests is that young people feel that if enough young people are concerned, and become involved, they become empowered to promote change," says Dr. Frank Sommers, consulting psychiatrist to the East York Board of Education, and one of the doctors involved with the Children's Mental Health Group, which conducted the study.

"In my work I've talked to many young people, in classroom situations, and many indicate they don't expect to live out their normal lifespan. I think politicians have an enormous responsibility to make sure young people have faith in their futures. Otherwise there will be an epidemic of cynicism in youth."

For some young people, the pursuit of peace is an activity that must be participated in if we are to survive.

From left, Leslie Charbon, Savarina Allevato, and Karen Ruttimann joined the Toronto Disarmament Network's youth committee to work for peace.

People involved in peace movements around the world have traditionally been young. Sommers says that young people who get involved usually stay involved as they grow older.

"It seems that once you've received baptism into the peace movement, you become more willing to continue the commitment as you grow older."

The message has changed only slightly over the years. Instead of marching with banners that say ban the bomb, young people interested in peace today crowd march routes carrying banners asking governments to refuse the cruise missile. For some groups, the issue is disarmament and a stop to the arms race. For others, it's education through outreach programs to make others aware of what the situation is. Some believe that more arms give us more protection against war.

But whatever the message, the players'

profile remains basically the same. They are young, concerned, and committed to the one thing they think really matters—helping to make sure peace survives in their lifetimes, and their children's.

Savarina Allevato, 25, says that she is involved, through TDN, because she can help do something about the threat of nuclear war.

"Peace is the Number 1 issue facing young people today," she says. "We can fight for jobs, and better education, but what's the point unless we also fight for peace?"

Too often, she says, young people feel they can't get involved because they aren't old enough to vote. Allevato says high school students can get involved by discussing the issue in school, and by starting petitions, and asking for help from other organized peace groups.

"We'll help them, and give them ideas," she says. "Young people who want to get involved should talk to other young people who are sensitive to the issues, and share ideas. Then they can contact TDN youth, and we'll help any way we can."

Allevato says it's sometimes hard for young people to get involved because they don't know how to find the support systems.

"We're not taught how to find a way to get involved," she says. "Even though there may be a lot of things we don't like, it's not easy for young people to be taken seriously, or listened to. It's hard to organize youth because they don't often feel what they are saying is as important as what adults are saying."

Leslie Charbon, 20, who is also involved with Youth Corps and TDN, says young people have a special quality that lends itself to celebration.

"Celebrating peace is much more positive than worrying all the time about war," says Charbon.

READING AND REACTING

1. List the reasons Fruman gives regarding why young people feel compelled to demonstrate.

2. In groups, discuss the effectiveness of approaches used by young people to change "the threat of war to the promise of peace."

REACHING OUT

1. a) As a class, discuss your feelings about the threat of nuclear war.

   b) Express your perception of the degree of control you can exert over your world.

   c) Determine how your generation can improve the chances for survival.

   d) Poll students in your school to find out their feelings on the likelihood of a nuclear holocaust in their lifetime. Present your findings in a graph.

2. Explore the level of active commitment to peace in your community and report back to the class.

3. a) Survey older relatives, parents, and friends to find out what concerned them most as teenagers and what they fought to change.

   b) As a class, determine the issues that most concern students in your school and discuss the most effective ways of bringing about change.

   c) Compare the feelings of the two "generations" regarding issues and how to deal with them.

4. Write a letter to your grandchildren in which you express your hopes and concerns for their future, including the legacy that your generation will leave for them.

1. Assume the role of an entrepreneur in the 21st century. You have carefully analysed business opportunities and have identified a project that you would like to invest in. Prepare a business plan to present to a banker to convince her or him to finance your enterprise.

a) Describe the product or the service that you intend to market.

b) Draw up a strong marketing plan.

c) Outline the operational and management systems.

d) Provide a detailed financial plan—state the amount of money you intend to invest and indicate the size of the loan that you require from the bank. Explain the financial viability of your enterprise through graphs and charts.

e) Have a group of classmates assume the role of bankers. Present them with copies of your business plan and do an oral presentation. Use overhead transparencies and flip charts to display your financial data.

f) After your presentation, find out how many bankers have decided to give you the financial support you are looking for.

2. Organize and run a campaign for a public office, based on a platform of peace and friendly co-existence with all countries. Prepare your speeches, posters, campaign publicity materials, and press releases for radio and television. If you have access to a VTR, prepare a five minute "meet the candidate" program to support your efforts. As part of your planning, itemize an itinerary that will assure that you achieve maximum exposure to the voters. Be sure to recognize in your written material the need to use different strategies to appeal to different kinds of voters.

3. Build or draw a model of your community in the year 2001. Consider such aspects as transportation, waste disposal, and land and building use. In a written report defend your design and explain in detail how the plan would work. Describe the construction materials used and any special features of interior design.

4. Read a major work by a futurist writer such as Alvin Toffler or Herman Kahn. In a written report summarize the writer's vision of the future and provide a critique in which you consider how credible this vision is.

▶ STUDENT GUIDE

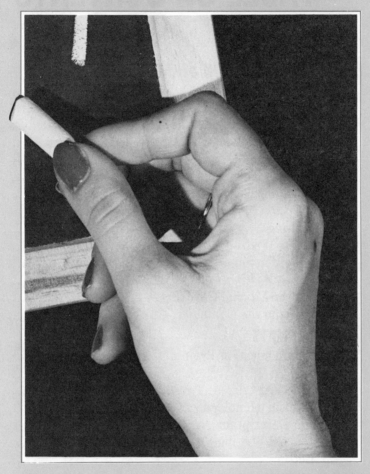

The Student Guide provides a description of such communication strategies as brainstorming and the writing process, as well as a glossary of such modes of expression as letter to the editor, script, and résumé.

▶ Student Guide
Table of Contents

▶ **Communication Strategies**

▶ **Formats**

► Communication Strategies

► Brainstorming

The brainstorming process is used to generate many ideas. The process can be used either individually or in groups. People in business use the brainstorming process to quickly and creatively generate ideas or to solve problems. The technique can be used just as effectively in the classroom. When you brainstorm in a small group, make sure all group members are comfortably seated; appoint one member to record all the ideas generated; set a time limit to the session and make sure you keep to the limit.

Brainstorming aims at producing a quantity of ideas. No idea suggested is ever rejected during a "brainstorm" session. In fact, the more radical an idea at this stage of the process, the better. Frequently, an idea suggested by one contributor will serve as a catalyst to suggest another idea to someone else. Contributors are continually "piggy-backing" on each other's ideas. In this way the improvement of ideas by others is encouraged. Ideas are only evaluated at the end of the brainstorming session.

► Group Work

Working in a group can be a rewarding experience; each person has the potential to contribute something unique to the process. In addition, ideas generated in a group are clarified, extended, and refined through discussion. Also, tasks can be divided between group members. For example, when researching a topic, each group member could look into one aspect of the topic, after which the group would get together to share whatever information was obtained.

The effective operation of a group depends on each member making a conscious effort to contribute, encourage, support, clarify, explain, question, analyse, piggy-back (see Brainstorming), and co-operate.

The following behaviours will detract from the effectiveness of the group: responding negatively without offering suggestions for improvement, ridiculing, intimidating, clowning, flirting, and blocking.

ORAL PRESENTATION

1. Assemble and organize data collected.
2. Represent appropriate types of information in graphic and table form.
3. Prepare visual displays.
4. Select the information you will present to the class, and arrange it in a logical order.
5. Make an outline to speak from.
6. Rehearse your presentation in front of a mirror, to a friend, or on a tape recorder.
7. Deliver your oral report.

Beginning: Move calmly to your position.
Arrange your material.
Pause.
Make eye contact with the audience.
State your intentions.

Middle: Maintain eye contact.
Speak loudly and clearly.
Move naturally.
Let your voice show enthusiasm.
Smile or frown at appropriate places.

Ending: Give your final summary and close firmly.
Pause.
Hold eye contact for a few seconds.
Collect your material and be prepared
to answer questions.

PROBLEM-SOLVING

Structured problem-solving involves four basic steps:
1) **Think about the problem**: Consider all aspects of the problem and clarify it in your mind.
2) **Devise a plan**: Develop a method for solving the problem.
3) **Carry out the plan**: Attempt to solve the problem, recording your findings so that you can monitor the process.
4) **Draw conclusions**: Based on your findings, develop a strategy for solving the problem, or suggest alternatives if possible.

QUESTIONING

Effective questioning involves the ability to ask relevant questions that show you are thinking about the subject and trying to learn more.

Test questions are those to which you already know the answer: e.g., at the scene of an accident, when you ask someone who is injured: "Did you hurt yourself?"

True questions elicit new information: e.g., "Have the police been called?"

Closed questions elicit a short response, and such questions often begin with "who," "where," "when," or "what." Use them to establish a fact or commitment, or to indicate a choice.

Open questions invite the speaker to expand his or her ideas. They show that the questioner is interested in the speaker's opinions and feelings. An interviewer is likely to ask open questions to find out as much information as possible.

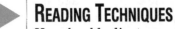

READING TECHNIQUES

You should adjust your reading to suit your purpose and according to the difficulty of the material.

Skim: Read over very quickly searching for specific detail.

Scan: Read through very quickly to get a general idea of the content.

Predict: Check title, subheadings, and visual material to anticipate what the material is about.

Check: Pause to compare what you are reading with what you predicted you would find.

Locate: Search the material for specific information that you have read.

Highlight: Use a marker or underline the sentences that contain the information you are seeking.

Organize: Identify in your mind or outline in a brief the organizational structure of the selection.

Remember: Choose facts that you will want to recall. Assist your memory by highlighting, making point-form notes, summarizing after blocks of reading, repeating to yourself, creating acronyms, or representing by graph or chart.

Evaluate: Pause as you read, and when you finish ask yourself: What meaning does this material hold for me?

RULES FOR CRITICISM

1. **Be tactful.** Most people's feelings are easily hurt. It is always wise, therefore, to *think* before you speak critically of someone. To be rude, cruel, unkind, bitter, or sarcastic in what you say about another person's efforts is not being *critical*; it's simply being small and petty. There's an old saying, "You can catch more flies with honey than with vinegar." Remember that proverb, and be thoughtful, courteous, and tactful in your criticisms.

2. **Be constructive.** Criticism is not mere faultfinding. It has a constructive meaning, too. The best criticism is that which builds up as well as tears down. You may pick out specific faults but you should also make definite, constructive suggestions for overcoming those faults. Your aim is to *help*, not *hurt*.

3. **Be definite.** Vague, general comments are often meaningless. To be helpful, you should make your criticism definite, accurate, and specific. Hurried and abrupt statements, such as, "I didn't

319

like the way he spoke," are too general. Instead, say, "His volume was well-regulated, but he spoke too rapidly and his enunciation was not clear."

4. **Be thorough.** Criticism that is complete and thorough is more helpful than that which is sketchy and hurried. There are more things to criticize in speaking than you realize. It isn't possible to comment on *everything* a speaker says or does, of course; nevertheless, it is wise to try to make as thorough an analysis of his or her efforts as possible.

Speaking and Listening Evaluation Checklist

The scales below are used to assess the speaking skills of the presenter and the listening skills of one student in the audience.

NAME OF PRESENTER ———————	High		Low
	3	2	1
Varies stress and tone for emphasis	3	2	1
Maintains eye contact and uses appropriate physical gestures	3	2	1
Speaks without excessive use of hesitations or stabilizers	3	2	1
Speaks at an appropriate pace	3	2	1
Speaks clearly and fluently, and is able to organize the message in a suitable sequence	3	2	1
NAME OF STUDENT LISTENER ———————			
Concentrates on speaker	3	2	1
Remains attentive without squirming or shuffling	3	2	1
Recognizes the main idea	3	2	1
Is able to recall appropriate details	3	2	1
Asks appropriate questions	3	2	1

Writing

The Writing Process

PRE-WRITING: At the pre-writing stage, you will compile a list of the topics you might like to write about, decide on the topic you will focus on, and clarify your ideas about that topic. Pre-writing involves the following processes:

Brainstorm in a small group to generate and explore ideas that may help you get started.

Make notes on everything that you might wish to deal with in your writing.

Organize your thoughts and information: Make an outline in which you consider the main points you want to communicate, how they can be best understood, and the order in which they should be presented. Your notes should prove very helpful at this stage.

Choose a voice: Determine who your audience is and what format and tone would be most appropriate.

WRITING A FIRST DRAFT: Be concerned with getting your ideas on paper or into the computer rather than with grammar and spelling. As you write, determine the sentence and paragraph structure that best reflects your outline.

REVISING: Re-read what you have written, considering in detail how it can be improved, and making any changes to that effect. At this stage of the process, you will be developing your ideas, refining your ideas, or even throwing out ideas and replacing them with new ones. Rewrite your draft as many times as it takes, making major changes in paragraphing, diction, and style, to ensure that your writing is as well-organized, clear, and interesting as possible.

POLISHING: Give your work a final check, correcting any errors in spelling, grammar, and punctuation. Any changes you make at this stage should be minor.

Conferencing

Conferencing is a process through which you look over your writing with a classmate or your teacher. Your conference-partner's task is to ask you questions that will help you formulate and clarify your thoughts and ideas, and to lead you to new directions, if necessary.

The following are some questions that could be asked during the conference:

—What is your objective in writing, saying, or doing this?
—What do you want to focus on?
—Who is your intended audience?
—How are you organizing your ideas?
—Is there something else you can add to expand on this idea?

The Writing Folder

Use a writing folder to help you organize your writing. Your writing should have three compartments:

In-Process Writing File:
Keep all the work that is still in draft form and needs revision in this compartment. Include all rough notes, outlines, or cuttings that you might use in your writing.

Personal Writing File:
In this file, you can include all the private thoughts that you have written about. You need not show the writing in this file to anyone else. On the other hand, you may want to use some of these pieces as a basis for future projects, or for refining.

Polished Writing File:
Keep all the completed, polished pieces in this file. You may choose pieces from this file for evaluation by your teacher.

Peer-Editing Checklist

As an editor, your task is to help the writer communicate his or her ideas as clearly and effectively as possible.

You should respond objectively to *how* the information and opinions are presented. Your editorial comments should be both constructive and supportive; they should aim to help the writer improve his or her ability to express ideas as a result of your friendly and honest feedback.

Use the checklist on the opposite page to help you edit:

Editor's Checklist

	O.K.	needs improvement	weak
1. Is the writer's purpose or thesis clear?	☐	☐	☐
2. Is the writer's intended audience clearly identified?	☐	☐	☐
3. Is the writer's format of writing appropriate for the purpose and audience?	☐	☐	☐
4. Does each paragraph adequately develop one main idea with sufficient and convincing supporting details?	☐	☐	☐
5. Are the ideas arranged in a logical order?	☐	☐	☐
6. Does each paragraph flow smoothly into the next?	☐	☐	☐
7. Does the writer use a variety of sentences?	☐	☐	☐
8. Does the writing have an effective introduction and conclusion?	☐	☐	☐
9. Is the word choice as precise, accurate, and descriptive as possible?	☐	☐	☐
10. Are there any problems with mechanics (spelling, punctuation, capitalization, grammar)?	☐	☐	☐
11. What are the strengths of writing?	☐	☐	☐
12. How might the writing be improved?	☐	☐	☐

USING THE COMPUTER

Word-processing software can simplify the writing process. The word-processor enables you to store data, and to rearrange, add, and delete what you have typed in, without having to re-copy your work every time you make a change. The computer can also help you in producing graphs, charts, and reports.

► FORMATS

► COMMUNICATION PROJECT

This project will involve several or all of the following modes of communication: speaking, listening, reading, writing, viewing, and presenting. The project will be integrated in a formal report, either written, spoken, or artistically portrayed for a well-defined purpose and audience. (See Report—Written; Oral)

► DEBATE

Two teams present arguments before an audience on both sides of a question. Each team researches the issue and develops an argument to convince the audience that its position is the most sound. After each side presents its argument, time is allotted for each team to respond to criticisms by the other team and to sum up the main points of its defence. The audience or panel of judges then votes on which side has presented the most convincing argument.

► EDITORIAL

An editorial is an article written by the editor of a newspaper or a magazine in which the newspaper editorial board's or editor's opinion on a topical issue is presented, and arguments are given supporting that position.

► INTERIOR MONOLOGUE

An interior monologue is a narrative in which one character expresses his or her innermost thoughts and feelings.

► JOB DESCRIPTION

A job description outlines the main features of a position within a company. Such features would include position, title, location, responsibilities and related duties, person to whom the employee would be responsible, education and experience requirements, and any special skills needed for the job.

POSITION TITLE
Accounts Payable Clerk

DIVISION/COMPONENT
CEPP - Canada

DATE
November 26, 1982

GRADE

DEPARTMENT
Finance

SECTION
Toronto

REPORTS TO: General Accounting Manager

DIRECTLY SUPERVISES (TITLE ONLY)
None

PRINCIPAL RESPONSIBILITIES
Performs the Trade Accounts Payable function for Toronto Operations according to established procedures and standards.

PRINCIPAL DUTIES:
- Prepare invoices for accounting entry and payment according to established procedures and policy, i.e. approval authority is being followed.
- Prepare payments in Canadian and foreign currencies.
- Provide keying support for trade payables.
- Maintain up to date filing of paid invoices.
- Maintain purchase order and receiving log.
- Reconcile supplier statements monthly.
- Maintain open payables files by invoices in alphabetical sequence.

RELATED RESPONSIBILITIES AND DUTIES:

- Handle supplier queries.
- Provide information required by other departments.
- Key in new vendor changes and additions.
- Maintain sequential file of new vendor forms.

SCOPE AND IMPACT (DIRECTLY CONTROLLED OR RESPONSIBLE FOR)

SALES/SERVICE DOLLAR VOLUME:
COSTS OR EXPENSES:
ASSETS:
PERSONNEL:
        N/A

MINIMUM EDUCATION/EXPERIENCE
REQUIRED:
    High School with 3 - 5 years experience

POSITION TITLE
    Administrative Assistant

DIVISION/COMPONENT
CEPP - Canada

DATE
September 5, 1983

DEPARTMENT
Finance

SECTION
Toronto

REPORTS TO:

GRADE

DIRECTLY SUPERVISES (TITLE ONLY)

PRINCIPAL RESPONSIBILITIES
    Provide a support function for the Finance section in the areas of typing, filing and secretarial duties.

PRINCIPAL DUTIES:
- Type, collate and distribute monthly performance package
- Type the monthly "Canadian Operations Consolidated Financial Summary" package.
- Type general correspondence for financial management staff.
- Distribute for mailing, signed accounts payable cheques.
- Distribute the monthly Computer Divisional/Departmental reports.
- Prepare monthly sales statistic report.

RELATED RESPONSIBILITIES AND DUTIES:

- Help with general filing during peak periods.
- Provide keying support during month-end closings.

JOURNAL WRITING

Your journal is for you to express what you are thinking, feeling, and learning. Writing about your ideas helps you to clarify and build on them. Don't worry about grammar or spelling at this point. Let your thoughts flow easily onto the page. You might want to record information or reflect on issues, conversations, and events of interest to you. Recording your observations about class discussions and projects may be useful preparation for doing assignments. Your teacher will provide possible entry points for your writing, but you are encouraged to write about something of your own choosing.

LETTER

STYLES

Full Block: All lines begin at the left margin.

Block: The return address, dateline, complimentary closing, signature, and title lines begin at the centre of the page. All other lines begin at the left margin.

Semi-Block: Block style is used with the exception that paragraphs are indented.

AMS Simplified: There is no salutation or complimentary close-up. In place of the salutation is a subject line in capital letters. Everything begins on the left margin, and there is no indentation.

PUNCTUATION

Open Punctuation: No punctuation marks follow any line other than the sentences in the body or a line that ends with an abbreviation.

Mixed Punctuation: Place a colon after the salutation and a comma after the complimentary closing.

Closed Punctuation: Every line ends with a mark of punctuation.

TYPES

Letter of Application/Cover Letter: accompanies and sums up the contents of a résumé, states the position you are applying for, and explains why you are qualified to fill it.

Letter of Request: asks the receiver to grant a request.

Letter of Confirmation: follows up a previous communication to confirm the details of an arrangement or agreement, such as for the date, time, and place of an interview.

Thank-you Letter: is a courteous follow-up to someone who has rendered you a service in the form of a short message which expresses your appreciation.

AMS Simplified

return address (13 lines from top of page)
xxxxxxxxxxxxxxxx

date (5 lines below return address)

address lines (5 lines below date)
xxxxxxxxxxxxxxx
xxxxxxxxxxxxxxx
xxxxxxxxxxxxxxx
xxxxxxxxxxxxxxx

subject (3 lines below address)
body (2 lines below subject)
xxxxxxxxxxxxxxxxxxxxxxxxxxxxxxxxxxxxxxxxxxxxxxxxxxxxxxxx
xxxxxxxxxxxxxxxxxxxxxxxxxxxxxxxxxxxxxxxxxxxxxxxxxxxxxxxxx

xxxxxxxxxxxxxxxxxxxxxxxxxxxxxxxxxxxxxxxxxxxxxxxxxxxxxxx
xxxxxxxxxxxxxxxxxxxxxxxxxxxxxxxxxxxxxxxxxxxxxxxxxxxxxxx
xxxxxxxxxxxxxxxxxxxxxxxxxxxxxxxxxxxxxxxxxxxxxxxxxxxxxx

signature (7 lines below body copy)

reference initial (2 lines below signature)

attachment/enclosure (2 lines below reference initial)

copy (2 lines below attachment/enclosure)

Semi-Block

return address (13 lines from top of page)
xxxxxxxxxxxxxxxx

date. (5 lines below return address)

address line, (5 lines below date)
xxxxxxxxxxxxxxxx,
xxxxxxxxxxxxxxxxx,
xxxxxxxxxxxxxxxxx.

salutation, (3 lines below address)
body (2 lines below salutation)
xxxxxxxxxxxxxxxxxxxxxxxxxxxxxxxxxxxxxxxxxxxxxxxxxxxxxxx
xxxxxxxxxxxxxxxxxxxxxxxxxxxxxxxxxxxxxxxxxxxxxxxxxxxxxxxx

xxxxxxxxxxxxxxxxxxxxxxxxxxxxxxxxxxxxxxxxxxxxxxxxxxxxxxx
xxxxxxxxxxxxxxxxxxxxxxxxxxxxxxxxxxxxxxxxxxxxxxxxxxxxxxxx
xxxxxxxxxxxxxxxxxxxxxxxxxxxxxxxxxxxxxxxxxxxxxxxxxxxxxxxx

close, (2 lines below body copy)

signature (7 lines below close)

reference initial (2 lines below signature)

attachment/enclosure (2 lines below reference initial)

copy (2 lines below attachment/enclosure)

Full-Block

xxxxxxxxxxxxxxxx
xxxxxxxxxxxxxxxx
xxxxxxxxxxxxxxxx
xxxxxxx

xxxxxxxxxxx

xxxxxxxxxxx
xxxxxx
xxxxxxxxxxxxxxxxxx
xxxxxxxxxxxxxxxx
xxxxxxx

xxxxxxxxxxxxxxx
xxxxxxxxxxxxxxxxxxxxxxxxxxxxxxxxxxxxxxxxxxxxxxxxxxxxx
xxxxxxxxxxxxxxxxxxxxxxxxxxxxxxxxxxxxxxxxxxxxxxxxxxxxxx
xxxxxxxxxxxxxxxxxxxxxxxxxxxxxxxxxxxxxxxxxxxxxxxxxxxxxx
xxxxxxxxxxxxxxxxxxxxxxxxxxxxxxxxxxxxxxxxxxxxxxxxxxxxxx

xxxxxxxxxx

xxxxxxxxxxxxxxxxx

xxx

xxxxxxxxx

xxxxxxxxxxxxxx

Block

return address (13 lines from top of page)
xxxxxxxxxxxxxxxx

date (5 lines below return address)

address lines (5 lines below date)
xxxxxxxxxxxxxxxx
xxxxxxxxxxxxxxx
xxxxxxxxxxxxxxx
xxxxxxxxxxxxxxx

salutation: (3 lines below address)

body (2 lines below salutation)
xxxxxxxxxxxxxxxxxxxxxxxxxxxxxxxxxxxxxxxxxxxxxxxxxxxxxxx
xxxxxxxxxxxxxxxxxxxxxxxxxxxxxxxxxxxxxxxxxxxxxxxxxxxxxxxx
xxxxxxxxxxxxxxxxxxxxxxxxxxxxxxxxxxxxxxxxxxxxxxxxxxxxxxxx

xxxxxxxxxxxxxxxxxxxxxxxxxxxxxxxxxxxxxxxxxxxxxxxxxxxxxxxx
xxxxxxxxxxxxxxxxxxxxxxxxxxxxxxxxxxxxxxxxxxxxxxxxxxxxxxxx

close, (2 lines below body copy)

signature (7 lines below close)
reference initial (2 lines below signature)

attachment/enclosure (2 lines below reference initial)

copy (2 lines below attachment/enclosure)

LETTER TO THE EDITOR

The 'letters to the editor' section of a newspaper or magazine usually appears on or near the editorial page. Readers are invited to express their opinions on a particular issue or in response to an article that appeared previously in the publication. Letters to the editor must be addressed specifically to the editor of the publication rather than to an individual or organization referred to in the letter.

MEMORANDUM (MEMO)

A memo is a written message—usually short—which is intended for use within the organization. It is useful for maintaining contact between departments, conveying information, and for keeping written record of oral communication. A standard memo should clearly state the date, subject, sender, and receiver of the memo.

REPORT

ORAL

An oral report should take into consideration the originality and organization of content, the vocabulary, grammar and pronunciation reflected in language use, and delivery. In order to communicate your message effectively, you need to consider the tone and volume of your voice, your enunciation, and the rate at which you speak. Your delivery checklist should also include preparation, poise, posture, and audience contact.

WRITTEN

A written document includes the following parts: title page, abstract, table of contents, body, and appendix or bibliography.

Title page: An indication to the audience of what topic the report will be covering.

Abstract: A statement summarizing the main points in a text.

Table of Contents: A list of the components of the report in sequential order and where they are to be found.

Body: The form in which the information you have gathered is presented.

Appendix: That which is added to the end of the report for further information.

Bibliography: Notations which show references that were used to research the topic, usually alphabetically listed. The bibliography lists the author's name, the name of the document, publisher, and date of publication. Style of reporting the reference varies according to whether the source is a book, magazine, or other source.

Memorandum

Holt, Rinehart and Winston of Canada, Limited.

TO EXECUTIVE COMMITTEE & DEPARTMENT MANAGERS

FROM MARGUERITE CLIFFORD   DATE MARCH 6, 1986.

RE: SEMINAR – REPORT WRITING

A Report Writing I Seminar will be held on Thursday, March 27, 1986. This Seminar will be of interest and benefit to all employees who have occasion to prepare reports and/or memos.

The seminar will be held in the Board Room at 9:00 a.m. and will last for approximately 3 hours. Tony Luengo will be the Instructor for this Seminar.

Report Writing II, a follow-up to this Seminar, will be held during the week of April 28, 1986. All participants of Report Writing I should attend the follow-up Seminar.

Relevant material will be sent to all participants prior to the course.

Would you please provide me with a list of all participants from your Division/Department by Tuesday, March 11, 1986.

Résumé/Curriculum Vitae

A résumé is a summary of information about yourself to help a potential employer assess your qualifications for a job. The résumé is usually organized under the following headings: personal data; work experience; education; special qualifications relating to a specific job description; interests or hobbies; and references.

Maria Sayles
512 Centre Street
GREENVILLE, Ontario

Telephone: 496-3300

POSITION DESIRED: Legal Secretary/Assistant

Work Experience:

1974 - 1976
June - Sept.

PRIVATE SECRETARY to Vice President of Imperial Insurance Co., Greenville, Ontario.

Duties: Handled all correspondence, scheduled appointments, transcribed minutes of meetings, was generally main assistant.

1972 - 1972
Jan. - April

SECRETARY for sales and marketing managers of Piko Plastics Ltd., Greenville, Ontario.

Duties: Placed advertising, reviewed all invoices, made up much of the correspondence, reviewed contracts for correctness in detail, did filing and some statistical work.

1971 -1971
June - Dec.

RECEPTIONIST for United Nickel Works, Greenville, Ontario.

Duties: Answered telephone, greeted clients, typed invoices and other copy work.

Education:

1976 - 1977

LEGAL SECRETARIAL/ASSISTANT course
Stanley Institute, Greenville, Ontario

STUDY AREAS: Law Office Organizaiton, Law and Business Organization, Real Estate, Litigation & Divorce, Wills & Estates, Corporate Law.

Shorthand speed 120 w.p.m. Typing speed 62 w.p.m.

PERSONAL DATA SHEET

Name: Robin K. O'Reilly

Address: 90 Breaker Avenue
TORONTO, Ontario

Telephone: 961-3043

Education: Bering Institute, Toronto
ELECTRONICS TECHNICIAN COURSE

Areas of Study: Electrical/mechanical/electronic drafting, equipment servicing, digital and integrated circuits, computer circuits, Fortran programming, computer applications.

Completed correspondence course in RPG and COBOL PROGRAMMING at Bering Institute.

Secondary school subjects included DRAFTING & ELECTRONICS.

Work History: JUNIOR DRAFTER--special project during summer of 1976.
United Steel Works, Côte Rouge, Quebec.

MACHINE OPERATOR--stove pipe production; May 1975 to September 1975.
Greenville Pipes, Greenville, Ontario.

SALES CLERK--two nights per week during school years (1975 - 1977) selling electrical and electronic components.
Steathroy Radio & Electronics Co.,
Toronto, Ontario.

Personal Interests: Stage technician at school's drama club in charge of lighting. Worked on special exhibit which showed the basic workings of a computer at high school open house.

Available: Immediately.

ROLE-PLAY

When you role-play a situation imagine yourself in the place of another person, so that you can act out how that person might feel, think, and react.

SCRIPT

A script is a format for writing a scene between two or more characters which is to be acted out, such as on T.V., radio, stage, or film. A script is set up so that each character's lines are listed in the order in which the character would speak them. Every time a character speaks, the character's name appears on a new line, followed by a colon, then the speech. The script should also include directions as to how the set should look, what sound and visual effects should be used, and how the characters should appear and move.

VISUAL AIDS

An oral presentation should include visual aids to help convey your ideas. Transparencies, blackboard and flip charts, slides, videotapes, and tape recorders can all be used effectively to emphasize points. Charts and graphs are useful for showing statistical information. Displays should be easy to see from a distance, simple, and should not detract from the flow of your presentation.

Aid	Materials and Equipment Required
Transparency	transparencies, frames, marking pens, overhead projector, screen
Blackboard	board, chalk, brush, coloured chalk
Flip Chart	chart, marking pens, easel
Tapes	tape-recorder or video cassette recorder
Posters	bristol board, marking pens, tacks or clips

LINE GRAPH

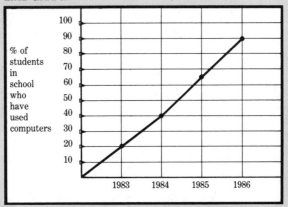

Simple line graphs can be used to show changes over a period of time. Relationships can be shown by using two lines.

FLOW CHART

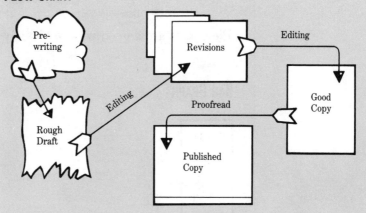

Flow charts illustrate the process by which things get done.

ORGANIZATIONAL CHART

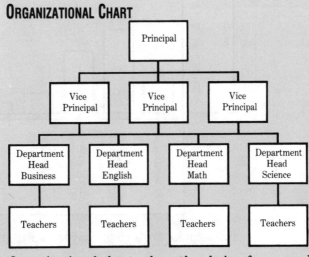

Organizational charts show the chain of command.

PIE CHART

Gabrielle's income

Pie charts are a good way to visually represent percentages.

BAR GRAPH

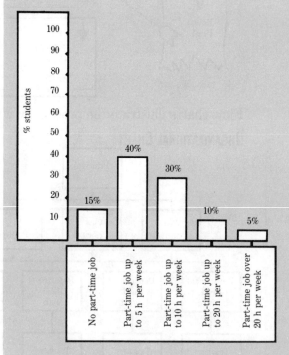

Bar graphs are a clear way to represent comparative figures.

► Acknowledgments

The Muscle: By Barry Callaghan. From *The Black Queen Stories* by Barry Callaghan, © 1982. Reprinted by permission of Lester & Orpen Dennys Publishers Ltd., Canada.

'Soften' Is Password to Better Social Contact: Reprinted by permission from *Making Contact* by Arthur C. Wassmer, published by The Dial Press, copyright © 1978 by Arthur C. Wassmer.

Watch What You're Saying: From *The Royal Bank Letter*, Published by the Royal Bank of Canada.

A Little English Is a Dangerous Thing: © 1985 Bill Bryson.

Now Listen Here!: Originally published in CTM: The Human Element, 1981. Reprinted by permission of Robyn Peterson.

Working in the Field: Previously published in *Homemaker's* Magazine. Reprinted by permission of Rona Maynard.

For Adults, Schooling Never Stops: By Theresa Tedesco, August 15, 1985, *The Globe and Mail*, Toronto.

Are You Looking for a Job?: Excerpted from *The Job Search Companion* © 1984 by Ellen J. Wallach, published by The Harvard Common Press, Boston.

Eight Steps to Get the Job You Want: Excerpted from *The Job Search Companion* © 1984 by Ellen J. Wallach, published by The Harvard Common Press, Boston.

How to Figure Out What You Want: Excerpted from *The Job Search Companion* © 1984 by Ellen J. Wallach, published by The Harvard Common Press, Boston.

Where Are You Going?: Excerpted from *The Job Search Companion* © 1984 by Ellen J. Wallach, published by The Harvard Common Press, Boston. *Choices*: Puts World of Work at Your Fingertips is reproduced with permission from Canada Systems Group.

Application Forms: Employment: Reproduced with permission of the Ontario Human Rights Commission.

How to Write a Sure-Hire Résumé: From *How to Turn an Interview into a Job* by Jeffrey G. Allen. Copyright © 1983 by Jeffrey G. Allen. Reprinted by permission of Simon & Schuster, Inc.

30 Action Verbs for a Winning Résumé: From *How to Turn an Interview into a Job* by Jeffrey G. Allen. Copyright © 1983 by Jeffrey G. Allen. Reprinted by permission of Simon & Schuster, Inc.

Want Ads: Originally titled, Want Ads—Employment Opportunities. Robert Garrison has worked as a School-teacher; Commercial Pilot—Airplanes; Welding/Fabrication; and Logging-Faller on the B.C. coast.

The Right Way to Write a Cover Letter: From *How to Turn an Interview into a Job* by Jeffrey G. Allen. Copyright © 1983 by Jeffrey G. Allen. Reprinted by permission of Simon & Schuster, Inc.

Student Cover Letter: Reprinted by permission of Tilla Seh.

How to Sell Yourself: Complete title, *How to Sell Yourself in the First Four Minutes of Meeting Someone New* from *The Four Minute Sell* by Janet G. Elsea. Copyright © 1984 by Janet G. Elsea. Reprinted by permission of Simon & Schuster, Inc.

A Successful Interview: Dos and Don'ts for a Successful Interview from *Family Circle*—Back to Work Handbook by Joyce Denebrink.

The Day of the Job Interview: From *Family Circle*—Back to Work Handbook by Joyce Denebrink.

A Thank-you Letter: Originally titled, A Thank-you Letter: It Often Makes the Difference from *Family Circle*—Back to Work Handbook by Joyce Denebrink.

Employer Looks for Attitude, Appearance: From *The Toronto Star Syndicate*, May 9, 1985, Letter to the Editor by Rene Jansen in de Wal, Steve Donaldson and Brian Burgess, University Painting and Improvements. Reprinted by permission of the authors.

20 Reasons Why People Don't Get Hired: From *Family Circle*—Back to Work Handbook by Joyce Denebrink.

from **A Mortal Flower**: By Han Suyin © 1965. Reprinted by permission of Jonathan Cape Ltd.

First Job: By Howard White. From *The Men There Were Then*, Pulp Press, 1983. Reprinted by permission of Howard White.

Relief Locations Manager: From *Groceries*, University of Pittsburgh Press, Pittsburgh, PA. Copyright 1976 by Herbert Scott.

You Can Make "That Damn Job" Better If You Try: By Wade Roberts, Knight-Ridder Newspapers.

Time Flies by in a Muddle If You Don't Learn to Manage It: By Helen Bullock. Reprinted with permission—*The Toronto Star* Syndicate.

Who Called This Meeting?: By Rosa Harris-Adler (*City Woman* Magazine—Holiday 1984).

The Neutral Enemy: By Don Bailey. This story first appeared in *Cross-Canada Writer's Quarterly*, 1985. Reprinted by permission of Don Bailey.

Respect Is Key in Worker Satisfaction: By Sandro Contenta and Brian McAndrew. Reprinted with permission—*The Toronto Star* Syndicate.

Smoking: Clearing the Air: Canada and the World, Maclean Hunter Ltd.

Office Pollution: Canada Wide/Pauline Comeau.

Workers' Health—At Risk: By David Bennett. Reprinted with permission of *Canadian Labour*, newsmagazine of the Canadian Labour Congress.

Job-Sharing: Good Outweighs Bad: By Margot Gibb-Clark, July 26, 1985, *The Globe and Mail*, Toronto.

The Students' Guide to On-the-Job Rights: By Leslie Fruman, July 12, 1985. Reprinted with permission—*The Toronto Star* Syndicate.

Should You Go into Business for Yourself?: From *Introduction to Canadian Business* by Brian Owen. Reprinted by permission of Allyn & Bacon, Inc.

Fast-Tracking with Those Who Have Made It: By Blake Harris. Reprinted from Canadian Business Life, Dec. 1984, with permission from the Better Business Bureau of Metropolitan Toronto Inc.

Investigate Franchises: By Eugene Ellmen, April 30, 1985, The Canadian Press.

Learning Skills to Climb the Corporate Ladder: By Marianne Tefft. With permission of *The Financial Post*.

A Little Bit of Romance Is Offered by 'Replicars': By Linda Kirby, Sept. 14, 1983. Courtesy The Canadian Champion.

Restaurant Is His Investment in the Future: By Leslie Fruman, March 5, 1985. Reprinted with permission—*The Toronto Star* Syndicate.

Day-Care Venture a Risk That Paid Off: By Leslie Fruman, July 23, 1985. Reprinted with permission—*The Toronto Star* Syndicate.

Fitness Consultants Run Family Business: by Leslie Fruman, April 26, 1985. Reprinted with permission—*The Toronto Star* Syndicate.
Kettle Creek Canvas Company: By Joyce Carter, June 18, 1985. *The Globe and Mail*, Toronto.
Teen Takes a Flyer on Business Venture: By Leslie Fruman, July 19, 1985. Reprinted with permission—*The Toronto Star* Syndicate.
The Fragile Bonds of Friendship: By Virginia Corner, October 5, 1985. Reprinted with permission—*The Toronto Star* Syndicate.
How Money Problems Wreck Romance: Reprinted by permission of The Putnam Publishing Group from *Love and Money* by Carol Colman. Copyright © 1983 by Carol Colman.
Charity: First printed in *The Fiddlehead*. Reprinted by permission of Mike Barnes.
Key Turns, House Is Empty: by Ellen Roseman. *The Globe and Mail*, Toronto.
The Rink: By Cyril Dabydeen. First printed in *The Fiddlehead*, #143, Spring 1985, The Observatory, University of New Brunswick. Reprinted by permission of the author.
Horse: © Douglas Glover 1981. By permission of Douglas Glover.
A Planet for the Taking: By David Suzuki. Reprinted by permission of David Suzuki.
Stress Bad If Wrongly Handled: By Dr. W. Gifford Jones, *The Globe and Mail*, May 19, 1983. Reprinted by permission of the author.
How Stress Hurts You: The Canadian Institute of Stress. Reprinted with permission.
How Your Job Rates on the Stress Scale: The Canadian Institute of Stress. Reprinted with permission.
Check Your Stress Count: The Canadian Institute of Stress. Reprinted with permission.
Teen Tobacco Addiction Linked to Stress: The Journal, Addiction Research Foundation, Toronto, Ontario.
How Marijuana Affects Your Ability to Cope: Reprinted with permission from *Marijuana: Answers for Young People and Parents*, Toronto: Addiction Research Foundation, 1984.
Two Fishermen: By Morley Callaghan. Reprinted by permission of Don Congdon Associates, Inc. Copyright © 1934 by Morley Callaghan. Renewed 1961 by Morley Callaghan.
The Interview: Previously published in *Going for Coffee: Poetry on the Job*, Harbour Press, 1981. Reprinted by permission of Margie Marks.
Sexual Harassment Case No. 8: Reprinted with permission of the Ontario Human Rights Commission.
Computers Zero in on Our Bad Work Habits: By Carey English, Sept. 21, 1985. Reprinted with permission—*The Toronto Star* Syndicate.
Risk Taking Can Give You a Healthy High: By Olivia Ward. Reprinted with permission—*The Toronto Star* Syndicate.
Robots That Make Robots Are Here and Machines That Think May Be Next: By George Brett, February 17, 1985. Reprinted with permission—*The Toronto Star* Syndicate.
Head of the House: By Timothy Perrin. Reprinted by permission of the author from *City Woman* Magazine, Fall 1985.
Low Pay, Lack of a Job Carry No Stigma in Society of 2010: By Lorne Slotnick, October 10, 1985. *The Globe and Mail*, Toronto.
Future Promises More Leisure Time but Less Money: By Mark Kingswell, October 21, 1985. *The Globe and Mail*, Toronto.
The Feeling of Power: By Isaac Asimov. Copyright © 1957 by Quinn Publishing Co., Inc. First appeared in *If: Worlds of Science Fiction*. From the book *Nine Tomorrows*. Reprinted by permission of Doubleday & Company, Inc.
In the Next War: By Robert Priest. From *This Magazine*, June 1984.
The Horses: By Edwin Muir. Reprinted by permission of Faber and Faber Ltd. from *The Collected Poems of Edwin Muir*.
Extinction Is Forever: By Louise Lawrence, from *Out of Time* ed. by Aidan Chambers, reproduced by permission of the author.
We Teenagers Feel the Older Generation Left Us a Poor World: Letter to the editor: Kitty R.
Young People Strive for Peace: By Leslie Fruman, March 21, 1985. Reprinted with permission—*The Toronto Star* Syndicate.
Rules for Criticism: Some Rules for Good Criticism, abridged and adapted from *The Art of Speaking* by E.F. Elson and Alberta Peck, © Copyright, 1952, by Ginn and Company. Used with permission. Every reasonable effort has been made to trace the owners of copyrighted material and to make due acknowledgment. Any errors or omissions drawn to our attention will be gladly rectified in future editions.

ILLUSTRATIONS

Doug Guildford: pp. XVI, 333, 334; Thom Sevalrud: pp. XVII, 104-105, 252, 282, 285, 289; Vladyana Krykorka: page 1; Richard da Mota: pp. 5, 8-9; Barbara Klunder: pp. 14, 15, 16, 17, 27, 28; Peter Nagy: pp. 37, 268-269; Laurie LaFrance: pp. 68, 193, 294; Leonard Aguanno: pp. 87, 89; Bruce Archer: pp. 94, 95, 96; Wojtek Gorczynski: pp. 115, 117, 120, 239, 243, 245; Shauna De'Andrea: page 187; Michael Reinhart: pp. 201, 205; Clive Dobson: pp. 211, 214, 216, 297, 300, 304; Robert Johannsen: pp. 276-277.

PHOTOGRAPHY

Four by Five Photography Inc.: pp.1, 21, 22-23, 31, 60, 73, 79, 93, 108, 133, 135, 139, 143, 146, 151, 181, 222, 227, 249, 255, 259, 261, 263, 291; *The Globe and Mail*, Toronto: pp. 45, 173; Paul Newberry: pp. 51, 179, 197; The StockMarket Inc.: pp. 100-101; 161, 312; *The Toronto Star* Syndicate: pp. 124, 126, 169, 170, 171, 174, 311; Canapress Photo Service: page 152; Better Business Bureau: pp. 156, 157, 158; *Financial Post*/Peter Redman: page 165; Milton Champion: pp. 167-168; CBC/Fred Phipps: page 220; Miller Services/Harold M. Lambert: page 315; Luke Golobitsh: pp. 334-335.

CARTOONS

The Far Side cartoon is reprinted by permission of Chronicle Features, San Francisco: page 130; Garnotte cartoons, LES ENTREPRISES CULTURELLES: pp. 54, 58; Jeff MacNelly, Reprinted by permission: Tribune Media Services: page 229; Schulz, © 1985 United Feature Syndicate, Inc.: page 322.